Paul Tschetter

Princeton Theological Monograph Series

K. C. Hanson, Charles M. Collier, and D. Christopher Spinks,
Series Editors

Recent volumes in the series:

S. Donald Fortson III, editor
Colonial Presbyterianism: Old Faith in a New Land

Christian T. Collins-Winn
*"Jesus Is Victor!": The Significance of the Blumhardts
for the Theology of Karl Barth*

Bernie A. Van De Walle
*The Heart of the Gospel: A. B. Simpson, the Fourfold Gospel,
and Late Nineteenth-Century Evangelical Theology*

David Hein
Geoffrey Fisher: Archbishop of Canterbury, 1945-1961

Linden J. DeBie
*Speculative Theology and Common-Sense Religion: Mercersburg
and the Conservative Roots of American Religion*

Paul Tschetter

The Story of a Hutterite Immigrant Leader, Pioneer, and Pastor

Rod Janzen

☙PICKWICK *Publications* • Eugene, Oregon

PAUL TSCHETTER
The Story of a Hutterite Immigrant Leader, Pioneer, and Pastor

Princeton Theological Monograph Series 114

Copyright © 2009 Rod Janzen. All rights reserved. Except for brief quotations in critical publications or reviews, no part of this book may be reproduced in any manner without prior written permission from the publisher. Write: Permissions, Wipf and Stock Publishers, 199 W. 8th Ave., Suite 3, Eugene, OR 97401.

Pickwick Publications
A Division of Wipf and Stock Publishers
199 W. 8th Ave., Suite 3
Eugene, OR 97401

www.wipfandstock.com

ISBN 13: 978-1-60608-134-1

Cataloging-in-publication data:

Janzen, Rod A.

Paul Tschetter : the story of a Hutterite immigrant leader, pioneer, and pastor / Rod Janzen.

Princeton Theological Monograph Series 114

xii + p. 304 ; 23 cm. Includes bibliographical references and indexes.

ISBN 13: 978-1-60608-134-1

1. Tschetter, Paul. 2. Hutterite Brethren—Great Plains—History. 2. Hutterite Brethren—History—19th century. 3. Hutterite Brethren—History—20th century. I. Title. II. Series.

Manufactured in the U.S.A.

Contents

Tables and Illustrations / vii

Acknowledgments / ix

1. Introduction: Paul Tschetter, the Hutterite Joshua / 1
2. The Hutterites / 9
3. Growing up in Ukraine / 25
4. The Journey to North America / 48
5. Immigration / 84
6. A New Life in Dakota Territory / 113
7. Paul Tschetter and the Hutterite Colonies / 131
8. Leading the Neu Hutterthaler Church / 142
9. The Evangelical Alternative / 172
10. The Final Years / 189
11. The Legacy of Paul Tschetter / 218

Appendix A: Paul Tschetter's Summer 1873 Diary / 227

Appendix B: Neu Hutterthaler Church Record Book, 1875–1919, Narrative Sections / 267

Appendix C: Paul Tschetter's Letter of Petition to President Ulysses S. Grant, August 8, 1873 / 285

Appendix D: Ulysses S. Grant's Response to Paul Tschetter's Petition, September 5, 1873 / 287

Appendix E: Hutterite Memorial, 1874–1974, Bridgewater, South Dakota / 288

Bibliography / 289

Index / 299

Tables and Illustrations

Tables

- 3.1 Paul Tschetter Family Tree / 28
- 3.2 Maria Walter Tschetter Family Tree / 39
- 8.1 Ministers Ordained by Paul Tschetter, 1884–1918 /
- 10.1 Hutterian Surnames: Sioux Falls (South Dakota) Telephone Directory, 2007 / 214
- 11.1 Prairieleut Hutterite Congregations in North America / 220
- 11.2 Prairieleut congregations of the Krimmer Mennonite Brethren Conference / 222

Maps

- 2.1 Hutterite Settlements in Europe, 1528–1879 / 21
- 5.1 Great Plains Railroad Lines and Laid Track, 1874 / 96
- 6.1 Paul and Maria Tschetter Extended Family Land Claims and Residential Plan / 116
- 7.1 Hutterite Colonies, 2009 / 140

Figures

- 2.1 Heinrich Bartosik, "Velke Levare Mill" painting, 1935 / 16
- 3.1 Paul Tschetter, 1873 / 38
- 4.1 Lohrentz Tschetter, 1873 / 52
- 4.2 Paul Tschetter's Diary / 55
- 4.3 First page of Paul Tschetter's Diary, 1873 / 56
- 4.4 Paul Tschetter Diary, Handwriting Sample / 58
- 4.5 John F. Funk / 65
- 4.6 Chris Janzen, "Ulysses S. Grant and the Hutterites," painting, 2004 / 81
- 5.1 Bon Homme Colony, 1875 / 102

6.1   United States General Land Office Deed with Paul Tschetter's Signature, April 5, 1877 / 118
6.2   Loading Manure with a Pitchfork / 120
6.3   Emil Tschetter (Paul Tschetter's Grandson) with a Team of Horses / 122
6.4   Jacob W. and Susanna Tschetter Farm House / 125
6.5   Tschetter School District Elementary School Building / 129
8.1   Neu Hutterthaler Church Original Building, circa 1890 / 147
8.2   Paul Tschetter's First Sermon Book / 161
8.3   Paul Tschetter's First Sermon Book, title page / 162
8.4   Jacob W. Tschetter and Susanna Decker Wedding Photograph, 1899 / 167
8.5   Traditional Shawl worn by Katherina Wollman Decker / 168
9.1   The Salem Krimmer Mennonite Brethren Church, 1917 / 177
10.1   Paul and Susanna Tschetter Decker and Family / 205
10.2   "Big Paul" Tschetter / 206
10.3   Joshua M. and Maria Tschetter Hofer / 207
10.4   Jacob W. and Susanna Decker Tschetter Family / 208
10.5   Joseph W. Tschetter / 209
10.6   North Carolina KMB Mission Church, 1919 / 210
10.7   Andrew A. and Barbara Tschetter Stahl / 211
10.8   Christian and Justina Tschetter Hofman Family / 212
10.9   David W. and Anna Glanzer Tschetter Family / 213
10.10   Raditschewa village, Ukraine, 2005 / 216
10.11   Hutterite-constructed Residence, Johannesruh Village Site, Ukraine, 2005 / 217
11.1   Christian and Justina Hofman House where Paul Tschetter was Living at the Time of his Death / 219

Acknowledgments

THIS BOOK COULD NOT HAVE BEEN WRITTEN WITHOUT THE AS-
SISTANCE and contributions of many people. South Dakota State University administrator, Wesley Tschetter, and Hutterite-Mennonite Centennial Committee president, Norman Hofer, have been especially helpful in providing original documents related to the Paul and Maria Tschetter family.

Wesley Tschetter provided a treasure trove of unpublished, often handwritten, manuscripts from his private collection. He also assisted in locating many of the photographs included in the book. Norman Hofer offered original and secondary source materials, including taped interviews with older Hutterians. Non-communal Hutterite historian Arnold M. Hofer (1916–2005), provided the original motivation for working on this biography while California genealogist Alan Peters helped trace the various Tschetter family lines. Colorado writer, Nancy Peterson gave the author handwritten notes from conversations with Paul Tschetter's grandson, Paul G. Tschetter (1907–1998), while, before his death, Paul G. talked openly about his grandfather in private conversations with the author. California State University geographer Stuart McFeeters created the maps published in the book.

Many communal Hutterites, and especially Forest River Colony German Teacher, Tony Waldner, were helpful in filling in gaps in the Tschetter family biographical record. South Dakota folklorist, Reuben Goertz (1918–1992) entertained the author with controversial stories on South Dakota Hutterian topics that provided important contextual understandings. Goertz also gave the author access to his private collection of hundreds of books and documents that are now in the possession of the Center for Western Studies, Augustana College, Sioux Falls, South Dakota.

Mennonite archivist Dennis Stoesz as well provided invaluable background information that guided the author through relevant files at the Archives of the Mennonite Church, Goshen, Indiana. Kevin

Enns Rempel provided similar assistance at the Mennonite Brethren Historical Library and Archives, Fresno, California. Thanks as well to Tim Waltner, publisher of the Freeman *Courier* for granting access to relevant newspaper records and to Jeremy Waltner for his photographs of the Paul Tschetter diary.

Special recognition is also extended to Pine Hill Press and its publisher, Joe Mierau, as well as his predecessors, who in the past century supported the publication of dozens of books dealing with Hutterite-related topics and issues. A quick glance at this book's footnotes and bibliography make it clear that the publications of Pine Hill Press were essential to the completion of this work.

Special thanks as well to John Wipf, who has provided strong support for this project, as well as Wipf & Stock editor, K. C. Hanson, typesetter Patrick Harrison, and graphic artist Kristen Bareman.

All Bible references in this book are taken from the *New Jerusalem Bible* (New York: Doubleday, 1998).

Abbreviations

AMC	Archives of the Mennonite Church, Goshen, Indiana
CHB I	*The Chronicle of the Hutterian Brethren I*
CHB II	*The Chronicle of the Hutterian Brethren II*
GRANDMA	Genealogical Registry and Database of Mennonite Ancestry
HHMA	Heritage Hall Museum and Archives, Freeman, South Dakota
HMCC	Hutterite Mennonite Centennial Committee
KMB	Krimmer Mennonite Brethren
MennEncy	*Mennonite Encyclopedia*
MennLife	*Mennonite Life*
MQR	*Mennonite Quarterly Review*
NHCRB	"The Neu Hutterthaler Church Record Book." Edited by David P. Gross and Arnold M. Hofer
NJB	New Jerusalem Bible
WTC	Wesley Tschetter Collection, Brookings, South Dakota

Aerial photograph of the Paul Tschetter homestead near Bridgewater, South Dakota, circa 1950. The large barn, built by Tschetter, is the only original building pictured and this is the only known photograph of a Paul Tschetter-constructed building. Photograph courtesy of Norma Jean Tschetter Parlier.

1

Introduction

Paul Tschetter, the Hutterite Joshua

The pure word of God,
We shall share and teach,
With all sincerity and diligence,
So it goes into the heart.[1]

—Paul Tschetter, 1873

BEGINNING IN THE AUTUMN OF 1874 AND CONTINUING FOR THE NEXT five years, 1267 Hutterites emigrated from the Russian Empire to the southeastern corner of Dakota Territory. Many purchased government land along the James River, the longest non-navigable waterway in the United States, as it wound its way south and east to the much larger Missouri River, in what is now Hutchinson County.

The Hutterites left their homes in the fertile farmland of the Ukrainian steppes due to Russian Government policies decreed by Tsar Alexander I in 1870. These new laws threatened religious freedoms and took away a number of political and educational rights. In response the Hutterites looked for a more pleasant habitation and eventually chose the North American mid-section as their destination. Here they sought to make a new start, thousands of miles away from the Eastern European homelands they knew so well, in a place half-way across the world.

When they arrived in the Dakotas the Hutterites divided into two main factions. The first group, comprising about 425 people, formed three colonies that practiced community of goods, following historic Hutterite practice. These are the Hutterites who are most well-known today. In 2009, their 49,000 descendents live in 480 North American communal colonies.

---

1. Paul Tschetter, hymn #2, stanza four, 1873. HHMA.

The remaining Hutterite immigrants, about 842 people, decided to live more individualistically on private farms, the way that most Russian Hutterites had lived since 1819, when communal life was discontinued at Raditschewa, Ukraine. In North America the noncommunal group observed traditional Hutterian religious and cultural practices but they did not live in communal villages. Today this larger Hutterite group is not well known but in the late nineteenth century it was led by the pioneer pastor Paul Tschetter, the subject of this book.

During the late nineteenth and early twentieth centuries, Paul Tschetter was the most influential noncommunal Hutterite leader in the United States. He was the leading Hutterite promoter of emigration from Ukraine to the United States and like Joshua in the Exodus account, Tschetter was one of twelve delegates who were sent to "spy out" the North American continent for possible Hutterian settlement. Like Joshua, Tschetter returned from his exploratory journey with a positive report and less than two years later he led his people into the "promised land."

In the summer of 1873, members of the Russian Hutterite community were talking seriously about re-settlement. Hearing that a delegation of ten Russian Mennonites had been commissioned to investigate agricultural and political conditions in North America, Paul Tschetter and his fifty-four year-old uncle Lohrentz joined the group bringing the Anabaptist delegation to a total of twelve.

Toward the end of that four-month long expedition the Tschetters, along with Mennonite minister Tobias Unruh, held a face-to-face meeting with President Ulysses S. Grant at his summer home on Long Island. Here Paul Tschetter presented a handwritten request for religious and social privileges, including the right to be exempted from military service. Grant's response was non-committal, but the meeting established a personal relationship that advocates of immigration used on their return to convince members to leave their homes in Eastern Europe half way across the world.

Paul Tschetter's 1873 travel diary includes insightful comments on European and American life in the 1870s as well as a window into the heart and mind of a late nineteenth-century Hutterite leader. An English translation of the diary is included in Appendix A. Although the diary was published in the 1930s, twelve original hymns interspersed within the journal were not included. Two of the Tschetter hymns have been translated and are published in this book.[22] Short sections of many of the remaining hymns are also included as well as evaluated. Like the diary narrative, the songs provide important insights into the Hutterite mindset of the time.

One of the Tschetter hymns, for example, is a theological reflection on the meaning of the destructive Chicago Fire of 1871. The hymn was written by a distraught Tschetter while he was sitting in a Chicago hotel room and it includes pointed assessments of nineteenth-century urban life. Tschetter viewed the devastating fire as God's judgment on human sin and immorality in what he continued to view as a very corrupt city.

Paul Tschetter's meeting with President Grant is especially striking. It shows the powerful influence of financier Jay Cooke and the Northern Pacific Railroad (Cooke arranged the meeting with Grant). It also reveals an Eastern European Anabaptist *modus operandi* that recognized the importance of personal meetings with important government officials. This was the reason for unsuccessful Hutterite attempts (in 1872) to see the Russian Tsar and his advisors in St. Petersburg. That a relatively uneducated German-speaking minister with pacifist inclinations might find anything in common with the cigar-smoking Civil War general is difficult to comprehend. But Grant impressed the Tschetters with his casual appearance, informality and general openness. There was little pomp and circumstance and if this meeting was anything like the one Mennonites Cornelius and Peter Jansen held with Grant earlier that same summer, the general regaled them with stories about growing up on a farm to which they could easily relate.

On his return to Ukraine in August 1873, Tschetter actively promoted emigration to the west. He successfully convinced nearly the entire Hutterite population (communal and noncommunal) to leave Ukraine. Tschetter was convinced that this was God's will for his people. In the new Dakota Territory homeland Tschetter provided leadership for the noncommunal Hutterite churches established there. He gave spiritual and organizational direction from the time of his arrival in 1875 until his death in 1919. Tschetter led worship services, guided theological debates, gave advice and counsel to members, and administered church discipline.

---

2. All twelve hymns will be published (in German and English) in a forthcoming collection of Paul Tschetter's written works.

In the late nineteenth century Tschetter also found time to reflect once again on why the Hutterites had left Ukraine in the 1870s, leaving a lengthy statement, "Why We Had to Leave Russia," that he placed inside the Neu Hutterthaler Church record book. A translation of this statement and other narrative sections of the Neu Hutterthaler record book are published in Appendix B.

Paul Tschetter was committed to traditional Hutterite theological, ecclesial, and cultural beliefs and practices. In Dakota, he led a tightly-knit ethno-religious society with a strong sense of purpose and destiny. Hutterite traditions had developed over the course of 350 years as the often-persecuted group established residence in different parts of Eastern Europe. These conventions, along with a history of harassment, gave members a strong sense of collective identity. Sacred sermons, martyr hymns, and a distinctive dialect were all important to the retention of this social specificity and Paul Tschetter was deeply committed to keeping everything as it was. An important question was whether these traditions could be maintained for long, however, in a very different social and political environment.

In Dakota Territory, the communal Hutterites established three colonies: one on the Missouri River west of Yankton, the other two overlooking the James River in Hutchinson County. Colony members believed that true Christians should live communally and they actively sought converts among their noncommunal friends and relatives.

While the communitarians were establishing colonies, members of Tschetter's larger noncommunal Hutterite group homesteaded on private land and organized their own churches and house congregations. In North America they accepted the name *Prairieleut* (Prairie People) since, unlike the communalists, most of them purchased land on the open prairie instead of constructing settlements along rivers or creeks. Later generations of noncommunal Hutterites called themselves "Hutters" to provide additional differentiation.

Paul Tschetter served as the ordained elder of the Neu Hutterthaler Prairieleut Church, but he was also recognized informally as a kind of "bishop" over all of the noncommunal Hutterite congregations. In Dakota his primary goal was to maintain the teachings and practices of the Hutterite ancestors. This was not an easy undertaking.

On one side Tschetter was confronted by the colonies where hundreds of Hutterites lived communally, constructing a way of life that was attractive not only for theological and historical reasons but for reasons of economic and social security. Paul Tschetter faced the constant lure of a Christian community that provided collective material support and strong spiritual resources for pioneers struggling to make a living on an undeveloped frontier and in the midst of a major economic depression (the Panic of 1873). At the same time some communalists were enticed by the individual freedom of life on the prairies. Dozens of Hutterian individuals and families thus moved back and forth across the communal/noncommunal divide, some joining one of the colonies; others choosing a more individualistic life on the prairies.

During the first few decades in the United States, visits to the colonies were common since noncommunal Hutterites had many friends and relatives who lived there. This led to dating relationships and many marriages across the communal/noncommunal divide, with accompanying residential and ecclesiastical implications. Communal/noncommunal contacts also led to many business contacts and relationships. The Wolf Creek and Old Elmspring Hutterite colonies, for example, built flour mills where many Prairieleut took their grain to be ground after the fall harvest. Many noncommunal Hutterites purchased shoes from colony shoemakers.

Paul Tschetter was not a communalist, but he visited the colonies often and he held communal Hutterites in high regard. Colony Hutterites might question the Prairieleut lack of *Gelassenheit*: yielding one's entire life and property to God. But early on there was little difference between the two groups theologically or culturally. Church services were identical, all Hutterites spoke the Austrian Hutterisch dialect and members dressed in the same plain garb. Communal Hutterites in turn admired the deep religious commitment of Paul Tschetter. He was held in such high regard that if Tschetter had decided to start his own communal faction he would likely have had little difficulty attracting a large number of followers.

What Paul Tschetter did not anticipate was that another religious group, the Krimmer Mennonite Brethren (KMB), would present a second attractive alternative for members of the noncommunal Hutterite community. Preaching a "born-again" Christianity that emphasized the "assurance of salvation" this highly evangelistic group attracted hundreds of members from the noncommunal Hutterite churches in the late nineteenth and early twentieth centuries. Tschetter was impressed with the spiritual vitality of the KMBs and the group's commitment to high moral standards but he believed strongly in the sacred power of the traditional Hutterite sermons and did not appreciate what he thought were overly-emotional and individualistic expressions of the Christian faith. Tschetter also did not like KMB prohibitions on alcohol use and the denomination's openness to musical instruments, informal and emotional worship services, and more modern dress.

Paul Tschetter thus found himself positioned between two appealing religious alternatives; communal Anabaptism in the Hutterite colonies and evangelical Anabaptism in the KMB congregations. But he did not sway to either side, instead taking a middle path; the path of traditional yet noncommunal Hutterianism with a community-based, mediational approach to God and continued adherence to conservative worship, dress and lifestyle. Tschetter felt that his charge was to hold things together in the middle, in the independent noncommunal Hutterite churches, even though outward signs confirming an elect spiritual state were more discernible in the colonies (institutionally) and in the KMB congregations (emotionally).

People that were struggling to make a living on unplowed, virgin land, with unpredictable climate and novel social patterns, wanted economic and spiritual protection. Paul Tschetter asked members of the Prairieleut congregations to find security in Hutterian traditions without giving up private property or turning their backs on the cultural, ecclesial and theological past.

For this difficult task Paul Tschetter brought forth the charismatic and spiritual power of his personality and all of the faith that he could muster. Although Tschetter was willing to take risks if religious principle dictated, he was not a natural innovator. Tschetter was most comfortable defending things as they were. But in response to attacks from the right (the KMBs) and the left (the colonies), Tschetter was often forced to find creative ways to promote a traditional way of living that did not incorporate community of goods yet emphasized the importance of prayer and holy living.

Tschetter had many problems to contend with. In addition to communal and evangelical religious alternatives, the powerful pull of American life, with its democratic and egalitarian traditions, its vibrant spirit of individualism and patriotism, enticed many members to subvert church rules and regulations and to question historic theological positions. Some Hutterians left the Anabaptist fold altogether.

The North American social, economic and political situation was highly tenuous. Paul Tschetter responded by advising young males against military service, excommunicating members who smoked tobacco or purchased musical instruments and admonishing young women to cover their heads. As Tschetter took these increasingly unpopular positions he found more and more people leaving the Prairieleut churches.

Paul Tschetter arrived in Dakota Territory in the spring of 1875. He homesteaded on land near the town of Bridgewater and for most of the next forty-one years he lived in a house that he built himself. Throughout his ministry Tschetter was unsalaried and had to hold down a full-time job to provide necessary economic support. Paul and Maria Tschetter and their children planted wheat, oats and barley and always maintained a large garden. Tschetter relied heavily on Maria, who took on the primary responsibility for nurturing their many children as well as performing many domestic and farm-related functions.

In addition to farming Tschetter delivered sermons on Sunday mornings, visited parishioners in their homes on Saturday evenings and Sunday afternoons, and provided counsel to those who visited him at his home. Tschetter made decisions about church policy and church discipline and at the Neu Hutterthaler congregation he also served as church custodian. For fulfilling all of these obligations Tschetter was deeply respected. Even during the final four years of his life (from 1915 to 1919) when Tschetter was living in the home of his now-KMB daughter, Justina, Neu Hutterthaler church members often dropped by to ask his advice on important matters.

What follows is the story of one man's attempt to maintain historic but noncommunal Hutterite understandings amidst the constantly changing social and religious climate of the American frontier. This Hutterite Joshua led his people into a chosen exile across the Atlantic Ocean to a new promised land. But once there it was hard to convince church members to keep their eyes away from the varied forms of spiritual expression that awaited them. Ultimately non-Hutterite and even non-Anabaptist churches attracted many of Tschetter's members in a continually flowing stream that ultimately affected all but one of his sons and daughters.

Paul Tschetter did not waver, however, holding the line on everything from opposing gun ownership to the American involvement in World War I. As a result, at the time of his death six large churches, as well as a number of house congregations, continued to observe historic yet noncommunal Hutterite practices. This important explorer and pioneer preacher demonstrated in his own life, in the life of his immediate family and in the life of the entire Prairieleut community, how difficult it is for any ethnic or religious group to establish the same kind of society with the same belief patterns in the United States as in the community it left behind. The story of Tschetter's battle against assimilation in its many forms is the focus of this book.

2

The Hutterites

> We are very much like the Dakota Sioux. It is not for nothing that we have settled in their land, land that was taken away by other whites. Like the Sioux, we strive not for self-expression or self-interest... All is one and one is all.[1]
>
> —from Frederick Manfred, *Sons of Adam*, 1983

THE HUTTERITES WERE ESTABLISHED AS A COMMUNAL CHRISTIAN SOCIETY in the 1520s as part of the Anabaptist movement in Austria and southern Germany. Like most Protestants, Anabaptists recognized the Bible as the Word of God and emphasized salvation by faith and a direct relationship with God.[2] They criticized what they viewed as unbiblical teachings and practices in the Roman Catholic Church, reducing the sacraments from seven to two (baptism and the Lord's Supper) and refusing to recognize the ecclesiastical authority of the Pope.

But unlike other Protestant groups most Anabaptists preached a code of love and non-resistance following the teachings and example of Jesus. The Anabaptists believed literally in the concept of the "priesthood of all believers" and they designed a democratic, congregational church structure. Anabaptists also introduced a Christological approach to biblical interpretation that gave prominence to the New Testament and especially to the Gospels. They instituted rigid ethical requirements and, following the New Testament Book of James, they believed that faith without works is a dead faith. Anabaptists also taught that the

---

1. Manfred, *Sons of Adam*, 302.

2. Important introductory works on Anabaptist history and thought include the following: C. Snyder, *Anabaptist History and Theology*; Dyck, *An Introduction to Mennonite History*; and J. Denny Weaver, *Becoming Anabaptist*.

church and the state should be separate. As a result they were viewed as political dissenters and social revolutionaries.

The 1520s-era radicals called themselves "Brethren in Christ" or simply "Christians." Their enemies called them "Anabaptists" ("re-baptizers" in Greek) to signify the group's opposition to infant baptism, using the same designation given to heretical Donatist Christians in the fourth century. Anabaptists did not recognize child baptism and they "re-baptized" adherents upon their confession of faith. This was a serious offense in all sixteenth-century Catholic and Protestant jurisdictions. Believer's baptism contradicted the orthodox teaching on original sin and threatened the social order since citizens could theoretically decide not to be baptized and might separate themselves from the morality-instilling influence of the church. Anabaptists also believed in a Lord's Supper that was purely symbolic. Throughout Europe "Anabaptism" was a crime punishable by lengthy imprisonment or death.

Some Anabaptists went further by establishing Christian communes. The communitarian expression of Christianity had deep historical roots, beginning with the Early Church in Jerusalem and continuing with Roman Catholic and Eastern Orthodox monastic communities for the next 1500 years. Communal Anabaptists believed that Jesus and his disciples, as well as the earliest Christians, all lived communally and that a life without private property was inspired and ordained by the Holy Spirit on the Day of Pentecost as described in the Book of Acts.

Communal Anabaptists believed that they were helping to revive God's original vision for humanity; the classless paradise that was originally given to Adam and Eve, the way of life that God was re-creating for the elect in heaven. To some extent sixteenth-century Roman Catholics understood this way of thinking recognizing the more spiritual character of those who lived communally as clerics in separation from the world. Twenty-first-century priests and nuns continue to live communally and to give primary attention to God and the work of the church. Along with the practice of celibacy, community of goods ensures that financial wealth does not accumulate within a church leader's nuclear or extended family. Communal Anabaptists, however, believed that all Christians should live without private property—not only those who served in ministerial offices.

As a purely economic system, Christian communism was attractive to many destitute peasants and social revolutionaries in the early 1500s.

As Leonard Gross writes, "The Hutterian way was a way to eternal salvation, but also a way out of material poverty for many."[3] For this reason, Marxist philosopher Friedrich Engels later described the Anabaptists as proto-communists.[4] But sixteenth-century communitarians were committed to the Christian faith and many people joined Anabaptist communes in specific anticipation of the end of the world, which they believed was prophesied in the Books of Daniel and Revelation.[5]

In the 1500s, community of goods as a biblically-based social and economic system attracted many people but few communes lasted more than a few years. The Hutterites were the only communal sixteenth-century Anabaptist group that established stable, long-lived colonies.[6] They did this by institutionalizing organizational structures founded upon a singular interpretation of the theological concept of *Gelassenheit*: the subjugation of the individual to God not only personally and directly but *through* the community of believers.[7] As Leonard Gross describes it, Christian salvation was transformed into a total "way of life."[8]

The Hutterites took their name from an Austrian hat maker (*Hutter*) and one-time gun-carrying Peasants War religious and political activist named Jacob Hutter. In 1535, now a pacifist, Hutter became the leader of a group of communal Anabaptist refugees who had established a settlement near Austerlitz, Moravia. Once described as a man who donned a "trimmed beard" and wore "a tanned leather coat," Hutter had come to believe that true Christianity could only be expressed through community of goods.[9] As he wrote in a letter to Moravian authorities, "He [God] led us together to serve Him in unity and to show that God himself is one and undivided."[10]

---

3. L. Gross, *Golden Years*, 48.

4. Krieger, ed., *The German Revolution*.

5. Von Schlachta, "'Searching through the Nations,'" 30–31.

6. Important sources for the early Hutterian movement include the following: Stayer, *The German Peasant's War*; Packull, *Hutterite Beginnings*; L. Gross, *Golden Years*; and Hutterian Brethren, eds., *CHB I*; and Hutterian Brethren, eds., *CHB II*. Important sources for Hutterite religious and cultural traditions are: Hostetler, *Hutterite Society*; Hostetler and Huntington, *Hutterites in North America*; and Kraybill and Bowman, *On the Backroad to Heaven*.

7. Robert Friedmann, *Hutterite Studies*.

8. L. Gross, *Golden Years*, 61.

9. Packull, *Hutterite Beginnings*, 242.

10. Hutter, *Brotherly Faithfulness*, 171.

Hutter's successors continued to emphasize that true Christians must live without private property. Peter Riedemann emphasized this teaching in the 1540s. His *Account of Our Religion, Doctrine and Faith* became the Hutterite confession of faith.[11] The communitarian position was supported by Hutterite leader Peter Walpot in the 1560s and 1570s and by Andreas Ehrenpreis in the following century.[12] In his writings, Walpot contrasted the separated non-worldly life of the Christian commune with the "saved" lives of those spared by God in Noah's ark.[13] Hutterites were unapologetic about their viewpoints. A Hutterite sermon from the seventeenth century describes noncommunal "Christians" disdainfully in the following manner:

> As soon as the pigs are brought home from the field and driven to the trough [i.e. as soon as most church members leave a worship service and go back to their private homes] one hears and sees how they grunt, whine and scuffle, step into the trough, slobber and squeal so that others dare not approach ... One cannot see any more evidence of rebirth in them than in a dog.[14]

Jacob Hutter himself was burned at the stake in 1536 after government officials first tortured him by pouring brandy into his wounds.[15]

The Hutterites were not well-loved by religious or political leaders and they suffered intermittent persecution and harassment into the 1550s. As Jacob Hutter explained, "Because we serve Him, do His will, keep His commandments, and leave behind all sin and evil, we are persecuted and despised by the whole world and robbed of our goods."[16] But by mid-century the Hutterites were able to find somewhat secure places of refuge in Moravia, where they had established their first communal villages in the 1520s, and in Slovakia, where they first formed a community in 1546. In both regions members of the landed nobility sought industrious farmers, craftsmen, educators and physicians. At

---

11. Riedeman, *Confession of Faith*. The most recent translation of Peter Riedemann's confession of faith is Friesen, ed., *Peter Riedemann's Hutterite Confession of Faith*.

12. Von Schlachta, "'Searching through the Nations,'" 27–49.

13. Robert Friedmann, ed., "Michael Waldner's *The Reestablishment of Communal Life among the Hutterites in Russia*," 150.

14. Hans Friedrich Kuentsche, in J. Anderson, "The Pentecost Preaching of Acts 2," 280–81.

15. Packull, *Hutterite Beginnings*, 255

16. Jacob Hutter, *Brotherly Faithfullness*.

least temporarily they granted Hutterites the freedom to practice their unique religious beliefs with little interference.

During the sixteenth-century Hutterites were some of the most active and successful evangelists in the Anabaptist movement and missionaries were sent across the center of the European continent. Hutterites did not, however, attract many members from among their Moravian and Slovakian neighbors. Most converts came from the German states, Switzerland and Austria. This softened the cultural impact of residence in Eastern Europe and caused the Hutterites to retain a strong south German ethnic and linguistic identity. Much of the mission-minded intensity of the early Hutterites was based on End Times speculation duplicating the eschatology of South German Anabaptists like Hans Hut, many of whose followers joined the Hutterites.[17]

In 1538 Hutterite Caspar Braitmichael began to record the history of the Hutterite people by placing it in the context of general church history. This account is known as the *Chronicle of the Hutterian Brethren*.[18] Over the years it became a living document that was updated regularly by different writers within the community. For historians the Chronicle is an invaluable original source. For Hutterites it ensures a sense of historical identity across the centuries. It includes a record of events, year by year, with letters from missionaries, theological commentary and a variety of original source materials. Eventually published in two large volumes the Chronicle carries Hutterite history through 1873, providing important first and second-hand accounts of historical events.

From 1563–1578 the Hutterites experienced a "golden period" when they prospered economically and experienced little harassment. This was the age of the largest and most successful evangelistic efforts in various parts of German-speaking Europe as well as northern Italy. During this time the Hutterite population grew to as many as 40,000 people with members living in more than seventy communes in Moravia and Slovakia.

In addition to farming the Hutterites developed a number of successful and highly regulated industries that included pottery and cutlery. Hutterite pottery in particular was known for its quality, artistic simplicity and practicality. Its production followed the Italian *faience* tradition brought into the community by expert artists and craftsmen.

17. Snyder, *Anabaptist History and Theology*.
18. *CHB I* and *CHB II*.

Persons from a variety of professional backgrounds joined the Hutterite villages providing a number of important human resources and abilities. There were coppersmiths, weavers, wagon makers, clockmakers and tanners. An apprenticeship system was organized and the Hutterites became models of economic success. Members of the Moravian nobility consulted Hutterite physicians.

The Hutterites also developed a model educational system that included the first "kindergarten," or what was more like a "pre-school." Peter Walpot's "School Regulations," developed in 1578, were progressive for the time period and include a detailed discussion of curriculum and pedagogy. Walpot implores teachers to "not always go to the rod" when discipline is needed.[19]

The years of Hutterite prosperity continued into the seventeenth-century but came to a halt during the Thirty Years War (1618–1648) when Protestant and Catholic armed forces moved back and forth through Moravia and Slovakia, ransacking the Hutterite communities almost at will. The Thirty Years War wreaked havoc on the Moravian communes, leading to a Hutterian diaspora that was accompanied by the death of hundreds of members. Gertrude Huntington notes, "Famine gripped the lands, and the large colony storehouses and barns of the non-resistant Hutterites were plundered and hoarded."[20] Catholic-Protestant tensions also led to increased religious intolerance. In 1622 the Catholic leaders of the Holy Roman Empire demanded that all Anabaptists (in twenty-four separate communities) leave Moravia.[21]

Now Hutterites found themselves scattered all over Europe and many suffered continuous harassment in their new places of residence. Hundreds of members rejoined one of the state churches, usually Roman Catholic. Others moved to Dutch/Low German Mennonite communities in Prussia, where, according to genealogist Alan Peters, they introduced surnames with the suffixes "er" and "el," (for example, "Penner" and "Harder").[22] Other Hutterites moved to one of the Slovakian Hutterite villages, where conditions were better, or to Transylvania,

---

19. Maendel, "Historical Guidelines."
20. Huntington, "Hutterite Faith and Community," 329.
21. Penner, *Die Ost und Westpreussischen Mennoniten*, 176.
22. A. Peters, "Unraveling the Origins," 3–4. Peters suggests that the Hutterite surname "Heyn," for example, may have been transformed into the Mennonite surname "Hein."

where a Hutterite community was established at Alwinz in 1621. At one time 3000 Hutterites were in residence at the Sabatisch (Slovakia) community.

As a result of the war and ensuing economic and social disorder, the Hutterites gave up communal life in Slovakia in 1685, and in Alwinz, Transylvania, five years later. The Hutterites maintained other religious and cultural traditions, but they continued to decrease in size due to unrelenting religious persecution (especially in Slovakia) and significant economic problems. During the leadership of Elder Andreas Ehrenpreis (1639–1662), hundreds of sermons, the Hutterite *Lehren*, were composed to encourage those that remained to stay faithful and not to forget the central tenets of the faith.[23] The *Lehren* are exegetical reflections on lengthy Bible texts. They are considered to be specially inspired by the Holy Spirit, and eventually they were the only sermons preached (i.e. read) in Hutterite church services. This continues to be the case in Hutterite colonies in the 2000s.

Also important to Hutterites was a collection of hymns or *Lieder* that were sung at church services and on other social occasions. Of the 347 songs in what became the largest Hutterite songbook (*Die Lieder der Hutterischen Bruder*)[24] one-eighth were written by early leader Peter Riedemann. There are also songs by noncommunal Anabaptist leaders Felix Manz, Balthasar Hubmaier, and Hans Hut. The *Lieder* are sung according to dozens of different melodies, many of which are fifteenth- and sixteenth-century German folk tunes and Lutheran chorales.[25] Forty of the original melodies are sung by Hutterites in the 2000s. The *Lieder* remind Hutterites of the steadfastness with which persecuted ancestors remained true to the faith. Many also focus on Jesus' death and resurrection and the Day of Pentecost.[26]

An infusion of new spiritual vitality occurred in 1767 when communal life was re-established at Kreuz (Transylvania) with the encouragement of a small number of ex-Lutheran converts who had fled to Transylvania from the Carinthian province of Austria. These people, with surnames like "Kleinsasser," "Waldner," "Glanzer," and "Hofer," accepted the revolutionary communal mandate after reading or hearing

---

23. J. Anderson, "The Pentecost Preaching of Acts 2."
24. Hutterian Brethren, eds., *Die Lieder*.
25. H. Martens, *Hutterite Songs*, 291–95. Interview, November 2005.
26. Ibid., 296.

Figure 2.1 Heinrich Bartosik, "Velke Levare Mill," painting, 1935. Photograph courtesy of Henry Bartosik.

it in Hutterite sermons. Without the Carinthians communal life may have died as a central Hutterite concept. By this time there were few Hutterites alive who had any personal experience of communal life.

This communitarian development corresponded, however, with a renewed effort on the part of the Roman Catholic Church to convert all Protestants. With the exception of sixty-seven persons, forty-eight of whom were new Carinthian members, all of the remaining Hutterites in Slovakia and Transylvania recanted and joined the Catholic Church. Interestingly, the Hutterite Catholics continued to maintain a separate cultural identity into the twentieth century as a German-speaking minority group called *Habaner*. In this group the surname "Tschetter" was carried forward into the twentieth century.[27] A 1935 painting of a Hutterite-constructed mill in the Habaner village of Velke Levare (formerly Gross Schutzen) appears below. The painter, Heinrich Bartosik,

---

27. Henry Bartosik, correspondence, January 2005. Bartosik is the son of Heinrich Bartosik who in 1934 produced the painting of the grist mill shown in Figure 2.1. In March 2005 Bartosik donated the painting to a museum in Malackky, Slovaka, which holds a large Hutterite archival collection. The painting appears on the cover of the 2005 issue of *Communal Societies*, the biannual publication of the Communal Studies Association.

said that growing up he had many acquaintances with the last name "Tschetter."[28]

The Hutterites were originally comprised of a number of Central European ethnic groups, presenting a sometimes difficult organizational challenge with a plethora of languages and cultural traditions. But over the years their unique religious beliefs caused commune residents to develop a peculiar sense of Hutterite people-hood. As evangelistic efforts ended in the seventeenth century, the Hutterites gradually became a distinctive ethnic group as they married almost exclusively within what was a very small religious society. By the late nineteenth century only twenty Hutterite surnames were found in the membership: a mix of "Old Hutterite," Carinthian, and Mennonite appellations. The Hutterites indeed are one of the only new ethnic groups to emerge (in a genetic and cultural sense) during the past five hundred years and they may therefore be compared to ethno-religious groups such as Orthodox Jews and Molokan Christians.[29]

In 1767 those few Hutterites who refused to recant and who were committed to communal Christianity fled to Wallachia in present-day Romania, where they lived for three years until March 27, 1770, when Turkish armies moved into the area. The Hutterite refugee group included a man named Lohrentz Tschetter. Lohrentz was Paul Tschetter's great-grandfather.

In later years Paul's parents and grandparents likely told many stories about the difficult days on the run when Lohrentz Tshetter and others had to forage for food, at times eating the bark of trees and seeking shelter in the forest. Fortunately, in 1770, a Russian nobleman, Count Rumiantsev invited the Hutterites to establish a communal village on his estate in Ukraine. He also granted the Hutterites a number of privileges, including religious freedom, exemption from military service, and the authority to manufacture goods for public sale.[30] This site, called Wishenka ("sour cherry" in Ukrainian), was located 150 miles northeast of Kiev on the Desna River. One hundred and twenty-three Hutterites established community of goods there, but Count Rumiantsev died in

---

28. Henry Bartosik, correspondence, June 2006.

29. The best work on the Molokans continues to be P. Young, *Pilgrims of Russia-Town*.

30. Waltner, ed., *Banished for Faith*, 64. Part of this book includes Waltner's translation of the second volume of the Hutterite Chronicle.

1802 and his heirs tried to turn the Hutterites into serfs with few remaining privileges.³¹

In 1802, a Hutterite appeal to the Russian Government led to an offer of crown land about sixteen miles north of Wishenka, also along the Desna River. Once again Hutterites were given special privileges. Now 202 members strong, the Hutterites relocated to village called Raditschewa, where they farmed the land and re-established a number of crafts industries, producing pottery, clocks, hats, cabinets and fine linen.³² The Hutterites also built two schoolhouses for different age groups and they operated two distilleries, which produced 61,500 liters of spirits annually.³³

There were continuous economic problems at Raditschewa, however, due to insufficient farmland for the number of people living there. A resulting focus on industrial production led to business relationships with non-Hutterites and the development of a more capitalistic mindset among many managers and foremen. A few of the industries became so large that, for the first time in Hutterite history, non-Hutterites (in this case Ukrainian peasants) were hired to provide a sufficient labor force.³⁴

Industrial development and insufficient farmland at Raditschewa led to a variety of ideological and personal conflicts. Eventually there was also division of opinion on the necessity of community of goods. Elder Johannes Waldner stood on the communitarian side of this debate with his assistant minister, Jacob Walter, on the noncommunal side. In 1818, a group of 143 disaffected Walter supporters left the community completely, moving temporarily to the Chortitza Mennonite settlement, 558 miles south. This was the first time that a group of Hutterites had decided to give up communal life for reasons unrelated to religious persecution.

Unfortunately for those that remained, a terrible fire destroyed most of the Raditschewa buildings in the following year (1819). The fire started when "a hot hoop of a newly constructed wooden barrel" contacted a "thatched roof overhanging above a door frame" while the barrel was rolled out of the shop,³⁵ On return visits in 2003 and 2005,

31. Hostetler, *Hutterite Society*, 116.
32. *CHB II*, 606.
33. Ibid., 610.
34. Waltner, ed., *Banished for Faith*, 102.
35. W. Tschetter, "Reflections on the Life of Paul Tschetter," 9. WTC.

Wesley Tschetter (a great-grandson of Paul Tschetter) discovered that the 1819 fire is still part of the institutional memory of area residents. It is mentioned in the village's history book that was published in 1999.[36]

The economic and social disruption caused by the Raditschewa fire led the Johannes Waldner group to give up communal life as well. This unexpected development brought members of the noncommunal Walter faction back from south Ukraine and the two groups temporarily formed a unified church. After all material possessions were equitably divided, members lived as individual families with only the orchards, woods, cellars (where food was preserved), and a few buildings held communally. Nearly destitute in an economic sense, the Hutterites had to start all over again.

There were thus two periods in Hutterite history when the group did not live communally: from 1690–1767, due to religious and political persecution, and from 1819 until 1859, for economic and ideological reasons. But there were always some Hutterites who remained devoted to the communal imperative, and communalism continued to be emphasized in many of the sermons. Nonetheless, for a combined period of 117 years (within a 169 year time span), Hutterites did not live communally and this phenomenon created a structural and religious foundation for a Hutterite church that could function with private property. This is the group that Paul Tschetter eventually led.

Noncommunal Hutterianism in Eastern Europe might more accurately be described as "semi-communal" since many members lived in two-family residences, planted and harvested together, and shared grazing land as well as some community businesses, including brick factories and distilleries. Noncommunal Hutterites lived in traditional villages with houses built close together and there was much personal interaction on a daily basis. All other uniquely Hutterian theological, ecclesial, and cultural traditions were retained. The noncommunal Hutterites spoke a Tirolean-Carinthian dialect (Hutterisch) that was interspersed with words from the various regions where Hutterites had lived, and they married almost exclusively within the group. Dress patterns as well were unchanged and represented simple peasant styles. Men wore beards while women covered their heads with scarves.

---

36. Kuleshov, ed., *History of Raditschewa*. WTC. Wesley Tschetter bought a copy of this book during a visit to Raditschewa in May 2003.

In terms of religious belief and practice, all Hutterites recognized the 1542 confession of faith and they read the *Lehren* at church services. No other sermons were composed or delivered in any noncommunal Hutterite church services. The *Lehren* typically begin with lengthy readings from the Bible, followed by detailed commentary and many practical examples from daily life. Twenty-first-century Hutterites continue to view the sermons as semi-sacred documents that are specially blessed by God even though most of the sermons were written before 1700.

The Hutterite sermons carry an Anabaptist message with a New Testament focus. The teachings and life of Jesus and the apostles, for example, override Old Testament understandings and/or significantly re-interpret the latter. Hutterites believe that the *Lehren* continue to speak to important religious issues, even in the 2000s. Because many of the *Lehren* carry a communal message, this emphasis was always present even during times when the Hutterites did not live communally.

In the noncommunal years, the Hutterites also continued to sing the traditional *Lieder*, which, like the sermons, were only available in a limited number of hand-written collections and were never published. Each minister made personal copies of both the sermons and the hymns that were used in church services. Here the words to each hymn were "lined out" (read out loud) before worshipers started singing, since none of them had their own personal copies. Hymn tunes as well were passed on by oral tradition.

After the fire and the discontinuation of communal life, things were never the same at Raditschewa. Particularly noticeable was the deterioration of the Hutterites' once-excellent school system. In the 1970s, when Arnold M. Hofer prepared 1870s-era genealogical records for the book *Hutterite Roots*, he found that names on official documents were often signed with an "x."[37] Jacob A. Tschetter (a nephew of Paul Tschetter) wrote the following in his family history:

> Now they were poor ... they had no schools. There was much illiteracy and many never actually learned to read or write. Grandfather [Jacob Tschetter] was one of them ... yet he was a man with a brilliant, keen mind.[38]

---

37. Arnold M. Hofer, interview, July 1993. The book cited is HMCC, eds., *Hutterite Roots*.

38. Jacob A. Tschetter, "Family History," WTC. Jacob A. Tschetter was a son of the Rev. John Tschetter (a brother of Paul Tschetter).

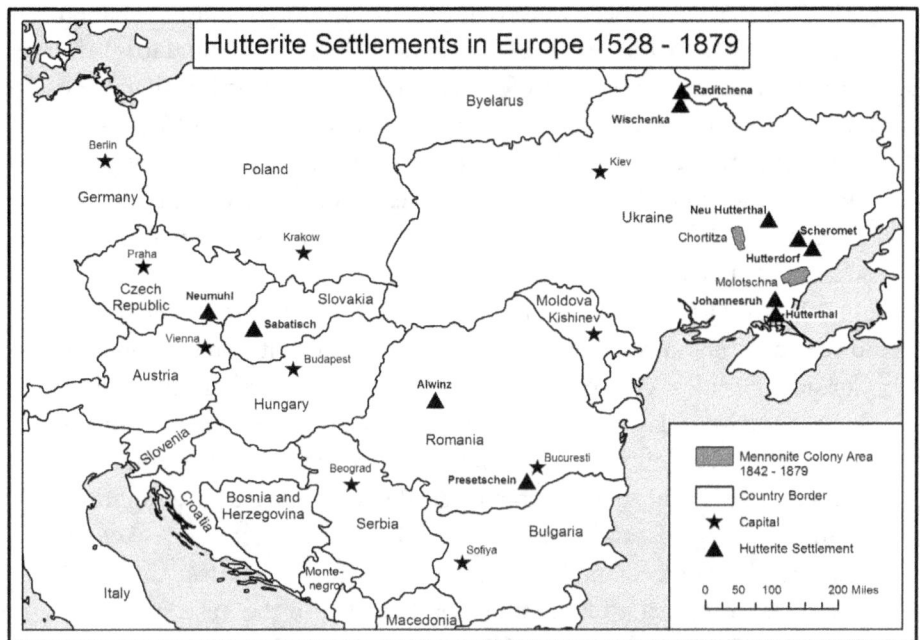

Map 2.1 Hutterite Settlements in Europe, 1528–1879.
Map courtesy of Stuart McFeeters.

Wesley Tschetter notes that when the young men raised at Raditschewa reached adulthood in the 1850s and 1860s, "they were not able to carry on the traditional leadership, ministerial and business functions of the community if the function required literacy."[39] Between 1819 and 1842, an entire generation was raised without a solid educational system. This created a leadership gap and caused Hutterites to develop a sense of intellectual inferiority when they (later) compared themselves to the Russian Mennonites. This is likely the reason that in the 1860s and 1870s, some Hutterite ministers (for example, Paul Tschetter) received their ordinations from Mennonite church leaders. It is the reason why Mennonites like John Warkentine and Jacob Janzen were asked to teach in Hutterite village schools.

Economic enterprises also suffered as a result of the Raditschewa fire. The loss of important tools for example, led to the discontinuation of the pottery, blacksmithing, weaving and tanning trades. Many related skills were lost in the ensuing years. When the moved southward in the

39. Wesley Tschetter, interview, May 2004.

1840s, Hutterite villagers were required to hire Mennonite craftsmen to construct their houses in order to meet demanded standards. The abandonment of communal life at Raditschewa also, ironically, made already small farming acreages more problematic. By the 1840s, the average Hutterite family owned about forty acres of land, not enough to support seven or eight people. Hutterite leaders appealed to the Russian Government for more land but they were not successful in obtaining additional allocations.

As early as 1834, concerned and desperate Hutterite leaders began to seek advice and assistance from the Mennonite entrepreneur Johann Cornies. Cornies chaired the influential Agricultural Improvement Society and served as a Russian Government-appointed member of the Supervisory Council for Government Lands.[40] He visited the Hutterites at Raditschewa and in 1842 convinced them to move as a total group to an undeveloped rural area near the Molotschna Mennonite Colony, where Cornies owned and leased a number of private estates. About 415 Hutterites, comprising fifty families, participated in the mass migration to an area 600 miles southwest of Raditschewa in the Melitopol district of the Ukrainian province of Taurien, a region just north of the Black Sea.

Mennonites from Prussia began to settle in the Black Sea area in the late eighteenth-century at the invitation of Tsarina Catherine the Great. By the 1840s they had established dozens of villages on the Dnieper River north of the Sea of Azov in two major colonies: Chortitza and Molotschna. Ethnically Dutch, Flemish and North German, the Mennonites had the same Anabaptist theological roots as the Hutterites but they had never lived communally.

The Black Sea Mennonites prospered in Ukraine by establishing successful farming operations. They constructed a collection of semi-communal villages where farm land was owned privately (initially in equitably divided strips) with commonly held meadows where cattle grazed. The Mennonites operated their own school systems and even controlled local government institutions in an interesting reversal of their historic commitment to the separation of church and state.

Johann Cornies helped the Hutterites in many ways. In addition to finding land for the migrants, he arranged for a 15,000 ruble advance from the Russian Government.[41] Cornies also offered grain

---

40. *CHB II*, 632.
41. Ibid., 637.

from government storehouses. In return, Cornies insisted on controlling many aspects of Hutterite life, even specifying the way that houses were constructed and advising what crops to grow (just as he was doing for Mennonites).[42] The helpful but authoritarian Cornies interfered in Hutterite social life as well, something that was not always welcomed, especially after the Hutterites repaid government loans in full within the required four-year time period.

The first Hutterite village established in south Ukraine, Hutterthal, was located near the Tashchenak River. It was named and designed by Cornies, who personally coordinated its construction. Cornies' estate was located only a few miles east of the Hutterthal site so he was able to intervene in Hutterite life almost at will. The Hutterthal village eventually consisted of forty-six well-constructed dwellings although many residents spent the first year living in temporary sod structures.

The basic design of the second village, Johannesruh (named after Cornies), consisted of one wide main street, with houses constructed on each side, just like Mennonite villages in the Molotschna and Chortitza colonies. Houses were placed fifty to sixty feet back from the public street and were made of brick. According to Arnold M. Hofer, "The houses were set back from the street so accurately that if the doors on both sides of all the houses were opened, one could see through the houses through the entire length of the village."[43] Each home owner was required to build a masonry fence and to place gate posts at the front of the street with ash trees planted alongside. The bricks were made by Mennonite master craftsmen in homemade kilns located in the Hutterthal village, where a brick factory was eventually constructed. Doors and windows were also constructed by Mennonite carpenters hired by Cornies.

Unlike in Mennonite and later Hutterite villages, the houses at Hutterthal were built for two families. This was done for practical reasons and in recognition of the communal past. There were many requirements, including the prescription that each Hutterite family plant and maintain at least two trees each year. At his own estate Cornies planted over 100,000 fruit and shade trees. Barns were constructed as attachments to each Hutterite house in the traditional European house-barn combination keeping livestock warm in the winter and always

---

42. Epp, *Johann Cornies*, 85–90.
43. HMCC, eds., *Hutterite Roots,* 109.

close by. A school constructed in the center of the Hutterthal village also served as a church meetinghouse.

Conditions in the Hutterite villages were not always ideal and included deep mud on non-paved streets in the spring after winter snows melted and before the once-frozen ground dried out. But for a period of more than thirty years the Hutterites found a place of refuge in south Ukraine near a large community of Mennonites. This is where Paul Tschetter was born.

3

Growing up in Ukraine

What will you do with the world? World is world and will remain world until the Lord will come and end it all.

—Paul Tschetter, 1873[1]

THE FIRST LISTING OF THE SURNAME "TSCHETTER" (ALSO SPELLED "Czeterle," "Zetterle," and "Tschetterle") in Hutterite records is found in the Chronicle in 1760, when a man named Tschetter (described as "one of the brothers") interrupts a Jesuit evangelist who is addressing a Hutterite congregation and calls him "blind" and "benighted."[2] "Man, you are so wrong," Tschetter insisted, "one can only pity you!"[3] This outburst led to Tschetter's arrest and his placement in a Jesuit cloister. Six years later, in 1766, the Chronicle notes that a Hutterite man named Abraham T. "Czeterle" (from Sabatisch) converted to the Roman Catholic Church after many years of imprisonment in a convent. This is likely the same man.

In 1764, a single sixteen-year-old man named Lohrentz Tschetter, described as a weaver, was also incarcerated. At some point released, he was re-imprisoned in 1766. But Lohrentz (born in Alwinz, Transylvania in 1748), did not recant and he accompanied the Hutterites the following year (1767) on their trek to Wallachia. He was one of only nineteen non-Carinthian Hutterites who helped resurrect communal life earlier that same year. The Chronicle records that in 1769, Lohrentz was "beaten by robbers" during the time the Hutterites were in Wallachia.[4]

---

1. J. M. Hofer, ed., "The Diary of Paul Tschetter," 123.
2. *CHB II,* 326. See also T. Waldner, ed., *Russian Record*.
3. *CHB II,* 326.
4. Ibid., 434.

Later Lohrentz was involved in negotiations with Russian Government officials as the Hutterites sought land and official privileges in Ukraine.[5] This Lohrentz, the once-imprisoned, non-recanting, refugee negotiator, was Paul Tschetter's great-grandfather.

Lohrentz's father (also "Paul Tschetter") initially "stayed behind" at Sabatisch and was probably one of the many Hutterites who converted to Catholicism.[6] But sixteen years later, in 1783, Paul, along with his brother Jacob fled to Alwinz (Transylvania) and rejoined the Hutterite Church there in order "to preserve the faith."[7] The Chronicle describes Paul and Jacob as two of "the most devout and highly regarded brothers.[8] But this was a difficult time to be a Hutterite. On his arrival in Alwinz, for example, Paul was immediately arrested and he recanted (for a second time?) due to threats made to his family. In 1784, when missionaries from the Wishenka (Ukraine) Hutterite community were sent to Alwinz to encourage Hutterites living there to join them in their new home, the emissaries stayed at Paul Tschetter's home.[9]

This sequence of events shows the troublesome times in which Hutterites lived in the late eighteenth century. Many Hutterites recanted more than once as a simple means of survival and to make sure that the authorities did not place their children in Catholic families. Yet many Hutterites retained private commitments to the Anabaptist Christian faith. They also maintained personal contacts with Hutterite friends and relatives who had escaped to the east. Eventually Paul Tschetter, along with wife, Judith, six children, and a few other families, made the journey eastward as well joining the Hutterite community at Wishenka.[10] Paul's brother, Jacob also fled to Ukraine, after first escaping from jail.

The Rev. Paul Tschetter thus came from a family that had faced unrelenting persecution and was constantly on the run. In Ukraine, the story of religious commitment in the face of political adversity was told often in the homes of almost every Hutterite family. Hutterites often compared themselves to the early apostles and they accepted the

---

5. Ibid., 452.
6. Ibid., 386.
7. Ibid., 452.
8. Ibid., 514, 515.
9. Ibid., 529.
10. Ibid., 533.

fact that true Christian discipleship always invited persecution and harassment.

Of the various Tschetter men who immigrated to Wishenka, only the aforementioned Lohrentz, the weaver and Hutterite communalist, had male heirs that survived infancy. Over 1,000 contemporary Hutterites who bear the surname "Tschetter" are thus the descendents of Lohrentz Tschetter and of one of his three sons, Lohrentz, Jacob or Paul.[11]

There continues to be mystery, however, about when the first person named "Tschetter" joined the Hutterite Church. Although the surname "Tschetter" is not found in the Hutterite Chronicle prior to 1760, oral history suggests that it existed among Hutterites much earlier. It is said that "Tschetter" was a recognized Hutterite name, for example, at the time the Carinthian contingent arrived from Austria in the 1750s. Contemporary Hutterites categorize "Tschetter" as one of the "Old Hutterite" surnames, as compared to family names that are of "Carinthian" or "Mennonite" background.

The surname "Tschetter" is also the only remaining Hutterite appellation that is probably of Czech or Slovakian ethnic background, though the spelling of the name ("Czeterle" or "Zeterle") was evidently Germanized by the Hutterites. In any case, the earliest Hutterite "Tschetter" probably represents one of the few Eastern European converts to the Hutterite faith, and the only Czechoslovakian family name that survived after the eighteenth century. Most other eighteenth and nineteenth-century Hutterites had mixed "old Hutterite," "Carinthian," and/or Mennonite ethnicity.

In 1795, for example, the thrice-widowed Lohrentz Tschetter married a Dutch/Low German Mennonite woman named Maria Isaak, who was originally from Prussia. Maria's family was one of a small number of Mennonite families who joined the Hutterites at Wishenka. The Rev. Paul Tschetter was the grandson of Lohrentz's son, Jacob, who married a woman named Anna Walter. Paul Tschetter was thus, in an ethnic sense, one-eighth Low German Mennonite.

Paul Tschetter's father, also "Jacob," was born at Raditschewa in 1816, as was his mother, Barbara (Kleinsasser) three years later (in 1819).[12] After moving south in the fall of 1842, the Tschetter family

---

11. Eichler, "Hutterian Surnames." Eichler, *Hutterite Genealogy*.

12. Important genealogical assistance was provided by the Genealogy Project Committee of the California Mennonite Historical Society, Fresno, California, and

Table 3.1 Paul Tschetter Family Tree.

Table courtesy of the Genealogical Registry and Database of Mennonite Ancestry (GRANDMA).

Generation 1	Generation 2	Generation 3	Generation 4	Generation 5
Jacob Tschetter Born 19 Dec 1816 #822 Radichev, Russia Marr 1 Dec 1835	**Jacob Tschetter** Born 13 Mar 1796 #210 Wischenka, Russia Marr 28 Nov 1815 Radichev, Russia Died 16 Dec 1855	**Lorenz Tschetter** Born 1748 #199 Alwinz, Transylvania Marr 6 May 1795 Wischenka, Russia Died 13 Feb 1808 Radichev, Russia	**Paul Tschetter** #56 _____ #57	
		Maria Isaak Born #195 Prussia Died 16 Dec 1839 Radichev, Russia	**Peter Isaac** #38976 _____ #38977	
	Anna Walter Born 9 Feb 1798 #534 Wischenka, Russia Died Abt 1889 South Dakota	**Darius Walter** Born 13 Sep 1774 #426 Sabatisch, Hungary Marr 11 Jan 1797 Wischenka, Russia Died 3 Jun 1850 Hutterthal, South Russia	**Jacob Walter** Born 20 Jun 1740 #417 Marr Died 13 Jul 1785 **Katharina Koller** Born #103 Died 20 Aug 1802 Radichev, Russia	
		Hester Kleinsasser Born 21 Jun 1778 #90 Wischenka, Russia Died 12 Nov 1838 Radichev, Russia	**Johannes Kleinsasser** Born 1723 #70 Marr 15 Feb 1777 Died 16 Oct 1779 **Anna Waldner** Born 10 Nov 1758 #89 Died 5 May 1821 Radichev, Russia	
Paul Tschetter Born 6 Oct 1842 #1241 South Russia Died 17 Nov 1919				
	Joseph Kleinsasser Born 5 Sep 1775 #112 Wischenka, Russia Marr 11 Jan 1797 Wischenka, Russia Died 23 Mar 1838 Radichev, Russia	**Matthias Kleinsasser** Born 1738 #72 Kleinsasserhof, Austria Marr 19 Oct 1771 Wischenka, Russia Died 27 Sep 1795 Wischenka, Russia	**Hans Kleinsasser** Born 1689 #68 Marr 30 Nov 1719 Died 30 Nov 1769 **Dorothea Selsacher** #69	
		Margaretha Wipf Died 19 Nov 1790 #109 Wischenka, Russia	_____ **Wipf** #35 **Gretel Zilchen** #36	
Barbara Kleinsasser Born 12 Aug 1819 #527 Radichev, Russia				
	Anna Koller Born Abt 1776 #350 Died 18 Mar 1820	**Andreas Koller** Born 1753 #349 Sabatisch, Hungary Marr Abt 1792 Sabatisch, Hungary Died 26 Sep 1790 Wischenka, Russia	_____ #0 _____ #0	
		Anna Wollman Born 1758 #254 Sabatisch, Hungary Died 21 Oct 1820 Radichev, Russia	**Jacob Wollman** Born 1730 #283 Marr 13 Oct 1784 Died 27 Feb 1810 **Assanath** _____ Died 15 Mar 1786 #284 Wischenka, Russia	

first established residence in the Mennonite village of Blumenort in the Molotschna Colony while waiting for the first houses to be constructed in what became the village of "Hutterthal." Blumenort is the place where Paul Tschetter was born.

Paul's father, Jacob Tschetter, is described as a tall man (over six feet in height) with very broad shoulders. He was illiterate because of the breakdown of the school system at Raditschewa, yet studious. Jacob knew a lot about biology and animal life as well as astronomy. He had a good memory, exercised appropriate judgment and had a "brilliant, keen mind."[13] According to daughter-in-law Anna Tschetter: "No matter how long a list of articles I gave him to bring home from town, he never forgot, but brought it all and knew the cost of every article he bought."[14] Jacob Tschetter was also remembered as a good storyteller. Grandson Jacob A. Tschetter recalled tales of bear hunts in the Ukrainian woods as well as many Bible stories. "Oh how we listened to him as he told us of the flood, the Joseph story and others," writes Jacob A.[15] Paul Tschetter likely heard many of these stories himself. Paul's father was also known as a man of "good moral character."[16]

Paul Tschetter's mother, Barbara Kleinsasser Tschetter, is described as a person "of very small stature" and as a good mother "with a deep affection to bring her children up in admonition to be good and God fearing."[17] She was "tenderhearted" and gave much attention to "the needy."[18] Jacob and Barbara Tschetter provided a strong religious foundation for their children.

In 1843, the Tschetter family left Blumenort and moved to the newly-constructed Hutterthal, a village located on Russian crown land that had been leased by Johann Cornies. Hutterthal was only twelve miles southwest of Melitopol, the regional administrative center and

---

the 2007 edition of the Genealogical Registry and Database of Mennonite Ancestry (GRANDMA). Another important source was genealogist Alan Peters; as well as Paul Tschetter descendent, Wesley Tschetter; Prairieleut historian Norman Hofer; and Hutterite German Teacher, Tony Waldner.

13. Mrs. J. W. Tschetter, *My Life Story*, 24.
14. J. A. Tschetter, *Family History*, 1.
15. Ibid.
16. Ibid.
17. Ibid.
18. Ibid.

was situated seventy miles southwest of the Molotschna Colony with its large population of about 15,000 Mennonites. Planning for the village began in February 1843 and the first houses were built in April.[19] Most of the Hutterites from Raditschewa, about 400 people, established temporary residence in this crowded village.

Hutterite descriptions of the land in south Ukraine indicate that it was level, semi-arid and fertile with a plentiful supply of grass for livestock. One liability was a lack of forest land, something to which Hutterites were not accustomed. During their sojourn in different parts of Eastern Europe they had always lived near woodlands. The Hutterite chronicler confirms that the land in southern Ukraine was "nothing but waterless steppe . . ." "As for woodland," notes the writer, "there was not so much as a bush."[20] Wood and stone that was required for the construction of buildings had to be transported from great distances and was thus very expensive. In his diary schoolteacher Peter Janzen (a Mennonite who joined the Hutterites in Ukraine) wrote that the Hutterites planted 1,200 trees during their sojourn in the Hutterthal village area.[21]

In the beginning Molotschna and Chortitza Colony Mennonites gave significant assistance to the Hutterites in terms of shelter, food and clothing. Johann Cornies authorized the provision of grain from Mennonite village storehouses and provided temporary employment for many Hutterite young people as maids and farmhands in the Mennonite villages. As noted, Cornies also required the use of Mennonite building patterns and styles in the newly constructed Hutterite villages. The demanding nature of Cornies' involvement is shown in the requirement that Hutterite homes have the same kind of sturdy Mennonite-designed window frames as were found in the Mennonite villages. At Hutterthal Mennonite craftsmen quickly transformed temporary sod residences into solid frame houses.

Cornies himself was one of the richest men in Ukraine and his Agricultural Improvement Society had major influence over crop selection decisions. Cornies was a member of the Russian Academy of

---

19. *CHB II*, 635.

20. Ibid., 643.

21. Peter Janzen, "Reise Nach Amerika," 193. A copy of the original Peter Janzen document, in handwritten German script, is in the possession of the Pearl Creek Colony, Iroquois, South Dakota.

Sciences and he oversaw a number of archeological excavation projects. Trusted by Russian Government officials, in 1843 Cornies was placed in charge of the entire Russian Mennonite school system.[22]

Cornies was a controversial figure, however, often at odds with Mennonite religious leaders who considered him intrusive, authoritarian and sometimes unethical.[23] Hutterites had the same love-hate relationship with Cornies. Without his assistance the Hutterites could not have established villages in south Ukraine. Many jobs also came via the Cornies connection. Dozens of young Hutterites served apprenticeships as wage-earners to local Mennonites. But even this development was not without its problems. Young Hutterites, for example, were required to board with Mennonite families and to sign formal employment contracts. Some did not like living away from their families and returned home leading Mennonite village officials to arrest and return them to their employers, who at times treated Hutterite workers as second class citizens.

Some Hutterites were even imprisoned for not fulfilling contractual obligations. Zacharias Walter from Hutterthal village said that his daughter was "shut up in a dark dungeon" for not wanting to stay with her employers.[24] In June, 1846, at Blumenort, there was a physical altercation between a Mennonite farmer and a young Hutterite laborer. As a result the Hutterite boy was punished for insolence by Mennonite villagers who hit him with a "birch."[25] Hutterites disagreed on how to respond to these situations, causing factions to develop at Hutterthal. Some people supported the Mennonite employers; others felt that the Hutterite workers were being mistreated.

Johann Cornies' view was that young Hutterites needed to learn modern farming techniques and trades and he expected them to adhere to agreed-upon contractual arrangements. He wanted young Hutterites to be less isolated, to interact with Mennonites, to eventually be assimilated into the mainstream Mennonite culture of south Ukraine. This is exactly what many Hutterites did not want.

Cornies also intervened in Hutterite social affairs insisting that the group give up its tradition of semi-annual arranged marriages.

22. Epp, *Johann Cornies*, 50.
23. Ibid., 25–26.
24. *CHB II*, 652.
25. Urry, *None But Saints*, 132.

Historically Hutterite parents and church leaders chose the young men and women that would be permanently joined together following a communal ethic that in theory did not recognize emotion-laden individual predilections. From the Hutterite perspective arranged marriages ensured that there were few unmarried members and that mature adults were involved in the spouse selection process. Cornies intervened when a young runaway bride appeared at his home in Ohrloff one evening, upset that she had been paired off with an older widower for whom she felt no attraction. There had even been a failed attempt to lock her into a house so that she and her new husband could get to know each other better.

Cornies intervened for humanitarian reasons, allowing the girl to reject her marriage vows. Cornies then hired her as his personal servant, ensuring that she was taken care of as well as kept apart from the Hutterite community. Then showing the extent of his political influence and authority, an angry Cornies told the Hutterites that the practice of arranged marriages had to end, abrogating a long-time Hutterite church-sanctioned custom. The Hutterites acquiesced, feeling they had no recourse at this difficult juncture in their history. The *Chronicle* notes, "For a long time afterward a wedding could not take place at Hutterthal until the girl had affirmed either to Cornies or to reliable people in the community that she willingly consented to the proposed marriage."[26] The end of arranged marriages occurred in 1846, only fourteen years before Paul Tschetter was married to the woman with whom he would spend the rest of his life.

At a very crowded Hutterthal village, where Paul Tschetter was raised, Hutterites were initially crammed into two-family structures. Separate housing was only introduced in 1853 after the village of Johannesruh was established two miles away. Johannesruh too was designed in accordance with established Mennonite guidelines, the houses positioned in rows on each side of a broad main street, with equal spacing between residences. The gabled side of each house faced the street, with the home's front entrance facing the back side of the next-door-neighbor's house. All of the structures were house-barn combinations, with the barns placed at the rear of the property. Cornies also required Hutterites to follow the Mennonite pattern of planting flower gardens in their front yards. In general as Peter Letkemann notes, the Hutterites

26. *CHB II*, 638–39.

were fully "integrated into the Mennonites' political, social and economic village structure."[27]

In the years that followed three more Hutterite villages were established, all more distant and located in Ekaterinoslav Province. These villages (*Dorfe*) were located east of the Chortitza (Mennonite) Colony and between 75 and 100 miles from Hutterthal and Johannesruh. The village of Hutterdorf was established in 1857, Neu Hutterthal (Dobritscha) in 1868, and Scheromet, a communal village, also in 1868.

With the exception of forced changes in marriage selection practices and building codes, however, other Hutterite cultural traditions and worship practices remained the same. Between 1842 and the 1870s, men dressed simply using hooks and eyes on their clothing instead of buttons. They wore high boots, coats with turned-down collars, and long beards that often hung "down to [the] navel."[28] Hutterite women wore simple long dresses and did not cut their hair, which they covered with dark scarves.

Hutterite culinary practices showed a preference for meat, dairy products, potatoes and breads but also included fresh fruits and vegetables. The most common beverage was *Pribs*, which was made by boiling water over roasted rye or barley. Eastern European Hutterites did not typically drink coffee. Popular Hutterite foods included *Gashtel* (dumpling soup), *Nukelen* (egg dumpling soup), *Griebenschmaltz* (goose or pork crackling spread) as well as string bean soup and pickled watermelon.

One of the most important developments in the new Hutterite villages occurred in 1859, when some Hutterdorf village residents resurrected communal life. This eventually led to the establishment of a separate communal village, Scheromet, ten miles south of Hutterdorf, in 1868. The immediate cause of the re-establishment of communal life was a vision given to the pastor Michael Waldner, in which a "spirit of God" told him in very blunt terms that Hutterites would end up in hell if they did not live communally. In his vision Waldner wrote that he "felt like he was flying" and that he had seen "heaven and hell and the damned," many of whom were his own Hutterite people.[29] Waldner

---

27. Krahn, ed., *From the Steppes to the Prairies*, 114.
28. *CHB II*, 654.
29. E. Bender, ed., "The Last Words of Michael Waldner," 355–57.

purchased the Scheromet land by selling property that he and his followers owned privately at Hutterdorf.

Hutterite communal traditions did not die easily and Russian Government officials were well aware that even the noncommunal Hutterite Church was different from the Mennonite Church. As a 1867 Russian Government report put it, "they strive for complete equality," noting that the Hutterites were "not distinguished from one another by lifestyle or any external details."[30] Mennonites, conversely, had significant social, economic, political and religious divisions between colony members.

In the Black Sea region, renewed interest in communal life preceded Michael Waldner's vision and was first promoted by the Hutterite minister George Waldner, who was influenced by the *Lehren*. As long as Hutterites used the historic sermons as their primary way of interpreting the Bible they were constantly faced with the communal imperative. Some Hutterite hymns also supported community of goods, as did the Chronicle, Hutterite epistles and many of the Ordnungen. The power of the written word was extremely important in Hutterite history and it often propelled communitarian modes of thought.

In 1848 at the Hutterthal village, George Waldner formally petitioned the Russian Government for a "majority vote" plebiscite that might lead to the re-instatement of community of goods.[31] Hutterites following the church elder Jacob Walter opposed this petition, as well as another that Waldner submitted in 1852, but communal life advocates did not rest their case.

Paul Tschetter thus grew up in the midst of ideological and interpersonal conflict, in a village (Hutterthal) where there were factions based on significant and ongoing differences of opinion about communal life, as well as the nature of the many personal and business relationships that had been established with Mennonites. Some Hutterite conflicts were family related. Other differences of opinion were founded on class considerations. According to Peter Letkemann, "The unprecedented prosperity experienced by the best Hutterite farmers soon stood in stark contrast to the poverty of their fellow craftsmen and wage laborers, and

---

30. *CHB II*, 646.
31. *CHB II*, 648.

produced bitter tensions in the community."[32] Oral history suggests that poorer Hutterites were the most interested in communal life.

In 1856, when Paul Tschetter was fourteen years old, a third George Waldner petition was finally accepted by the Russian Government. As a result, Waldner and thirty-three Hutterite families sold their land and established the Hutterdorf village, eighty miles north of Hutterthal and thirty miles from the Dnieper River in Ekaterinoslav Province. But community of goods was never successfully established at Hutterdorf. There were too many differences of opinion. Three years later, in 1859, Hutterdorf pastor Michael Waldner's vision led to the establishment of the first successful communal group. But even then not all Hutterdorf communalists recognized Michael Waldner's leadership! Another minister, Darius Walter established a second communal group in the same village in 1860.

Four years later, in 1864, a third communal group was formed in the Johannesruh village. They were joined by a few interested families from Hutterthal that moved into the community. The Johannesruh communal group was led by Jacob Wipf. By the mid-1860s, therefore, the Hutterite Church in Ukraine was divided into three small communal and one large noncommunal faction.

But in south Ukraine it was hard to practice full and separate communal life in the Hutterite villages due to restrictive Mennonite economic policies. Greater success was achieved in Dakota Territory when the struggle for survival on the frontier gave an early advantage to communal economic arrangements and there were fewer property, land use and building regulations. Gertrude Huntington writes, "The importance of migration to the reestablishment of community cannot be overemphasized."[33] Without migration communal Hutterianism may never have succeeded.

Paul Tschetter as a Young Man

Paul Tschetter was born on October 6, 1842 in the Mennonite village of Blumenort shortly after his parents established temporary residence there. Jacob and Barbara Tschetter and their children moved to the Hutterthal village the following year, in 1843. This is where Paul

---

32. Krahn, *From the Steppes to the Prairies*, 114.
33. Huntington, "Hutterite Faith and Community," 335.

Tschetter grew up. As a boy he attended the Hutterthal school that was opened on November 20, 1845, and where Mennonite Jacob Janzen served as schoolteacher.

Janzen was appointed by Johann Cornies who had "jurisdiction" over Mennonite and Hutterite village schools.[34] The workload was heavy. Initially Janzen taught ninety-one children during the day and conducted separate classes for adults in the evening. After his wife died in 1848, Jacob Janzen married a Hutterthal woman named Maria Waldner and joined the Hutterite Church.[35] Janzen was well-loved by his students as was the Mennonite schoolteacher, John Warkentine. Both of these men are mentioned often in Hutterian memoirs. Paul Tschetter's brother, John Tschetter described Warkentine as a "God-fearing" man who often had "tears" in his eyes when he discussed spiritual matters.[36]

Hutterite village schools were established following Mennonite educational models with a teaching manual provided by Johann Cornies. This document includes eighty-seven specific considerations and emphasizes a practical, rigorous and uniform course of study with a focus on ethical development.[37] Major emphasis is placed on reading, writing, arithmetic and German.[38] Musical instruction was also a required part of each school's curriculum. This introduced young Hutterites to songs with which they were unfamiliar.

Teachers in the Hutterite schools were licensed after first attending Mennonite training schools, worships and conferences. By the mid-nineteenth century these teachers were utilizing progressive child-centered pedagogical techniques that included peer tutoring and discouraged corporal punishment and verbal berating. Peter Letkemann notes that Mennonite schools were in general "the most spacious in the region," and were unique in their use of long rectangular tables instead of one or two-person seating arrangements.[39] School attendance was compulsory and gender inclusive and formal instruction was conducted in German.[40] The Molotschna Colony curriculum included the

---

34. Smith, *The Coming of the Russian Mennonites*, 40.
35. "Hutterite Marriage Records," in HMCC, eds., *Hutterite Roots*, 70.
36. John A. Tschetter, n.d., "John Tschetter Autobiography," 1. WTC.
37. Epp, *Johann Cornies*, 52–60.
38. Unruh, *A Century of Mennonites in Dakota*, 14.
39. Peter Letkemann, "Molochna 2004," 111.
40. N. J. Klassen, "Mennonite Intelligentsia in Russia."

following subjects: Reading, Grammar, Mathematics, Music, German, Geography, Nature Studies, Bible Stories and Church History.[41]

Little is known about what Paul Tschetter was like as a young boy. We have no idea what school subjects interested him or whether he ever got into trouble. When not in school, most Hutterite children assisted with farm work, gardening and household chores. Paul likely did the same. For most children, schooling did not extend beyond age twelve or thirteen, at which time boys and girls joined the agricultural or domestic work force, became apprentices in different trades or were sent to work in factories or homes in the Mennonite villages. Paul Tschetter's parents were farmers and he became a full-time tiller of the soil. Since a major Hutterite crop was winter wheat Tschetter probably knew a good deal about planting, weeding and harvesting this crop. He was also likely competent in carpentry, plumbing, taking care of livestock and butchering.

With regard to political alliances at Hutterthal, most members of Paul Tschetter's family took the Jacob Walter (noncommunal) side of the religious debate. During his growing up years Paul would have heard many arguments for and against communal life. He would have been keenly aware of the experiments taking place at Hutterdorf and Scheromet and the many Hutterite factions that had developed within a very small community of people.

In the only extant and known photograph of Paul Tschetter, taken in 1873, he is shown with a square face and a high forehead. Tschetter dons a full black beard as well as a coat with wide lapels and a round-collared vest buttoned to the neck.[42]

In the photograph Tschetter's facial expression is a stern one but this was the expected nineteenth-century pose. In later years Tschetter was more commonly attired in narrow black trousers and a black cap. According to grandchildren, Paul G. Tschetter and Justina Hofman Guericke, Paul Tschetter (unlike his father) was short of stature, standing about five feet, six inches tall. He weighed 150–160 pounds and

---

41. Maendel, "Historical Guidelines," 5.
42. Peterson, ed., *People of the Old Missury*, 93.

1842. — Ältester Paul Tschetter. — 1919.

Figure 3.1 Paul Tschetter, 1873.
Photograph courtesy of the Hutterite Mennonite Centennial Committee.

had "stocky legs."[43] With reference to personality Tschetter was known throughout his life as a person with great "drive, energy and will."[44]

On November 27, 1860, at age eighteen, Paul Tschetter married a seventeen year-old village girl named Maria Walter. Maria, born on July 23, 1843, was the daughter of Jacob and Maria Hofer Walter. Right before their marriage, following common Hutterite practice, Paul and Maria would have studied the catechism with one of the village ministers and been baptized upon their confession of faith.[45] The two were

---

43. Justina Guerke, "History of the Rev. Paul P. Tschetter," presentation for Paul Tschetter Family Reunion (1960). WTC. Peterson, ed., *People of the Old Missury*, 93. Paul G. Tschetter, "A Legacy," unpublished manuscript, 1987. A copy is in the possession of Nancy M. Peterson.

44. Paul G. Tschetter, "A Legacy." HMA.

45. Joseph W. Tschetter, "A Brief Biography of Paul Tschetter, 1842–1919" in JMH, 112.

Jacob Walter
Born 29 Jul 1815 — #744
Radichev, Russia
Marr 25 Oct 1837
Hutterthal, South Russia
Died 22 Apr 1883
Freeman, South Dakota

    Jacob Walter
    Born 23 May 1794 — #438
    Wischenka, Russia
    Marr 10 Nov 1812
    Radichev, Russia
    Died 23 Sep 1866
    Hutterthal, South Russia

        Jacob Walter
        Born 26 Jun 1770 — #424
        Sabatisch, Hungary
        Marr 9 Jan 1793
        Wischenka, Russia
        Died 9 Mar 1855
        Hutterthal, South Russia

            Jacob Walter
            Born 20 Jun 1740 — #417
            Marr
            Died 13 Jul 1785

            Katharina Koller
            Born — #103
            Died 20 Aug 1802
            Radichev, Russia

        Anna Glanzer
        Born 7 Nov 1775 — #164
        Wischenka, Russia
        Died 7 Mar 1819
        Chortitza, South Russia

            Paul Glanzer
            Born 1732 — #78
            Marr 1762
            Died 3 Mar 1813

            Barbara Hofer
            Born 1742 — #158
            Died 20 Sep 1807
            Radichev, Russia

    Barbara Koller
    Born Abt 1783 — #351
    Sabatisch, Hungary
    Died 15 Jul 1839
    South Russia

        Andreas Koller
        Born 1753 — #349
        Sabatisch, Hungary
        Marr Abt 1782
        Sabatisch, Hungary
        Died 26 Sep 1790
        Wischenka, Russia

            #0
            #0

        Anna Wollman
        Born 1758 — #254
        Sabatisch, Hungary
        Died 21 Oct 1820
        Radichev, Russia

            Jacob Wollman
            Born 1730 — #283
            Marr 13 Oct 1784
            Died 27 Feb 1810

            Assanath
            Died 15 Mar 1786 — #284
            Wischenka, Russia

Maria Walter
Born 23 Jul 1843 — #23827
Died 21 Dec 1915
Bridgewater, South Dakota

        Christian Hofer
        Born 26 May 1773 — #186
        Wischenka, Russia
        Marr 9 Jan 1793
        Wischenka, Russia
        Died 12 Apr 1797
        Wischenka, Russia

            Christian Hofer
            Born 1749 — #154
            Marr 19 Oct 1771
            Died 11 Mar 1802

            Barbara Miller
            Born 1754 — #131
            Died 6 Jan 1810
            Radichev, Russia

    Zebulon Hofer
    Born 9 Mar 1796 — #412
    Wischenka, Russia
    Marr 18 Nov 1817
    Radichev, Russia
    Died 23 Mar 1830

        Maria Pullman
        Born 1773 — #410
        Died 1 Jul 1833

            Joseph Pullman
            Died 1 Sep 1793 — #463
            Wischenka, Russia

            Judith Kuhr
            Died 2 Jul 1787 — #464
            Wischenka, Russia

Maria Hofer
Born 17 Jul 1821 — #880
Died 12 Jan 1867

        Hans Cornels
        Born 4 Feb 1776 — #589
        Przechowka, Prussia
        Marr 11 Jan 1797
        Wischenka, Russia
        Died 29 Jul 1812
        Radichev, Russia

            Jacob Cornelsen
            Born 26 Jan 1752 — #3699
            Marr 12 May 1771
            Died 12 Jun 1807

            Liscke Funcken
            Born 10 Feb 1754 — #3700
            Przechowka, Prussia

    Gretel Knels
    Born 10 Feb 1801 — #590
    Wischenka, Russia

        Suzanna Wurz
        Born 16 Jun 1778 — #290
        Wischenka, Russia
        Died 21 Apr 1808
        Radichev, Russia

            Christian Wurz
            Born 1754 — #138
            Marr 19 Feb 1777
            Died Jan 1792

            Gretel Stahl
            Born 1758 — #180
            Died 13 Aug 1800

Table 3.2 Maria Walter Tschetter Family Tree. Table courtesy of the Genealogical Registry and Database of Mennonite Ancestry (GRANDMA).

married by the Rev. David Hofer, along with three other couples.[46] Paul and Maria were not strangers to each other. They grew up in the same village, attended the same church and probably knew a good deal about each other's individual personalities as well as family connections.

To begin a formal relationship with Maria Walter, Paul likely followed the developing *Aufreden* tradition, whereby his parents and a friend approached Maria's parents to ask for her hand in marriage. This practice was based on the Old Testament Genesis account where a servant of Abraham stood in for him when his son Isaac asked permission to marry Rebecca. As the tradition advanced young Hutterite couples usually planned everything ahead of time so that there were few surprises.

Paul and Maria chose each other in somewhat unencumbered fashion. But they would have been keenly aware that this was a novel practice in Hutterite history; one that had only recently been introduced. This must have been talked about often by members of both of their families. Paul and Maria were surrounded by adults, including their own parents, who had been joined together in an arranged marriage structure. Even after Cornies ended arranged marriages, parents, grandparents, ministers and older persons continued to be actively involved in the spouse approval process. This is likely what happened in Paul and Maria's case.

In terms of family relationships, Paul and Maria were third cousins, but this was not unusual. In Hutterite colonies today the average husband and wife are more closely related than second cousins due to many years of marriage within a small group of people. Like her husband, Maria Walter had some Low German Mennonite background. Her maternal grandmother was a Mennonite woman named Gretel Knels (or "Cornelsen"). Her grandparents, Jacob and Liscke Funk, were Mennonites from Przechowka, Prussia, who joined the Hutterites when they were living at Wishenka. Maria's particular Walter family line was later referred to as the *Sepel* clan (Russian for "Joseph"), after one of Maria's brothers.

Oral accounts describe Maria as an intelligent woman with more years of education than her husband. She attended a Mennonite school for nine full (9-month) years.[47] Maria is described as "broad-faced,"

---

46. HMCC, eds., *Hutterite Roots*, 72.
47. Justina Guericke, "History of the Rev. Paul P. Tschetter," 2. Wesley Tschetter,

"big-boned" and small in stature.[48] Her personality is characterized as "kind" but "direct."[49]

Little is known about the bride and groom's first six years of marriage. But in 1866, at age twenty-four, Paul was chosen to be a minister at the Hutterthal Church. Historically Hutterites used the casting of lots procedure outlined in Peter Riedemann's confession of faith. This continues to be the way that communal Hutterites select ministers in the 2000s. When a pastor is required the church's male members nominate those within the congregation who are discerned to have appropriate spiritual gifts. These names are then placed into the lot. The lot-casting process varies, however, and often requires that a nominee receive a minimum number of votes before having his name placed into the lot. It is also typically expected that more than one individual will be nominated for the position.

Astrid von Schlachta questions whether Hutterite ministers were always selected by lot during the community's first years of existence.[50] Peter Riedemann, for example, wrote that having more than one nominee was not always necessary. According to Riedemann, "If, however, there is only one or just as many as needed, we need no lot, for the Lord has shown him or them to us."[51] But in the mid-sixteenth to early nineteenth centuries it became standard Hutterite practice to choose ministers by lot according to the model described above.[52] The practice continues not only with Hutterites but among the Old Order Amish and many other conservative Anabaptist groups.

With reference to casting lots, the Hutterites emphasize two Bible verses. In the Old Testament, Proverbs 16:33 states, "The lot is cast into

---

notes from interview with Emil Tschetter (n.d.). WTC.
48. Peterson, ed., *People of the Old Missury*, 95.
49. Paul G. Tschetter, "A Legacy," 2. HMA.
50. Von Schlachta, "'Searching Through the Nations,'" 34.
51. Peter Riedemann, *Confession of Faith*, 110.
52. There have been a few exceptions. In 1952, for example, a minister (Jacob Waldner) was chosen at Bon Homme Colony (Tabor, South Dakota) without casting lots. There were other nominees but the ministers present rejected them. Because of this unusual occurrence the Schmiedeleut Hutterite leadership ruled that in the future, if there was only one acceptable nominee, the process had to start over (Tony Waldner, interview, July 2005).

the fold of the garment, but the decision comes wholly from God."[53] In the Hutterite view God makes the final decision.[54]

In the New Testament, Acts 1:23–26 reads,

> Having nominated two candidates, Joseph known as Barsabbas (whose surname was Justus) and Matthias, they prayed, "Lord, you can read everyone's heart; show us therefore which of these two you have chosen to take over this ministry and apostolate, which Judas abandoned to go to his proper place." They then drew lots for them, and as the lot fell to Matthias, he was listed as one of the twelve apostles.[55]

Selecting ministers by casting lots is a powerful *modus operandi* since it is believed that God plays a direct and little mediated role in the process. To non-Hutterites it may appear that lot-casting is a random event but Hutterites believe that God is spiritually present in the church building when the lot is cast. It is a sacred procedure in which God makes the final determination about who will be one of his ministers, even if the person selected feels unworthy for the position. Swiss Mennonite leader Harold S. Bender wrote this about lot-casting in 1957, "It is one of the few times when direct divine action can be visibly experienced, at least to those who sincerely believe that God acts through the lot, and it therefore intensifies the religious experience of the group practicing it."[56] It is an extremely powerful ritual that bears similarities to the way

---

53. Proverbs 16:33. All Bible references in this book are taken from the *New Jerusalem Bible* (New York: Doubleday, 1998).

54. One Hutterite minister told the author that once he was selected, and reluctantly accepted the call to ministry, he was forced to act more maturely and to show greater concern for the spiritual well-being of other members. He accepted the fact that God had called him through the lot; he viewed this as a sacred mandate.

55. Acts 1:23–26.

56. Harold S. Bender, "Lot" entry, *MennEncy*, 3:443. According to Bender, the first step in selecting pastors in Swiss-American Mennonite churches, into the twentieth century, was to distribute slips of paper on which members nominated "candidates." Anyone receiving at least two votes was placed into the lot. The second step was to ask each candidate to come forward to pick a book or Bible from a selection placed on a table in front of the church. Prior to the meeting the Proverbs 16:33 verse was written on a piece of paper and placed inside one of the written works. As the candidates came forward, church leaders opened the books or Bibles selected until one contained the inscribed slip of paper. This led to immediate ordination. Lot-casting was practiced as late as the mid-1950s in many American Mennonite congregations although the nomination process was often revised so that only the names of the top two vote-getters were placed into the lot.

that Roman Catholics recognize the presence of the body and blood of Christ in the celebration of the Mass.

The lot selection process eliminates individualistic calls to ministry. A prospective Hutterite pastor cannot receive a direct call from God. It has to come through the community. The modern evangelical Christian disposition to view ministerial selection as a "God-to-prospective minister" calling followed by a "God-through-the-body-of-believers" confirmation is by contrast less community-oriented. Hutterite lot-casting also contains a vital democratic element due to the way that prospective ministers are nominated. In Hutterite colonies today candidates are required to receive a pre-determined number of votes in order to have their names printed on a slip of paper and placed inside a Bible. After a time of prayer, the lot is cast with the minister-in-charge selecting one of the Bibles.

During the Raditschewa and south Ukraine era (1802–1877), however, the Hutterite Church strayed from the traditional lot-casting approach and at times did not use it at all. It is unclear whether Paul Tschetter's own selection as minister followed a traditional lot-casting procedure but it is doubtful that it did. Hutterite oral history suggests that few if any ministers were selected by lot between the 1840s and 1870s. As noted, there was some precedent for this approach. In addition to Riedemann's confessional comment, the Hutterite Chronicle provides two examples of ministers selected by the "laying on of hands, followed by probation," with no lot cast.[57] In 1782, for example, Johannes Waldner received twenty votes while two other nominees received one or two votes. It was decided that the lot was not necessary.

In the 1860s the Hutterites were not far removed from the Raditschewa era with its extremely low educational levels. This led to a dearth of trained and literate leaders. After the 1819 Raditschewa fire male schoolteachers were not replaced when they retired.[58] An 1825 report indicates that the Hutterite school still functioned for boys and girls ages seven and older, and that reading, writing and practical crafts were part of the curriculum.[59] But those doing the teaching were older women with little educational background or experience. Most

---

57. CHB II, 661.
58. Ibid., 641.
59. Ibid., 624.

Hutterites interviewed believe that this is the reason that the lot-casting process was for a time discontinued.

With reference to selecting ministers, it is important to note that Dutch Low German Mennonites never chose ministers this way. Although Menno Simons referred to lot-casting in some of his writings, it was never used regularly by his followers.[60] The practice was thus relatively unknown in the Russian Mennonite community, with whom the Hutterites now had much association and who exerted considerable influence on them.

Official Hutterite church records state that Paul Tschetter was "elected" to be "Teacher of the Word" (*erwahlt Lehrer des Worts*) on January 30, 1866. The word "election" is the same term that is used to describe the ordinations eight years earlier of George Hofer, Michael Waldner and Darius Walter (at the Hutterdorf village church), with a period of "probation" following. Three men chosen for the ministry in 1857 (Martin Waldner, Peter Hofer, and Jacob Wipf) were also "elected" by "majority vote," which was followed by "probation" and "confirmation" of their callings.[61] Entries in official church records imply that the lot was not cast in these cases. Communal Hutterites re-established the lot-casting procedure after they immigrated to Dakota Territory in the 1870s.

But Paul Tschetter's story contains a few mysteries. Seven years after his ordination, for example, in a May 13, 1873, diary entry, Tschetter writes that among American Mennonites, "the ministers are elected, just as we do, and are finally chosen by lot (Acts 1:26)." Had "finally chosen by lot" taken on a new meaning or was Tschetter hinting at a difference in sacramental practice?

In any case Paul Tschetter was selected from within the Hutterthal congregation by people who knew him well. This exemplifies the Hutterite belief that it is important to know one's spiritual leaders; it is important to know something about their families, their general character and even their youthful indiscretions. This happened automatically when ministers like Tschetter were chosen from within the village church. Public knowledge about every member tended to keep those chosen to be ministers humble. Everyone knew their strengths and weaknesses intimately. Selection from within also showed that in

---

60. Harold S. Bender, "Lot," in *Mennonite Encyclopedia*, 3:399–400, 443.
61. *CHB II*, 664–65.

every congregation, however small, God could always find someone to serve as a spiritual leader.

Hutterite ministers were selected for life so Paul Tschetter knew that his call to pastoral leadership was not a short-term assignment. It was a very serious calling. This did not mean that he would not make some or many mistakes as he provided spiritual leadership. But the lifetime nature of his appointment meant that differences of opinion, controversial decisions and personal conflicts had to be worked through.

Although there were occasional love offerings, Hutterite churches did not pay their ministers regular salaries. Paul Tschetter was expected to have a regular job to support his family. Most Hutterite ministers at the time were farmers, and this was the occupation chosen by Tschetter. Throughout his life, in addition to a variety of ecclesiastical responsibilities, Paul Tschetter gave considerable attention to farming operations in order to make ends meet. This contrasted with the communal Hutterite system where individual financial loads were non-existent. Work was done collectively and all members, including ministers with special functions, worked and shared equally in the fruits of their labor. Communal Hutterite ministers could more easily than Paul Tschetter leave work responsibilities when pressing religious matters arose. Tschetter and other noncommunal ministers did not operate alone, however, since there were usually at least two or three ministers selected in every congregation.

Four weeks after being selected as a minister, Paul Tschetter delivered his first sermon at the Hutterthal schoolhouse, which also served as the village church. Tschetter preached (i.e. read) from the 1 Timothy 4 Hutterite *Lehr* text. Tschetter was formally ordained on July 10, 1866, by the Mennonite pastor Peter Wedel from the Alexanderwohl village (Molotschna Colony). Why a Mennonite minister, not a Hutterite pastor, presided over Tschetter's ordination is another biographical mystery. This was also the case for a few other Hutterite ministers during the south Ukraine period. They represent the first pastors in Hutterite history (after the early years) to be ordained by non-Hutterites.[62]

Why Tschetter was not ordained by Hutterite Elder Michael Stahl (who ordained other Hutterite ministers during the same time period) is difficult to explain. Stahl lived in Paul Tschetter's home village (Hutterthal) and was, in Russia, a leader among noncommunal

---

62. See also Justina Guericke, "History of the Rev. Paul P. Tschetter." WTC.

Hutterians. Factional differences at Hutterthal likely played a role in all church-related decisions. Yet in 1869, when Paul Tschetter needed an assistant minister at the Neu Hutterthal village, Joseph Wipf was ordained by Michael Stahl, not by a Mennonite minister, even though Neu Hutterthal was located ninety miles away from Hutterthal.[63]

Paul Tschetter's descendants uniformly attribute Tschetter's ordination by a Mennonite to the contemporary spiritual condition of Hutterites, general illiteracy and the fact that there were many gifted Mennonite ministers in the Molotschna and Chortitza colonies. During the 1860s and 1870s, the Hutterites selected a number of very young ministers and many of them were impressed with the superior education provided in the Mennonite-directed schools.[64] This perspective places a negative imprimatur on Elder Michael Stahl, who was known as a gifted and spiritually-minded individual. It is also true, however, that Michael Stahl himself was ordained (in 1857) by the same Peter Wedel who later ordained Paul Tschetter.[65]

In 1867, one year after ordination, Paul Tschetter performed his first marriage ceremony: for Daniel Stahl and Justina Tschetter. Later, in North America, Daniel and Justina left the noncommunal group and joined the communal Bon Homme Colony.[66] The following year, 1868, Paul and Maria and their children, Susanna (born in 1865), Paul (in 1866) and Jacob (in 1867), helped establish the Neu Hutterthal village about 90 miles north of Hutterthal, along with twenty other families.[67] The new village was established to deal with overpopulation at Hutterthal. Before giving birth to their daughter Susanna, Paul and Maria lost a son, a first "Jacob," who lived for only a month.

Paul and Maria's fourth child, Maria, was born at Neu Hutterthal in 1870. She was followed by Barbara in 1872 and Jacob W. (the second

---

63. D. P. Gross and A. M. Hofer, eds., "The Neu Hutterthaler Church Record Book," 2, 10. This document was translated into English in 1992 and is in the possession of the Hutterite Mennonite Centennial Committee (HMCC), Freeman, SD. Other sources for information about Tschetter's experiences in North America are Joseph W. Tschetter, "Introduction," in J. M. Hofer, ed., "The Diary of Paul Tschetter," 113; W. Tschetter, "Reflections on Paul Tschetter." See also Ernst Correll, "President Grant and the Mennonite Immigration from Russia."

64. Arnold M. Hofer, interview, May 2004.

65. NHCRB, 664.

66. Krause, *Tschetter-Waldner Families*, 241.

67. J. M. Hofer, ed., "The Diary of Paul Tschetter," 112.

"Jacob" died in 1873), in 1874. One can see that the Tschetters followed a common nineteenth-century practice of re-using the names of children who died at young ages. So Maria Tschetter ultimately gave birth to three sons with the "Jacob" name. Before the discovery of now-common antibiotics and inoculations, the death of young children was not unusual and it affected the lives of virtually every family. This caused people to view life as less predictable and more transitory than it is viewed in the twenty-first century. Concurrently death was not feared as much and was recognized by many Hutterites as a quick avenue to a different and better form of existence.[68]

---

68. Aries, *The Hour of Our Death*.

4

The Journey to North America

> As guided by the Lord's hand
> I must travel from this land
> Into a strange place
> To search for a homeland.[1]
>
> —Paul Tschetter, 1873

> He [the Devil] is also looking today,
> To seduce every person,
> To take into his evil nest,
> And into his power.[2]
>
> —Paul Tschetter, 1873

IN 1866, PAUL TSCHETTER WAS CHOSEN FOR A LIFE OF CHRISTIAN MINistry. He had started a family with spouse Maria, who soon had many children to care for. But radical changes were in store for members of the entire Hutterite community. It all started in July 1870, when Tsar Alexander II issued a *ukase* (edict) that announced new assimilationist government policies. These laws sought to bring non-Russian ethnic communities into the greater social, economic and political mainstream of Russian Empire life. The 1870 *ukase* proclaimed a program of Russification that instituted greater government control over the lives of all foreign inhabitants even if they had been living in the Empire for a long period of time. Most laws were to go into effect within five years, by 1875, and the process was to be completed by 1880. Since one clause of the edict stated that foreign groups that chose not to adhere to the

---

1. Paul Tschetter, hymn #3, stanza two (1873). HHMA.
2. Ibid., hymn #4, stanza three.

new laws would be allowed to leave the Empire, many Mennonites and Hutterites started looking elsewhere immediately.[3]

Up until this time both the Mennonites and Hutterites had benefited from *privilegium* granted by Catherine the Great in the late 1700s, formalized by her successor, Tsar Paul II, and adhered to by subsequent monarchs. These imperial edicts granted Anabaptists as well as German Catholics and Lutherans, and some Russian religious dissenters (for example, Doukhobors and Molokans), the right to live semi-autonomously and in relative isolation on the Ukrainian steppes. These regions had been conquered by Russia in the eighteenth century and were, at the time, sparsely populated by semi-nomadic ethnic groups. The Russian Government wanted settlers to develop the land and establish an economic and human presence. This is similar to what European countries did in North and South America with reference to the Western Hemisphere's indigenous peoples.

The terms of the *privilegium* granted the pacifist Hutterites and Mennonites exemption from military service as well as control of their own schools and local government (ironically including some policing responsibilities). The Anabaptists were allowed to use German as a semi-official language and were given the right to distill alcohol (a privilege historically reserved for the Russian nobility). In return the colonists agreed not to proselytize among members of the Russian Orthodox Church (i.e. most Russian Ukrainian peasants). Amazingly, the Mennonites and Hutterites did not contest this proscription. By this time both groups had become closed ethno-religious communities with little interest in evangelism. They rationalized this position by suggesting that God had called them to be Christian models, not missionaries.

Terms of the 1870 *ukase* meant that the Hutterites and Mennonites had to transfer control of their schools and local government to Russian Empire designates. Russian would be introduced as the primary language of instruction in schools and for government activities. Teachers had to be certified by the state. The latter qualification made Hutterites fear that their children might end up being taught by non-Anabaptist, perhaps Orthodox Christian, instructors. Most alarming to Mennonites and Hutterites was the termination of full exemption from military service, a stipulation that threatened their historic commitment to pacifism, a central belief. As Paul Tschetter put it in one his hymns,

3. Correll, "President Grant and the the Mennonite Immigration from Russia," 212.

> Christ the Lord commanded
> To love the enemy,
> Whoever betrays you; do them good.[4]

The new Russian laws were protested by prominent Mennonites who had government contacts in St. Petersburg. These entreaties were mostly unsuccessful and a requested hearing before the Tsar never materialized. Negotiations did eventually lead to significant policy changes that provided Anabaptist Church-funded alternatives to military service. These alternatives, discussed below, were not acceptable to the Hutterites.

As early as 1871, Paul Tschetter attended special meetings led by Elder Michael Stahl in the Hutterthal village school building.[5] Here there was significant debate about how to respond to the new government regulations. The following year, in February 1872, Tschetter joined Elder Stahl and Jacob Wipf as representatives of the noncommunal Hutterites on a seven-day visit to St. Petersburg, where they sought policy alterations on education and military service.[6] It is interesting to note that Michael Stahl and Jacob Wipf later became leaders in the communal Hutterite colonies in Dakota Territory.

While in the capital the Hutterite delegates were sent from one government official to another, wasting a lot of time and achieving almost nothing. Russian administrators told the delegates that they were not willing to let the Hutterites use German as the language of instruction in their schools. In response to requested military exemption they offered noncombatant service in the Army's "sanitation department."[7] Paul Tschetter wrote that one government official told them, "The Mennonites are not to be drafted to shed blood."[8] But military service in medical units was not acceptable to the Hutterites. Earlier, in 1853, some Hutterites had been forced to serve in this capacity during the Crimean War. One Hutterite, Sam Kleinsasser, received a gold watch from the Tsar for his "exemplary" service.[9] The Hutterites did not want to repeat that

---

4. Paul Tschetter, hymn #3, stanza eight (1873). HHMA.
5. NHCRB, 8.
6. NHCRB, 10.
7. NHCRB, 9–10.
8. NHCRB, 10.
9. D. Gross, ed., *Schmiedeleut Family Record*, 138. Schmiedeleut descendents do not know who inherited the watch.

embarrassing experience.¹⁰ Later as the Russian Government began to fear the loss of thousands of productive citizens, additional alternative service possibilities were offered, including work in civilian hospitals, fire companies, government forestry service and Crown-owned railways and factories.¹¹ By this time most of the Hutterites were preparing to leave for (or had already moved to) North America.

The February trip was followed by a second unsuccessful visit to St. Petersburg in the fall of 1872. This time Paul Tschetter stayed home and Michael Stahl was accompanied by Paul Gross and Peter Hofer.¹² This trip too was unsuccessful. What turned out to be a more important journey was undertaken from April to August, 1873, when Paul and his uncle Lohrentz joined a ten-person Russian Mennonite delegation to explore possibilities of settlement in the unpopulated central regions of the North American continent. In later years these men were often compared to the twelve "spies" that Moses sent to Canaan in the Book of Numbers account.

Preliminary arrangements for the North American journey were made by Russian Mennonite businessman, Cornelius Jansen and by American Mennonite leader, John F. Funk. There was also support from General Conference Mennonite leader Christian Krehbiel. Funk corresponded with Russian Mennonite leaders as early as 1871 and hosted an initial visit from four young Molotschna Colony men in 1872.¹³ Other settlement possibilities were also reviewed, including Turkestan, Russia's Amur Province, South America, Australia and New Zealand but none were as attractive as the United States and Canada.

In addition to theological and cultural reasons for emigration, many Mennonites were enticed by economic opportunities. American railroad companies, state and territorial commissions and the Canadian Government actively promoted these contingencies.¹⁴ For example, there was a significant shortage of land in the Molotschna and Chortitza colonies making it difficult for a majority of young Mennonites to purchase farms. Overpopulation and restrictive inheritance laws created a large landless (*Anwohner*) class of citizens, many of whom were eager

10. J. E. Hofer, "A History of the Neu Hutterthaler Church, 39. HHMA.
11. *CHB II*, 744.
12. NHCRB, 10.
13. Liebrandt, "The Emigration of the German Mennonites," 5.
14. Toews, "Non-resistance Re-examined."

Figure 4.1 Lohrentz Tschetter, 1873. Photograph courtesy of the Hutterite Mennonite Centennial Committee.

to improve their lot. A constant search for new areas of settlement led to the establishment of Mennonite daughter colonies that spread out for thousands of miles, from the Crimea to western Siberia. Hutterites were starting to experience a land shortage problem of their own and they did not want to emulate the Mennonite practice of establishing outpost settlements hundreds of miles away.

Among some Mennonites, emigration also expressed a new-found interest in evangelism. This was a special concern of break-away sects such as the Kleine Gemeinde, Mennonite Brethren and Krimmer Mennonite Brethren.[15] Since evangelism was prohibited in Russia it was difficult to adhere to Jesus' Great Commission. For Hutterites, interest in emigration followed some of the same lines of reasoning but unlike Mennonites, they acted collectively and there was no talk about missions.

Paul Tschetter hoped that another Hutterite minister might join him in the delegation to North America but no one was interested. Hutterite folklore suggests that Paul's 54-year-old uncle Lohrentz Tschetter went along to keep Paul company and because "he had

---

15. These Russian Mennonite sects were established in 1814, 1860, and 1869, respectively.

nothing better to do."¹⁶ He had no particular standing (except perhaps in a negative sense) in the Hutterite community. It is also said that Lohrentz had significant financial resources. In any case, Paul and Lohrentz Tschetter became the de facto representatives for all of the Hutterite villages, communal and noncommunal, as part of what the St. Paul *Dispatch* described as the Anabaptist "commission" from Russia, even though the Tschetters had not been officially selected to represent the communal Hutterite groups.¹⁷

Paul Tschetter was recognized for leadership abilities and for a resolute commitment to moral principles.¹⁸ In April, 1873, he was also only thirty-one years of age and full of curiosity about the world-at-large. Although he spoke no English, Tschettter had previously spent time in the city of St. Petersburg so he had some experience traveling to unfamiliar places.

In the Neu Hutterthaler (South Dakota) Church record book, Paul Tschetter later wrote that he requested specifically that someone from Hutterthal village join the delegation, giving a more broad-based representation and one that included a larger, more established community. But no one came forward.¹⁹ This was dismaying to Tschetter since his own village, Neu Hutterthal, consisted of only twenty families, yet he and Lohrentz were now representing one-sixth of the entire Mennonite/Hutterite delegation.

While Paul Tschetter was in North America, the communal Hutterite group sent its own separate delegation to St. Petersburg in a last ditch effort to secure a personal meeting with the Tsar. This delegation was comprised of George Hofer, Darius Walter, and Joseph "Yos" Hofer. We know a lot about this trip because "Yos" Hofer kept a diary, which Arnold M. Hofer discovered in the late 1980s. The 112-day excursion (from July 19–November 8) turned out to be no more successful than

---

16. Arnold M. Hofer, interview, July 1993.

17. Note in St. Paul *Dispatch* (June 5, 1873), in C. Hiebert, *Brothers in Deed to Brothers in Need*, 63.

18. W. Tschetter, "Reflections on Paul Tschetter." This presentation was based on interviews with a number of Paul Tschetter's grandchildren, including Emil Tschetter, Justina Guericke, and Maria Tschetter Hofer. WTC.

19. NHCRB, 10.

Paul Tschetter's earlier journey to the Russian capitol but it indicates that the communal group was not putting all of its eggs in one basket.[20]

In addition to the Tschetters, the twelve delegates to North America included the following Mennonite representatives: Leonhard Suderman, Jacob Buller, Tobias Unruh, Andreas Schrag, Jacob Peters, Heinrich Wiebe, Cornelius Buhr, Cornelius Toews, David Claassen, and Wilhelm Ewert.[21]

The Journey to the West

Many village residents came out to say farewell to Paul and Lohrentz on the day that they left Neu Hutterthal. Paul's parents, Jacob and Barbara cried and "clung to him until the last moment."[22] One of Lohrentz Tschetter's daughters "followed them until the faces they loved blurred into dots in the distance."[23] As Paul Tschetter put it, "So we left with a sad and troubled heart, only God knowing if I should ever see my loved ones again."[24]

Paul Tschetter kept a diary during his visit to the United States and Canada and it provides an important source for late nineteenth-century Hutterian thinking. The journal provides insights into European and American life from the perspective of a minimally educated Hutterite. It includes detailed reflections on American Mennonites, analysis of the unsettled lands and peoples of the North American mid-section, as well as deliberations on modern Western society. The diary contains everything from land fertility assessments to comments about Tschetter's personal health. The detailed account begins on Saturday, April 14 and continues through Friday, the 27th of July. It is the only diary account that Paul Tschetter is ever known to have kept. A latter-day reflection on the 1873 visit is found in a written statement Tschetter later prepared for the Neu Hutterthaler church book. Entitled "Report of Why We Had to Leave Russia"[25] this narrative provides Tschetter's most detailed analysis of the rationale for moving half-way around the world. It includes

---

20. A. M. Hofer, ed., *The Diaries of Joseph "Yos" Hofer*, July 1873 to November 1873 entries, 9–58.

21. Kaufman, ed., *General Conference Pioneers*, 44.

22. Peterson, ed., *People of the Old Missury: Years of Conflict*, 93.

23. Ibid.

24. JMH, "The Diary of Paul Tschetter," April 20 entry.

25. NHCRB, 10–17.

Figure 4.2 Paul Tschetter's Diary.
Photograph courtesy of Jeremy Waltner.

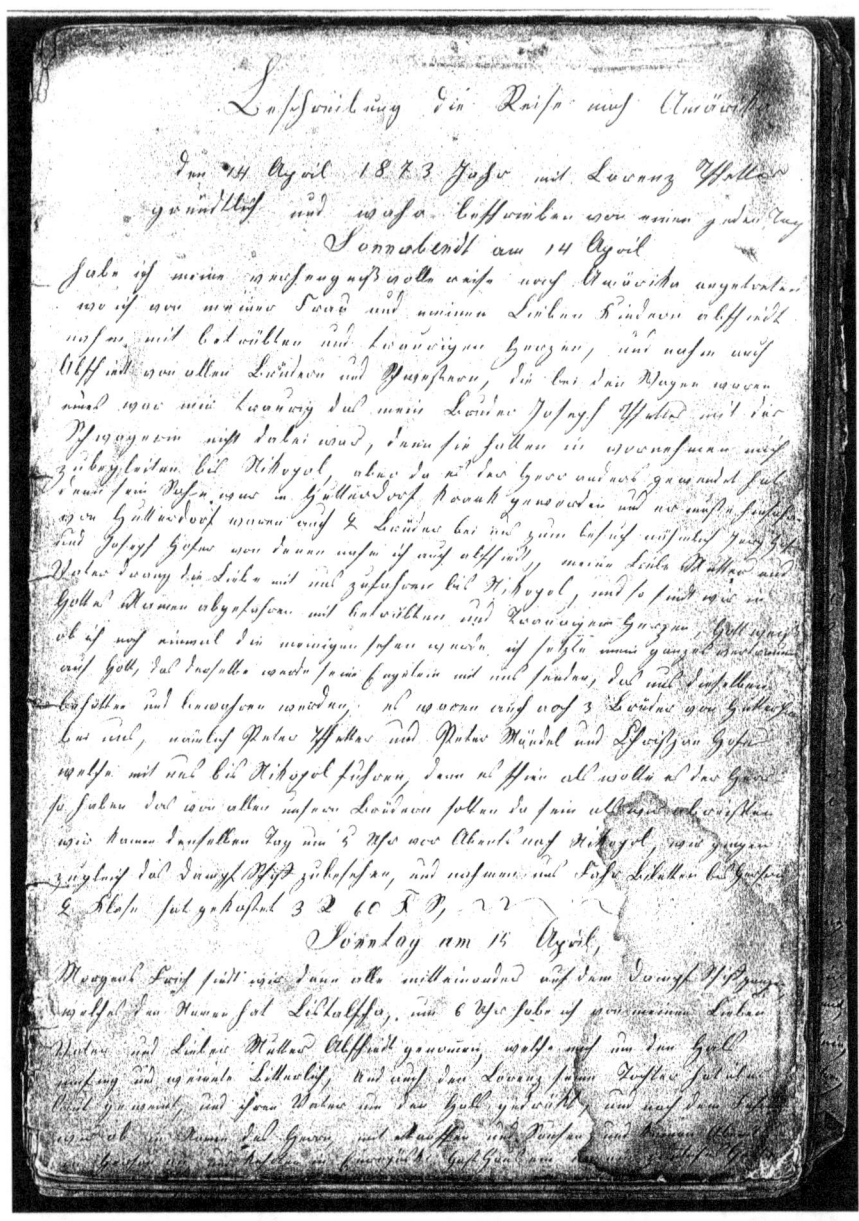

Figure 4.3 First Page of Paul Tschetter's Diary.
Photograph courtesy of Wesley Tschetter.

significant criticism of Russian Mennonite society. A copy of the report is included in Appendix B.

In his report, Tschetter notes that in southern Russia the Hutterite people found themselves economically dependent on a much larger Mennonite population. Mennonites also considered themselves intellectually and culturally superior to the Hutterites. Their influence on Hutterite theology, ecclesiology and culture was growing as the Mennonites provided teachers for Hutterite village schools and introduced an Anabaptist Christianity without communal roots and traditional Hutterite rituals. Mennonites had a different ecclesiastical structure and did not rely on centuries-old sermons. In general therefore Paul Tschetter believed that the Russian Mennonites were having a negative and at times secular impact on his people. This was an important reason for rebuilding Hutterite life in a new location.

Paul Tschetter's 1873 diary follows the Julian calendar dating system, and is thus twelve days behind the commonly used Gregorian calendar. This accounts for divergent dates in many Hutterian church records, historical accounts and personal correspondence. For purposes of discussing the 1873 tour this book uses the original Julian dating system, common in Orthodox Christian countries into the twentieth century.

The original copy of the Paul Tschetter diary comprises three small booklets in what has always been assumed to be Tschetter's handwriting. The diary is displayed in a simple manila folder, inside a glass-enclosed case, at the Heritage Hall Museum and Archives, on the campus of Freeman Academy (Freeman, South Dakota). In somewhat fragile condition, the diary is readable and mildew-free. Some of the pages show underlying handwriting indicating that the thrifty Tschetter (or whoever transcribed his notes) wrote over the top of a previous composition.

The writing that Tschetter did en route was most likely transcribed into a more presentable and readable form on his return to Ukraine. It is even possible that Tschetter did not copy the words that are found in the only extant copy. This is the conjecture of German scholar Albert Berg. In May 2004, the author was given permission to make a copy of the original, which was presented to Berg. He discovered that individual lines on two pages were originally positioned incorrectly; then scratched

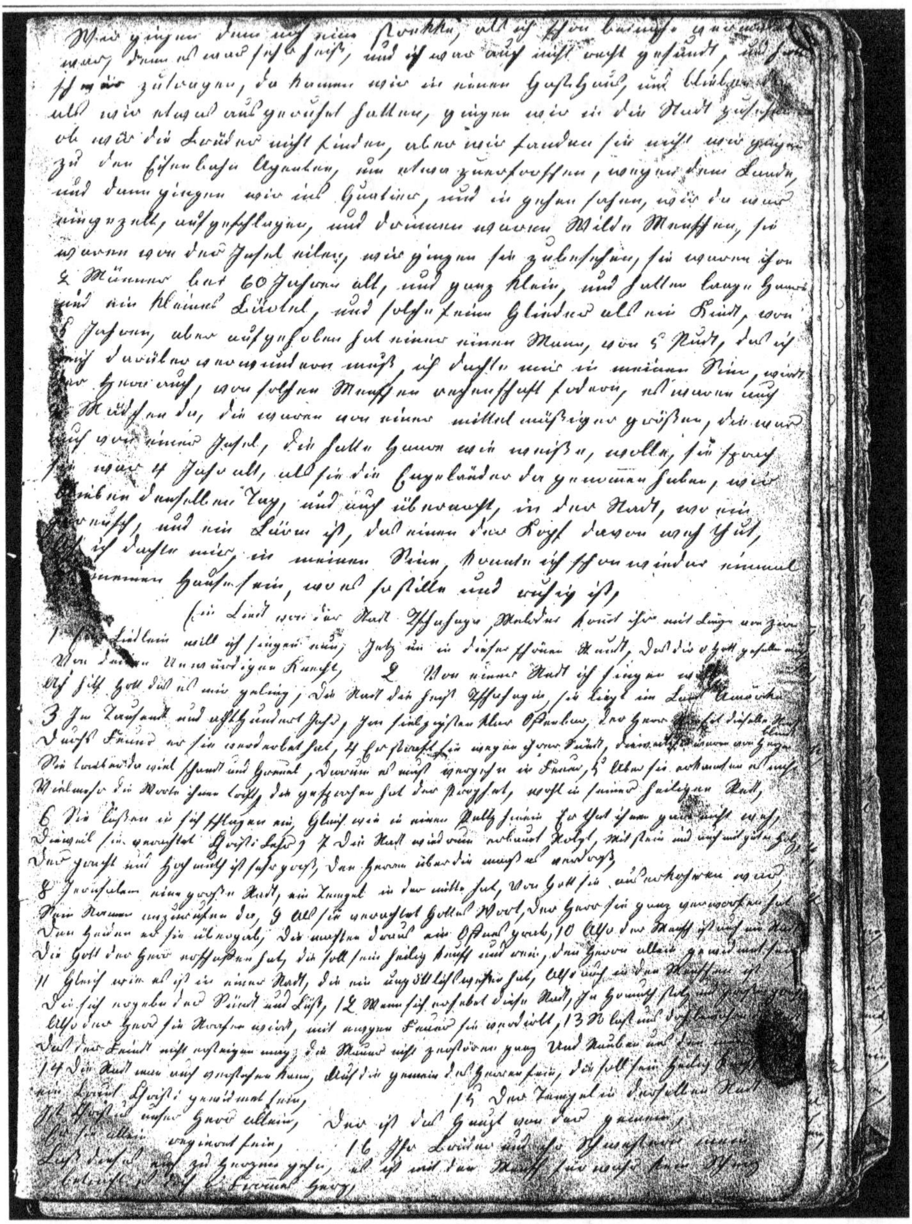

Figure 4.4 Paul Tschetter Diary, Handwriting Sample.
Photograph courtesy of Jeremy Waltner.

out.²⁶ Berg also found that Tschetter's "unique writing style" included the use of "speed writing" or abbreviated script.²⁷ Since Hutterite ministers were known to ask family members with good handwriting skills to transcribe copies of the Hutterite sermons, it is not unreasonable to assume that Tschetter did the same with his diary account.

The diary not only includes a day-by-day narrative but also twelve hymns composed by Tschetter during the trip. Eight of these hymns were for some reason written a second time, each placed in different parts of the diary. Tschetter provides both lyrics and suggested tunes for the hymns, which were likely never sung, except by Tschetter himself, and have not heretofore been translated. The hymns are significant because they represent the only known attempt at Hutterite songwriting since the seventeenth century.

Paul Tschetter's 1873 hymns range from ten to nineteen stanzas in length. He provides tune suggestions but it is sometimes difficult to determine exactly what he had in mind. For example, Tschetter often recommends the melody from a hymn entitled, "*O Gott du frommer Gott.*" This hymn, however, is sung with a variety of melodies by both Hutterites and Mennonites. In the 2000s, communal Hutterites sing the hymn using at least four different tunes.

In April 2005, sixty-seven Paul Tschetter descendents, led by great granddaughter Mary Ann Gross, sang four stanzas of one of Tschetter's hymns that had been translated into English. The rather didactic hymn was sung according to one of the melodies associated with the hymn "O Thank We Now Our God" (the melody suggested by Tschetter).²⁸ The first stanza reads as follows:

> God be with you
> And give you strength in all that you do.

---

26. Albert Berg, interview, February 2005. In May 2004, Heritage Museum archivist Duane Schrag granted permission to make a copy of the "original" diary.

27. Albert Berg, correspondence, May 2004.

28. Mennonite musicologist Helen Martens and Mennonite composer Larry Warkentin provided assistance in making determinations about hymn melodies referenced by Tschetter. Tony Waldner (Forest River Colony, Fordville, ND), indicated (in correspondence, April, 2005) that "*O Gott du frommer Gott*" is most commonly sung according to melodies also used for the hymns "*Spar deine Busse nicht*" and "*O Jesus susses Licht.*" This is the rendition composed by Johann Cruger in 1647 and later harmonized by Felix Mendelssohn in 1840. The Hutterites may have adopted the melody from Mennonites in Ukraine.

His Spirit shall guide you
On a level pathway.
Do not deviate
From God's Word and teaching.
Be steadfast and trust Him,
Build your lives only on Him.

This hymn encourages the maintaining of Christian traditions but it also contains a pietistic emphasis on the importance of inner transformation. It was written, as Tschetter indicates, "for J.M.," most likely Neu Hutterthal Village resident Jacob Mendel, who accompanied Tschetter to a meeting at Hutterthal village in 1872.[29] Mendel was the grandfather of Jacob J. Mendel, later a well-known South Dakota publisher.

In 1931 Jacob M. Hofer (whose wife, Maria Tschetter, was a granddaughter of Paul Tschetter), translated the Tschetter diary (minus the hymns) into English and it was published in the *Mennonite Quarterly Review* in back-to-back issues. The Hofer translation is found in Appendix A. At the time Hofer was a graduate student in history at the University of Chicago. What follows is an analysis of Tschetter's discoveries as found in his diary.

Spying Out the Land

Paul and Lohrentz Tschetter began their trip on April 14, 1873. With "prayer, sighing and weeping," they sailed down the Dnieper River to Kherson, then to the Black Sea port of Odessa.[30] From the outset the Tschetters were accompanied by two of the Mennonite representatives, Cornelius Toews and David Klassen, who represented the Kleine Gemeinde sect.[31] The delegates traveled through Poland to Germany, where they stopped briefly in Berlin. Tschetter observes: "We were strangers in a city where, no doubt, plenty of wicked people can be found."[32] On each day of the journey, Tschetter began and ended his waking hours with prayer. At the outset he also composed the following hymn, published here in its entirety:

---

29. HMCC, eds., *Hutterite Roots*, 90.

30. J. M. Hofer, ed., "The Diary of Paul Tschetter," 110.

31. The Kleine Gemeinde was a small Mennonite denomination established by Claas Reimer in 1812 as a conservative protest against the Russian Mennonite Church.

32. J. M. Hofer, ed., "The Diary of Paul Tschetter," 116.

In the year one thousand eight hundred,
In eighteen seventy-three,
In the month of April,
We were disturbed in our quietness.

Guided by the Lord's hand,
Now I must travel from this land
Into a strange place,
To search for a new homeland.

I did not go because of the flesh,
Because Jesus has forbidden this,
I gave myself to the will of God,
Whatever God wants, I will be happy.

I entrust to Him all of me,
My body and soul,
Because He gave them to me,
He will take care of my needs.

I entrust to Him my wife and child,
Heaviness was in my heart and soul,
And it lasted for a long time,
It is a heavy concern.

But if I truly consider,
This is not of much real importance,
Because I am following Christ's teaching,
He will be honored.

Christ, the Lord, commanded,
To love the enemy,
Whoever betrays you, do them good,
Christ, the Son of God, also tells us this.

The devil thought,
He could deceive by the snake's gift,
Like Adam in paradise,
Perceive this with great diligence.

Do not let yourself be seduced quickly,
And entrapped in sins and hell,
Stay firm to the good every time,
That you inherit blessedness.

> So I end this little song,
> That I write with pureness of heart,
> Consider what is right every time,
> Do not let yourselves be deceived by evil people.
> Amen.

The Tschetters arrived in Hamburg, Germany on April 20 and they stayed there for three days, waiting to board the ship that would take them across the Atlantic Ocean. Paul Tschetter writes that he was aware that a large community of Mennonites resided in Hamburg and he even "purchased a book on Menno Simons."[33] But he did not visit local Mennonites, nor did he even agree to meet with one of their ministers, the Rev. Karl Roosen, because as he put it, "[I] feared that I might get into an argument with him, for I knew that he was an unsound Mennonite."[34] German Mennonites were more liberal on theological and lifestyle issues and had a close working relationship with the state. Members wore modern dress and commonly served in the military and Tschetter wanted to have nothing to do with them.

Throughout his historic journey, whether on trains traveling across the European and North American continents or on board ships sailing across the Atlantic Ocean, Tschetter writes constantly about the crowded conditions, the "great noise and bustle in and about" and he often complains about the "worldliness" of other passengers.[35] More positively, Tshetter writes that there was usually plenty of food to eat. Tschetter also regularly communicates concern for his family in Ukraine. In one of his hymns he exclaims,

> I entrust onto Him my wife and child,
> They will be protected from evil.
> He is the true father alone,
> Who guards His children.[36]

In his diary, Tschetter expresses a general distrust of cities, places where he says that there are "no doubt, plenty of wicked people."[37] "Stand firm to the good every time," Tschetter admonishes, confronting squarely

---

33. Ibid., 118.
34. Ibid.
35. Ibid., 116.
36. Paul Tschetter, hymn #3 (1873). HHMA.
37. J. M. Hofer, ed., "The Diary of Paul Tschetter," 116.

the many temptations of urban life.[38] While in Hamburg, Tschetter walked through the main hall of a five-story inn where some boys and girls were dancing. In his diary entry Tschetter instructs that "they should rather pray than dance."[39] This statement is reminiscent of Hutterite Joseph "Yos" Hofer's comments about St. Petersburg, written in the same year (1873). Hofer notes, "Yes, here there is nothing to see than a lot of bustle and noise ... everything here is running toward hell."[40]

On his journey Paul Tschetter suffered frequently from intense headaches (probably migraines), which were at times almost incapacitating and caused him to spend a great deal of time in whatever private spaces he could find. Tschetter also had many intestinal problems, some of which were possibly stress-related, although in later years he blamed them on seasickness."[41]

After boarding a ship at Hamburg, the Tschetters, Klassen, and Toews, now joined by the delegates Heinrich Wiebe, Cornelius Buhr and Jacob Peters, sailed up the Elbe River to the North Sea and into the English Channel. At Le Havre, France they boarded the *S.S. Silesia* and sailed across "the great and wild Atlantic Ocean."[42] The delegates spent the next thirteen days "swimming around on the stormy ocean," an experience that included the sighting of icebergs near Iceland.[43] They arrived in New York City on May 7 and the distraught Tschetter expressed great joy that he was now "relieved of the godless rabble with whom I was obliged to spend such a long time on the ocean."[44]

In New York City, Tschetter may also have had his picture taken. If so, this violated Hutterite teachings against the making of graven images. Paul Tschetter always opposed the taking of photographs and he battled against the practice for most of his life. Yet there is one extant photograph of the Rev. Tschetter that was taken when he was visiting the United States. Written accounts (based on oral history) as well as interviews (past and present) indicate that the photograph was taken in New York City. This might have occurred on arrival or during a second

38. Paul Tschetter hymn #3 (1873). HHMA.
39. J. M. Hofer, ed., "The Diary of Paul Tschetter," 117.
40. A. M. Hofer, ed., *The Diary of Joseph "Yos" Hofer*, 20.
41. J. M. Hofer, ed., "The Diary of Paul Tschetter," 117.
42. Ibid., 110.
43. Ibid., 120.
44. Ibid., 122.

visit to the city at the end of the summer when Tschetter was waiting to meet President U.S. Grant. In any case, hundreds of copies of the photograph are in circulation.

There is no way to definitively explain how and why Tschetter allowed himself to be photographed. Maybe it was a visa or passport requirement at the beginning or end of the trip. Hutterite folklore says that he took it on a whim. In an often-told story, grandson Paul G. Tschetter said that the photograph was not required; that Lohrentz convinced his nephew to take it.

Paul G. Tschetter said that his grandfather later threw the photograph overboard on the journey back across the Atlantic Ocean. According to this account, which is part of Hutterian folklore, the three delegates encountered a very bad storm at sea and, like Jonah in the Old Testament, the Rev. Tschetter thought God was punishing everyone on board because of his own idolatrous indiscretion. "We are the Jonahs on this ship," he exclaimed to Lohrentz and threw what he thought was the only copy of the photograph overboard. The seas calmed immediately.[45]

According to this and other accounts, the continued existence of the Paul Tschetter photograph is credited to Lohrentz Tschetter who is said to have held back at least one copy of the photograph. On arrival at Neu Hutterthal village, Lohrentz pulled the photograph out of a coat pocket, showed it to his nephew and started laughing at him. If this story is true, all later copies came from Lohrentz's facsimiles.

In his diary, Paul Tschetter's only comment about photographs is found in a June 6 (1873) entry where he says that an unnamed man wanted to photograph the twelve delegates in Winnipeg before they set off on an excursion westward. Tschetter writes, "As we were about to leave with our wagons (west of Winnipeg) a man came carrying a tripod with a box and glass on top."[46] Tschetter notes that this was "not to my taste, because I do not like to have my picture lying around in all parts of the world. But what will you do with the world? World is world and will remain world until the Lord will come and end it all."[47] This statement implies that Tschetter allowed his picture to be taken a second time under duress but there is no known copy of this photograph if it was in fact taken.

45. Paul G. Tschetter, interview, July 1998.
46. J. M. Hofer, ed., "The Diary of Paul Tschetter," 203.
47. Ibid.

Figure 4.5 John F. Funk.
Photograph courtesy of the Archives of the Mennonite Church, Goshen, Indiana.

In Clarence Hiebert's book, *Brothers in Deed to Brothers in Need*, Paul and Lohrentz Tschetter's names, spelled incorrectly as "Farl" Tschetter and "Corcar" Tschetter, are printed to the right of a formal portrait of about twenty people standing on the main deck of the *S.S. Silesia*.[48] The caption includes the Tschetters' somewhat correct ages as well as their occupations ("farmers"). But the Tschetters are not recognizable in the picture and the photograph is likely a generic one. Interviewed a few months before his death in 2006, Clarence Hiebert said that he could not remember why he had placed the Tschetter names next to this photograph.[49]

From New York City, the Tschetters and their original traveling partners Klassen and Toews (the others went on a side trip to Ontario) took a forty-six hour train ride to Elkhart, Indiana, where they contacted the Swiss Mennonite publisher John F. Funk on May 12. Funk had negotiated the delegates' travel arrangements with railroad companies on behalf of the Mennonite Board of Guardians, whom he served as treasurer.[50] The railroads provided free transportation and assisted the delegates in finding lodging.[51] Funk, a Mennonite minister, was the editor of the Mennonite *Herald of Truth (Herald Der Wahrheit)*, which was published in both English and German. He was also a leader in the "Great Awakening" movement in the American Mennonite Church, an effort that emphasized holy living, personal conversion, and practical piety. During the previous summer and fall (1872) John Funk had visited the plains states himself, primarily on the Northern Pacific rail line.[52]

Paul Tschetter stayed in Elkhart for eleven days. While there he attended Mennonite church services and was impressed with the religious vitality of the congregants; with their sermons and their general worship practices but he had at least one disappointment. "There was one thing that I did not approve," he notes, "and that was the fact that some of the women smoked and chewed tobacco."[53] Tschetter found Mennonite

---

48. C. Hiebert, ed., *Brothers in Deed to Brothers in Need*, 46.

49. Clarence Hiebert, interview, July 2005. Hiebert died in November 2005.

50. Ernst Correll, "Mennonite Immigration Into Manitoba: Sources and Documents, 1872, 1873," MQR (July, October, 1927), 202.

51. Liebrandt, "The Emigration of the German Mennonites," 5.

52. "John F. Funk's Land Inspection Trips." Funk's diary, dated June 3–July 26, 1873, is published in Clarence Hiebert, *Brothers in Deed to Brothers in Need*, 48–54.

53. J. M. Hofer, ed., "The Diary of Paul Tschetter," 123.

men doing the same. Tschetter was also disturbed by reddish-colored rugs in some Mennonite homes as well as wall-papered interiors, which to him showed materialistic indulgence. He also disliked the presence of mirrors, a clear sign of idolatry.

On Sunday, May 13, Paul Tschetter was asked to preach a sermon at an afternoon service at the Shaum Mennonite Church. At the beginning of the service he was asked to sit up front with the rest of the ministers. Tschetter selected the Hutterite sermon on 1 John 5:14–21, which he likely read from his own hand-copied *Lehren* book, which was completed in 1870, and which is presently in the possession of a descendent in South Dakota. Tschetter also brought along a collection of martyr hymns.

Two days later (on May 15) Tschetter delivered a second sermon, this time at a special Tuesday morning service at the Yellow Creek Mennonite congregation. Tschetter refers to Yellow Creek sermon as an "extemporaneous" one.[54] It is hard to know exactly what this means. Tschetter wrote that he preached the sermon with "as much as the Lord gave me grace, for it is customary here in America to preach from memory."[55] This tradition continues among the Old Order Amish. Unanswered is the question of whether Tschetter created his own sermon or simply preached as much of a particular Hutterite sermon as he could remember.

Another American Mennonite practice that displeased Tschetter was the use of musical instruments. According to Tschetter, one man "had a music box (actually an organ) in his house and he began to play the instrument." After listening to several pieces, Tschetter remarked, "the Apostle said, 'Speak to yourselves in Psalms and hymns and spiritual songs . . .'" In defense the Mennonite organist reminded Tschetter that the psalmist David had played the harp. Tschetter's counterattack was that David had also been a warrior and shed a good deal of blood and that this was against New Testament principles. According to Tschetter his adversary "became silent and did not say another word."[56]

Tschetter also disliked the American Mennonite acceptance of hunting, exclaiming at one point: "what a fine example of a non-resistant Mennonite" after one of the "gray-haired old ministers . . . emerged from

54. Ibid., 124.
55. Ibid.
56. Ibid., 127.

the woods, gun in hand."[57] In general Tschetter was more impressed with the Amish because of their more conservative dress, opposition to musical instruments and separatist ideology.[58]

On Sunday May 20, Tschetter was asked to preach in the Elkhart area for a third time and he selected the Acts 2 Hutterite sermon. One wonders how the Mennonite audience responded to this sermon's blunt criticism of noncommunal Christians and/or whether Tschetter passed over the sermon's strongest statements. While in Elkhart he also attended services at an evangelical church located near the home of John F. Funk. Tschetter was less than pleased with what he saw and experienced there. According to Tschetter, as the sermon progressed:

> The minister began to speak louder and louder and as I sat near the pulpit I was greatly bewildered; in fact I felt like running from the church. He marched back and forth behind the pulpit, once to this side and then to the other as if he were insane. He hammered on the pulpit with his fist, and pointing to his heart he cried, 'Herein must the Lord live.' At times he pointed toward heaven and then again down to hell, shouting like a mad man, for only a mad man could act like he did. His actions were not those of a minister of the Gospel but those of a general.
>
> Sometimes he praised everyone into heaven and then again he damned us all into hell. It is not in my power to describe this and my readers will doubt my statements, but it remains true nevertheless. I have been in many churches but have never witnessed the like. A comedy could hardly offer more entertainment.[59]

Tschetter ends this comment with the interesting conclusion that the minister "preached the truth but with great indiscretion and lack of judgment."

On the 22nd of May the delegation said farewell to Elkhart and headed west, the two Tschetters accompanied again by Klassen and Toews as well as John F. Funk, who served as a guide, interpreter and comrade for the next few weeks. In his diary Funk commonly refers to the delegates as the "Russians."[60] The delegates were also accompanied

---

57. Ibid.

58. The Amish, named after Jacob Ammann, divided from the Swiss Mennonite Church in 1693.

59. J. M. Hofer, ed., "The Diary of Paul Tschetter," 126.

60. "Diary of John F. Funk, June 3—July 26, 1873," in C. Hiebert, *Brothers in Deed to*

by C. B. Power, the Northern Pacific Railroad's chief land department agent. Another Northern Pacific representative, the German-speaking Michael Hiller, joined the group later, at Fargo, Dakota Territory.[61]

Since the rail line ran straight through the city of Chicago, the delegates spent a full day and one night there on the banks of an ice-filled Lake Michigan. While in the city Tschetter also composed a hymn entitled *Ein Lied von der Stadt Tschakaga*, which is a theological reflection on the Great Chicago Fire of 1871. It has been translated into English by the poet Jean Janzen and is published below:[62]

1. I will sing a little song
   Here in this strange city.
   May it please you, oh God,
   From your unworthy servant.

2. I sing about a city;
   With God's help I will do it well,
   This city called Chicago
   In the land of America.

3. In October of 1871
   The Lord punished this city
   Destroying her with fire,
   Judging her for her sins.

4. From their hearts, loose and distant
   Poured deeds of shame and horror.
   Therefore the fire poured over them,
   But they did not understand.

5. Even as they allowed
   The words of the Prophet
   In his holy speech
   To be beaten into them,

6. As though under their skin,
   Yet they found no rest
   Because they despised
   The teachings of Jesus.

Brothers in Need, 48–54.

61. Schell, *History of South Dakota*, 72.

62. A more in depth analysis of this hymn is found in R. Janzen and J. Janzen, "Paul Tschetter's Chicago Fire Hymn."

7. With pride they erected the city again,
   With rocks and fine wood,
   And with lofty splendor
   To the Lord's great displeasure.

8. For Jerusalem, that great city
   Is elected by God, the temple
   In the middle, that place
   Where we may call on his name.

9. When these despised God's Word
   The Lord abandoned them,
   Gave them to the pagans
   Who made of them an open grave.

10. A person is like a city
    Created by God the Lord
    Who must be holy and pure
    And faithful to the Lord

11. It is the same in a city
    Which has an ungodly heart
    As it is with the people
    Who surrender to sin and lust

12. When this city is exalted
    In prude and great splendor,
    The Lord will punish her again,
    Will ruin her with eternal fire.

13. So let us preserve the city
    That the enemy may not conquer it,
    The walls not be destroyed,
    The interior be protected.

14. For the city can also be understood
    To be the community of the Lord
    Who shall be holy, just and pure,
    The Bride consecrated to Christ.

15. The temple in this same city
    Is Christ our Lord alone,
    He is the Spirit of the community,
    The One who governs with excellence.

16. You my brothers and sisters,
    May this enter your hearts:
    There is no other security.
    Contemplate this, oh pious heart.

The Chicago Fire occurred in October 1871 and burned for two days. The fire originated in the vicinity of a cow barn near a cottage owned by a man named Patrick O'Leary, though there is no proof that the legendary account of his wife's cow kicking over a lantern started it.[63] But ultimately three hundred people lost their lives as a result of the fire and another 90,000 were left homeless. Property damage was estimated at about 200 million dollars and this included 18,000 buildings and about 28 miles of streets. The fire received national and international attention.

Between 1871 and 1873, however, the city of Chicago was re-built in remarkably rapid fashion with stone and steel making it clear that American urban industrial areas could respond quickly and successfully to disasters and simultaneously make significant improvements to infrastructure. The response to the Great Fire was thus a source of pride for the city of Chicago and for the United States as a whole. But this is not how Tschetter viewed it.

Paul Tschetter rode into Chicago by train on the evening of May 22, 1873. Feeling tired and ill Tschetter went immediately to the hotel where the delegates were to spend the night, deciding not to join the rest of them on a sightseeing venture. Later, while taking a private stroll on the Chicago streets Tschetter sighted many bizarre things, including "two wild and uncivilized men from a distant island caged up."[64] It seemed that everything Tschetter saw in Chicago was an indication of the debauchery of urban life. Even when he was in his hotel room, he was "surrounded by so much noise and tumult that my head ached."[65] These experiences likely influenced the lyrics of the "Chicago Fire" hymn. Ironically, Paul's son, Joseph W., later spent forty years establishing and leading a mission church in the downtown section of the same despised city.

---

63. Important sources for information about Chicago's Great Fire are the following: Ross Miller, *The Great Chicago Fire* (Chicago: University of Illinois Press, 2000); and Sawislak, *Smoldering City: Chicagoans & and the Great Fire, 1871–1874*.

64. J. M. Hofer, ed., "The Diary of Paul Tschetter," 198.

65. Ibid.

Tschetter's diary account shows that he knew that the city of Chicago had "nearly burned to the ground one and one-half years ago."[66] He was also aware of the re-building effort that had taken place, writing in his diary: "By this time [May 22] large portions of the city have already been rebuilt."[67] Tschetter saw this with his own eyes. But he did not view the project positively, noting in his diary that "according to all of these things the end of the world must be nigh."[68] He viewed rebuilding efforts as an example of materialistic obsession. It showed that secular-minded Chicagoans had learned little if anything from the great conflagration.

Paul Tschetter's "Chicago" hymn is a clear reflection of late nineteenth-century Hutterian thought. In Tschetter's opinion the fire was the direct result of the lifestyle of the people living there, of their "loose and distant" hearts and their "deeds of shame and horror." In response God had "judg[ed] her for her sins."[69] Tschetter was not impressed that the city was being re-built quickly, in many cases with better and more fire-resistant building materials. To him this showed only pride and arrogance. God would ultimately have to bring the city down again.

In the Chicago Fire hymn, Tschetter also compares the city of Chicago to the individual Christian and emphasizes the importance of maintaining personal purity in order to please God. He completes the hymn by instructing the Hutterite church, the *Gemein*, to be on guard against sinful powers.

After leaving Chicago the delegates visited St. Paul and Duluth, Minnesota, re-connecting with some of the Russian Mennonite representatives. A local newspaper mentioned the foreigners' visit while misspelling the Tschetter name as "Schetter."[70] In St. Paul some of the delegates also met with representatives of the Northern Pacific Railroad concerning land purchase issues as well as requested religious and cultural privileges. Leaving St. Paul the delegates traveled west to Fargo in Dakota Territory where all twelve delegates reconnoitered at the Mississippi river town.

66. Ibid.
67. Ibid.
68. Ibid.
69. Paul Tschetter, "The Chicago Fire Hymn" (1873). HHMA.
70. "The Mennonites: Arrival of a Delegation in the City Yesterday," in C. Hiebert, *Brothers in Deed to Brothers in Need*, 62.

In 1873 Dakota Territory comprised the present states of South Dakota and North Dakota. The area was not opened to non-Indian settlement until 1859 and was not recognized as a separate governing entity until 1861. During the next twelve years (1861–1873) the territory was the site of many attacks on settlers and railroad personnel as American Indians fought last ditch battles in defense of their traditional lands and way of life. The Northern Pacific Railroad only finished laying track from Fargo westward to the town of Bismarck in the spring of 1873.

The Northern Pacific Railroad hired an African-American cook for the Anabaptist expedition and, as C. Henry Smith notes, "For supper the first night on the prairie they had roast beef, potatoes, bread, butter, hominy, pudding, pie, and good coffee."[71] This was followed by a four-day journey on the Hudson Bay Company steamboat *Dakota*, motoring up the Red River to Winnipeg, a distance of 294 miles. John F. Funk wrote that a few "Indians" were also on board.[72] On one occasion the delegates held a church service on board.

En route Paul Tschetter paid close attention to the quality of the land they passed through. He was concerned about soil types, the presence of rivers or streams (for mill construction), the experiences of previous settlers, climate, water and feed sources and the existence of rail lines (to get products to market). The agricultural potential of much of the land seemed particularly suited for producing wheat and raising cattle. In the Fargo area, at the east-central border of the Territory, Tschetter found rich black soil that was two feet deep as well as abundant wild berries and lumber sources.

Tschetter was not as impressed with the Winnipeg region (later Manitoba), describing it (in a later manuscript) as "too far north and too cold."[73] In his diary Tschetter wrote, "Here and there one could see a miserable hut inhabited by Indians." He noted that "these Indians are quite civilized and would not hurt anyone" but he was not impressed with their way of life.[74] Winnipeg at the time was a small village with a population under 500 and accommodations in the area were primitive.[75]

---

71. C. H. Smith, *The Coming of the Russian Mennonites*, 62. Smith relied significantly on the account of Molotshna Colony delegate, Leonhard Suderman.

72. Funk, "Notes By the Way," October 1873, *Herald of Truth*. AMC.

73. NHCRB, 12.

74. J. M. Hofer, ed., "The Diary of Paul Tschetter," 200.

75. HMCC, eds., *A History of the Hutterite Mennonites*, 49.

John F. Funk later wrote: "It was altogether a pretty rough trip. The mosquitoes were thick at times, and we had to sleep on the floor...."[76] In his own diary delegate Leonhard Suderman noted that even "completely clothed, hats on our heads, with nets over our faces, it was still impossible to protect ourselves from these intruders."[77]

Seeing enough of Canada, on the ninth of June, the Tschetters, along with Wilhelm Ewert, Andreas Schrag and Tobias Unruh, left the other delegates (who wanted to spend more time there) and returned to the United States. Just south of the border the travelers were especially impressed with the Pembina area in the Red River valley, where Tschetter noted "beautiful land with black soil and an excellent growth of grass."[78] The delegates also saw thick "woods" that included oaks and poplars, "often so thick that two men could hardly reach around them."[79] Tschetter also cited plentiful water sources. It was in the Pembina area that Paul Tschetter composed a hymn that grandson, Paul G. Tschetter, entitled "The New Jerusalem."[80] "I want to sing about a city," Tschetter writes, "Her name is Jerusalem, and every Christian knows her."[81] Tschetter describes the new "Jerusalem" or heaven as a place where the streets are "decorated with pearls beautifully."[82] He also compares it to a "beautiful meadow."[83] When Leonhard Suderman visited this same area about a week later, he found plentiful supplies of wild currants, gooseberries and grapes as well as "black earth two feet deep."[84]

Previous visitors had also been impressed with the land in the northeastern corner of Dakota Territory. Russian Mennonite businessman Bernhard Warkentin, for example, toured the area in September, 1872, as part of an earlier Northern Pacific Railroad-funded excur-

---

76. John F. Funk, correspondence, June 27, 1873. John F. Funk Collection, Box 7. AMC.

77. Suderman, *From Russia to America*, 17.

78. J. M. Hofer, ed., "The Diary of Paul Tschetter," 204.

79. Ibid.

80. Paul Tschetter, hymn #8 (1873). HHMA. Paul G. Tschetter, "Monologue," tape, June 1989, Mitchell, South Dakota. HHMA.

81. Paul Tschetter, hymn #8, stanza one (1873). HHMA.

82. Ibid., stanza two.

83. Ibid., stanza six.

84. Suderman, *From Russia to America*, 24.

sion and his reaction was extremely positive.⁸⁵ John F. Funk was with Warkentin and was similarly impressed, noting the presence of wild cherries, strawberries and other garden products as well as good timber, corn and oats.⁸⁶ In an article in *Der Herold der Wahrheit*, Funk actively promoted settlement in the Pembina area.⁸⁷ As Tschetter put it in a hymn included in his diary:

> As I wandered through the wide forest,
> A thought came over me,
> How God so wonderfully,
> Created so many trees,
> Those stand so beautiful,
> Full of life strength,
> So preciously lasting,
> And so magnificent.⁸⁸

While crossing the prairies, the delegates spent the night in tents or in private homes. On many occasions Tschetter felt so ill that he stayed in his room while the others were out viewing land or sightseeing. One of his evening hymns reads as follows:

> The day has come to an end,
> The sun went down,
> The darkness is coming herein,
> The stars becoming visible ...
> Today You have protected me,

---

85. Schnell, "John F. Funk and the Mennonite Migrations of 1873–1885."

86. C. Hiebert, ed., *Brothers in Deed to Brothers in Need*, 48–54. Schnell, "John F. Funk and the Mennonite Migrations of 1873–1885," 71–72.

87. "The Russian Brethren," 168. *Der Herold der Wahrheit*. AMC.

88. Paul Tschetter, hymn #6 (1873). HHMA.

> From sin and lust,
> And from life's harm too.[89]

Along the way the delegates had a number of encounters with prairie settlers, who were in general eager to attract neighbors. General William Beadle, who traveled across Dakota Territory around the same time, wrote the following about the pioneers he encountered: "They were lonely, far from neighbors and denied by circumstances the social life that is so much better."[90] On one occasion in Moorhead, Minnesota, the delegates were offered lodging at the home of a German family, but a saloon was located in the same building. This bothered Paul Tschetter, so he, Lohrentz and Tobias Unruh crossed the Red River to the Fargo (Dakota Territory) side and found alternative lodging.[91]

The delegates also viewed land in southwestern Minnesota and visited the region near Sioux City, Iowa. But they discovered that reasonably priced government land was not available in these states.[92] Continuing southward the delegation looked at land between Omaha and Columbus, Nebraska but again they were not impressed. Paul and Lohrentz Tschetter had seen enough. While Wilhelm Ewert and Andreas Schrag continued to central Kansas, the Tschetters and Tobias Unruh went north.[93] According to Tschetter, "We decided to return to Dakota and meet the other brothers in two weeks at Moorhead."[94]

All in all, Paul Tschetter was most impressed with the land on the northern plains of Dakota Territory and he wrote that it reminded him of the Ukrainian steppes. Land prices were about three dollars an acre if purchased from the railroads and much less from the United States Government if it was homesteaded. These contingencies were attractive to Tschetter. He was especially interested in the Red River valley near Pembina and thought that the entire Hutterite community should settle there.[95] Tschetter continued to be concerned, however, about the lack of formal government assurances that Hutterites would be exempted from military service. Before making a final decision to immigrate he

89. Ibid., hymn #13.
90. Beadle, *Autobiography of William Henry Harrison Beadle*, 126.
91. J. M. Hofer, ed., "The Diary of Paul Tschetter," 208.
92. Ibid., 204.
93. Ibid., 212.
94. Ibid., 204.
95. Ibid., 211.

sought a face-to-face meeting with President Ulysses S. Grant so that he could request a personal and official guarantee. One might think that this was an impossible request but Northern Pacific Railroad agents told Tschetter that they could arrange a meeting.

Although he was a war hero Ulysses S. Grant held strong peace sentiments. In his Second Inaugural Address (in spring 1873) Grant proposed utopian one-world perspectives with statements like the following: "I believe that our great Maker is preparing the world, in His own good time, to become one nation, speaking one language, and when armies and navies will be no longer required."[96] In a speech given a few years later (in England in 1877), Grant, sounding like Karl Marx, railed against the evils of capitalism.[97] Most important, Grant was an active supporter of immigrant settlements on the sparsely populated prairies.

For Paul Tschetter it was important that the federal government provide confirmation of specific social and political rights. Otherwise there was no reason to leave Russia. This was especially consequential since the Tschetters had decided not to settle in Canada, where the government granted virtually every privilege the Mennonites who settled there requested.

So after fifty-two days of exploration, Paul and Lohrentz Tschetter, along with Tobias Unruh headed to the East Coast to see the President, stopping first in Elkhart, Indiana, where they stayed for five days.[98] Here, on July 15, Paul Tschetter preached his fourth and final American sermon, what he described as "the main sermon" in the church service. Tschetter was followed by Tobias Unruh, who preached a short sermon of his own. Tschetter read the Hutterite sermon on Colossians II but it was not well received. According to grandson Emil Tschetter, at one point the Rev. Tschetter looked up from the text and noticed that there was no one left in the meeting house.[99] In his diary Tschetter describes the situation this way: "The congregation was very small, but when the sermon was over there were even less. Hardly

---

96. A comprehensive study of Ulysses S. Grant is McFeely, *Grant: A Biography*.

97. Ibid., 462.

98. J. M. Hofer, ed., "The Diary of Paul Tschetter," 212.

99. Wesley Tschetter, notes from interview with Emil Tschetter, May 1984. WTC. According to Emil, Jacob M. Hofer spoke to an individual who was in attendance at the church where this incident occurred.

any were left except the ministers. Very likely the sermon was not to their taste."[100] Perhaps many in the Mennonite audience simply had difficulty understanding German. Afterward, Tschetter wrote, "I had such a headache that I had to lie down as soon as we reached home and did not eat anything that evening."[101]

The group left Elkhart the next day and on July 18, they arrived in Philadelphia, where they met Michael Hiller, the German-speaking Northern Pacific Railroad agent.[102] Hiller, who had accompanied the delegation on their trip from Fargo to Winnipeg, served as translator for the Tschetters in their meeting with President Grant, which was arranged by Northern Pacific Railroad trustee, Jay Cooke.

The Tschetters first appointment in Philadelphia was at Jay Cooke's office, at 10 A.M. on the 19th of July. This meeting included the consumption of "some very excellent wine."[103] Before the meeting Paul Tschetter met a group of Moravian Church members in the office lobby. Always ready to speak his mind, he engaged in a heated debate with the Moravians over the issue of female leadership in the church, which the Moravians supported and he did not.[104]

Paul Tschetter Meets Ulysses S. Grant

A meeting between the cigar-smoking ex-general and three unsophisticated, German-speaking pacifists is remarkably ironic and it shows the influence of the Northern Pacific Railroad on the Grant Administration. Jay Cooke was a well-known financier, land speculator and Republican Party fundraiser who had backed Grant's 1872 election campaign. Grant had even visited Cooke at his home in Philadelphia.[105] With regard to the involvement of Michael Hiller, Cooke wrote a letter of introduction, portraying the former as "an eminent German citizen of New York."[106] Cooke described the Tschetters and Unruh as "Mennonites

---

100. J. M. Hofer, ed., "The Diary of Paul Tschetter," 213.
101. Ibid.
102. Liebrandt, "The Emigration of the German Mennonites," 10.
103. J. M. Hofer, ed., "The Diary of Paul Tschetter," 215.
104. Ibid.
105. Harder, "The Russian Mennonites and American Democracy under Grant," 55.
106. Correll, "President Grant and the Mennonite Immigration," 146. Correll quotes a letter of introduction from Jay Cooke to U. S. Grant, dated July 31, 1873. The "Letter of Introduction from Jay Cooke, Trustee of the Northern Pacific Railroad, introducing

from Russia" and confirmed the desirability of attracting "thousands" of immigrants from this group.[107] Hiller later wrote Secretary of State Hamilton Fish that Jay Cooke and Company "represente[d] the Mennonite delegates by power of attorney."[108]

Paul Tschetter prepared for the meeting with Grant by drafting a handwritten petition in German stipulating various desired privileges. Tschetter had the draft translated into English and handed it over to Michael Hiller. The letter is published in full in Appendix C. Earlier that same summer, two other Anabaptists had also met with President Grant. This encounter included Russian Mennonite immigration advocate, Cornelius Jansen and his son Peter.[109] Peter Jansen's personal account of the meeting was published fifty years later, in 1921. Jansen recalled that he and his father were surprised that the executive mansion in Washington D.C. was "guarded by a single colored man, who not even displayed a sword!"[110] Jansen described President Grant as "a rather stocky, middle-aged man, with a closely cropped full beard and well shaped head, dressed in a rather worn black Prince Albert coat . . ."[111]

The young Peter Jansen was impressed that Grant had grown up on a farm and in the course of their conversation the President not only informed his guests that "he could hitch up and drive a team of horses as well as ever," but that during his younger years he had milked twenty cows a day, morning and evening.[112] But the real highlight of the meeting was when Grant introduced the Mennonite guests to the German-speaking General George Custer, who was accompanied by a delegation of American Indian chiefs. Exhibiting concurrence with contemporary popular opinion Jansen wrote: "Poor General Custer! Three years later

---

M. L. Hiller to President Grant," is found in C. Hiebert, ed., *Brothers in Deed to Brothers in Need*, 64.

107. Correll, "President Grant and the Mennonite Immigration," 146.

108. Ibid., 148.

109. Jansen, *Memoirs of Peter Jansen*.

110. Ibid., 35. Jansen later served as one of twelve United States commissioners to the World's Fair in Paris in 1900. He was appointed by President William McKinley, whom he helped nominate for President at the Republican Party National Convention in St. Louis, in 1896.

111. Ibid., 35.

112. Ibid.

[in 1876] he met his untimely death through the treachery of his red friends, whom he had always treated so well."[113]

Paul Tschetter assumed that he would need to travel to Washington D.C. to talk to the President but an appointment was scheduled instead at Grant's Long Island summer home. Arrangements took a while to work out causing the delegates to delay their trip home. But they were insistent on seeing Grant so they waited for nine days in the New York city area, spending most nights at Michael Hiller's home, six miles south of the city, as well as a few nights in the city itself.[114]

While waiting on Grant the delegates continued negotiations with railroad agents about land prices but also had a good deal of free time, which Tschetter did not necessarily appreciate. As he put it in his diary on July 26: "Oh how I abhor life in the city. All the noise and music make me so disgusted, that I can hardly stand it."[115] One evening while walking through different parts of New York City Paul Tschetter got lost and wandered around for a number of hours before he could find his place of lodging (in this case at a "church mission").[116]

According to Hutterian folk tradition, Paul Tschetter's uncle, Lohrentz, did less worthy things in his own spare time, avoiding boredom by seeking out various forms of entertainment. Some stories have him spending time in taverns; others in places of less repute. In his diary, Paul Tschetter almost never mentions Lohrentz. But dozens of slightly different yet consistently racy verbal accounts tell the story of a man of questionable character. As a result many Hutterians, who believed they knew the whole story about Lohrentz, his drinking and lack of interest in institutional religion, were upset that a commemorative marker was placed near his grave during the 1974 Hutterite-Mennonite Centennial celebration in South Dakota.[117]

In any case, on July 27, the delegates and Michael Hiller "took the steamer [once again] for New York City, walked through a part of the

---

113. Ibid., 36.
114. J. M. Hofer, ed., "The Diary of Paul Tschetter," 215.
115. Ibid., 216.
116. Ibid.
117. R. Janzen, *The Prairie People*, 239. This comment is based on interviews with many older Prairieleut, all of whom requested anonymity, as well as local historian Reuben Goertz, who was interviewed in July, 1993.

Figure 4.6 Chris Janzen, "Ulysses S. Grant and the Hutterites," painting, 2004. Photograph courtesy of Chris Janzen

city, and boarded a second ship to Long Beach . . ."[118] Here they took a train to lodgings that had been arranged for them about a mile and a half from Grant's home. They arrived at Grant's residence at 8 P.M. and were finally able to sit down with the President.[119]

This surprising encounter between three men with little formal education, social status or material wealth and the Civil War hero is captured on canvas by Chris Janzen and is shown in Figure 4.6. It is hard to imagine that pious individuals like the ministers Paul Tschetter and Tobias Unruh would feel comfortable meeting with a man with a reputation for crude language, racy stories and a good cigar.[120] But sacrifices had to be made for the sake of the Gospel.

The Tschetter-Grant painting depicts a confident, larger-than-life President Grant, a man not known for a conservative lifestyle, seated at the same table as the spiritual-minded Rev. Tschetter. The cannons sur-

118. J. M. Hofer, ed., "The Diary of Paul Tschetter," 217.
119. Boese, *The Prussian-Polish Mennonites*, 62–63.
120. McFeely, *Grant: A Biography*. See also Grant, *Personal Memoirs*.

rounding Grant illustrate his military background as well a reputation for ruthless "total war" tactics during the recently ended American Civil War. The dove above the Tschetters illustrates Hutterite/Mennonite pacifist traditions; the Bible in Tschetter's hand, the minister's religious commitments. Note as well the expression of boredom on the face of Lohrentz Tschetter, the uncomfortable demeanor of Tobias Unruh and the animated involvement of Michael Hiller, the Northern Pacific Railroad translator, seated at the end of the table. Tschetter later complained that Grant did not speak German. He was surprised that the President of the United States would not have at least a rudimentary understanding of this important language.

The petition that Paul Tschetter presented to Grant included a variety of requests that were reviewed at the meeting. In addition to military exemption, Tschetter's petition seeks permission to settle in separated, self-governing communities, to use the German language, to have control over schools and to be exempt from jury duty and the taking of oaths in legal proceedings. Tschetter also asked for the freedom to leave the United States whenever desired.

According to Tschetter, President Grant "received us in the most friendly manner" and suggested "patience" with regard to the petition.[121] Tschetter's diary includes nothing else about the meeting. In the Neu Hutterthaler church record book, Tschetter adds that Grant told them that he could not respond immediately because "he could not speak German," using an excuse that is not noted in the diary.[122] In a letter from President Grant to Secretary of State Hamilton Fish dated one day after the meeting, Grant wrote the following: "Of course no privileges can be accorded to foreign born citizens not accorded to all other citizens."[123] But he did not make an immediate decision about how to respond to the petition.

Their business completed, but too impatient to wait for an answer, the Tschetters left New York City on August 2. Jay Cooke pleaded for a quick response before their departure but he was not successful in obtaining one.[124] The Tschetters and Unruh therefore boarded the

121. J. M. Hofer, ed., "The Diary of Paul Tschetter," 217.
122. NHCRB, 15.
123. "U.S. Department of State, miscellaneous letters, August 1873, part 1," in C. Hiebert, *Brothers in Deed to Brothers in Need*, 65.
124. "Telegram from Jay Cooke to Hamilton Fish," in Correll, "President Grant

Cimbria and left the United States from Castle Garden.[125] According to Paul Tschetter's account in the Neu Hutterthaler church record book, the trip from New York City to Hamburg, Germany, took eleven days. Nine days later (on August 20), after traveling across the European continent, the Tschetters arrived safely at Neu Hutterthal village.[126] The entire trip had taken 132 days.

---

and the Mennonite Immigration," 148. The telegram is also found in C. Hiebert, ed., *Brothers in Deed to Brothers in Need*, 67.

    125. John F. Funk, diary entry, August 13, 1873. AMC.

    126. NHCRB, 15.

5

Immigration

> Fats said, "Yeh, bo, this is quite a town. Quite a town. Everybody in it is related. Fulla Hofers and Kleinsassers and Tschetters." Fats cleared his nose with a guggling sniff. "Yeh, an' when the Hofers get t'huffin', an' the Kleinsassers t'sassin', an' the Tschetters t'spittin' seeds, you got somethin'."[1]
>
> —from Frederick Manfred, *The Chokecherry Tree*, 1943

BY THE TIME PAUL TSCHETTER RETURNED TO UKRAINE IN EARLY AUGUST, 1873, he was personally convinced that the Hutterites should move to the United States but he did not know how many people would agree with him. He called a general meeting in the Neu Hutterthal village to deliver his report and discern the will of the people. As Tschetter later wrote, "We called for a church meeting and reported everything word for word regarding how we found things in America."[2] Tschetter knew that not everyone wanted to leave and he expressed this concern in correspondence to John F. Funk as late as November 29, 1873.[3] Delegate Leonhard Suderman wrote that many Russian Mennonites viewed "America" as a "haven for criminals." According to many, "only one who had his pockets full of loaded revolvers and expected to risk his ife, if need be, would dare to go America."[4]

Paul Tschetter and five of the Mennonite/Hutterite delegates also sent a letter of thanks to the American Mennonite community that

---

1. Manfred, *The Chokecherry Tree*, 198.
2. NHCRB, 15.
3. Paul Tschetter, correspondence with John F. Funk, November 29, 1873. Transcribed by Elizabeth Horsch Bender, John F. Funk collection (Historical Manuscripts: Mennonite Board of Guardians and Russian Immigrant Correspondence, Box 68), AMC.
4. Leonhard Suderman, *From Russia to America*, 2.

was published in the *Herald of Truth*. In this letter they recognized "the undeserved hospitality" provided by Mennonites, who had secured free railroad passes and hired guides and surveyors while they were in North America.

Sad personal news also awaited the Rev. Tschetter on his return. While he was gone Tschetter's six-year-old son, Jacob, had "died" Maria did not telegraph her husband with the news because of the difficulty of ensuring that the message would be actually be received, and in order to preserve him from undue stress.[5] Now, as they talked about what had transpired, Paul and Maria amazingly discovered that Jacob's death had occurred at the very moment that Paul Tschetter was attending a funeral service in Elkhart, Indiana.[6]

The Hutterites have always approached the death of young children with a certain measure of relief and thankfulness to God. Believing in the general innocence of young boys and girls, there is full confidence that at death they will be welcomed into heaven. Since eternal life contrasts favorably with the present world's "veil of tears," with its anticipated temptations and frustrations, death is not approached with a great sense of loss. As John Hostetler wrote about the Hutterites in 1974, "Children who die in their innocence are envied by adults, for they have been spared many temptations and the struggles of self-denial."[7] This viewpoint corresponds with the position held in theory by many if not most western Christians but in practice most people want to live as long as they can.

In late November, 1873, Paul Tschetter wrote John F. Funk that he was "glad" that his son had gone to a "calm place" due to the "bad" conditions that existed in the world.[8] In later years Tschetter wrote, "We don't begrudge him [Jacob] the rest but entreat him to the Lord our God, and I am assured that he will be a little angel in heaven."[9] This does not mean, however, that Paul and Maria did not suffer deeply as a result of the loss of their child.

Paul Tschetter's anxiety in the fall of 1873 was augmented by the Grant Administration's seemingly slow response to his petition.

5. NHCRB, 15. Anna Hofman Fisher, interview, May 2004.
6. Paul Tschetter, correspondence with John F. Funk, November 29, 1873. AMC.
7. Hostetler, *Hutterite Society*, 249.
8. Paul Tschetter, correpondence with John Funk, November 29, 1873. AMC.
9. NHCRB, 15.

Tschetter's letter to John F. Funk in late November, asked Funk to contact Michael Hiller on his behalf to see if any correspondence had been received. As Tschetter put it, "without these papers [confirming the privileges requested] we can't do anything."[10] In the same letter Tschetter notes in desperation that even without a response many Hutterites had already "sold" their Ukrainian properties.

In a letter from Tobias Unruh to Funk, also written in November, 1873, Unruh references a letter he had recently received from Tschetter. In the letter to Unruh, Tschetter expressed fear that Hutterite "children" would be "be given" to the Russian Government if something was not done by the "new year."[11] Tschetter was referring to the new educational and military requirements that Unruh, in his letter to Funk, agreed were "horrible" and "threaten[ing]."

In reality Grant had responded to the Tschetter request rather quickly; in early September. But his response did not get to Tschetter until months later. How this happened is not completely clear. In correspondence dated August 29, 1873, Michael Hiller personally requested a quick response from Secretary of State Hamilton Fish on behalf of the Tschetters and Unruh. Hiller asked Fish to send Grant's correspondence to him personally "in care of Messrs Jay Cooke and Co. in New York."[12] Fish then responded almost immediately on Grant's behalf, sending a letter directly to Hiller, who was asked to forward it to Paul Tschetter. Part of this letter, dated September 5, 1873, reads as follows:

> Since personal military service, citizenship obligations, jury service, and control over schools are all matters that fall under the jurisdiction of the various states. . . . the President says that he cannot exempt them from the laws of the states and the law to which other citizens are subject. As to the paying of substitute money for 50 years, that, too, is beyond his power of promising. It is true, however, that for the next 50 years we will not be entangled in another war in which military service will be necessary. But should it be necessary there is little likelihood that Congress would find justification in freeing them from duties which are asked of other citizens."[13]

10. Paul Tschetter, correspondence with John F. Funk, November 29, 1873. AMC.

11. Tobias Unruh, correspondence with John F. Funk, November 13, 1873. Box 68. AMC.

12. Correll, "President Grant and the Mennonite Immigration from Russia," 148.

13. Ibid., 149. C. H. Smith, *The Coming of the Russian Mennonites*, 74. Towne, *Jacob Hutter's Friends*, 39, 212.

The full text of Grant's response is contained in Appendix D. With regard to the most important request, military exemption, Grant casually suggested that the United States would not be involved in a conflict requiring military conscription for the next "fifty years," a rather optimistic and inaccurate prediction but one that Tschetter ultimately accepted. In any case it was not President Grant's idea to provide a fifty-year promise; his was a specific response to Tschetter's fifty-year guarantee entreaty. In a private note to Hiller that accompanied the official response, Fish showed greater honesty than was extended to Tschetter and Unruh. Fish wrote, "We *hope* not to be involved in a war during the next fifty years..."[14]

Throughout most of their history the Hutterites had been sojourners without a country they could call their own. They anticipated that true Christians would always have to suffer for the sake of the Gospel. The Hutterites relocated often, from Austria and Germany to Moravia and Slovakia in the 1500s; to Transylvania in the 1600s, then to various locations in Ukraine in the 1700s and 1800s. As Paul Tschetter put it in one of his hymns, "All faithful ones suffer on this earth."[15] The Hutterites did not thus anticipate that they would stay in one place for a very long period of time, not even in the United States. President Grant's fifty-year promise was sufficient and it was all that Tschetter had requested. Outside of the Slovakian non-Catholic Habaner community, not a single Hutterite living in 1873 had experienced life in one place for more than forty-one years. Not since the 1760s had any Hutterites lived in a place longer than that.

Why Hamilton Fish's September 5 response was not in Tschetter's hands as late as November, however, is perplexing. The Grant administration assumed that the Northern Pacific Railroad had passed it on to the delegates. Perhaps Fish's letter was not telegraphed but sent instead by the least costly shipping route, a process that could take weeks or months. Or maybe the telegram never got through to the Neu Hutterthal village. There is another possibility. Since Fish's letter did not offer support for most of Tschetter's requests (outside of military exemption) perhaps Hiller did not want Tschetter to see the letter right away, believing that this might forestall expected support for immigration. If the latter was what happened, it was certainly an effective ploy on Hiller's part. In the

14. Correll, "President Grant and the Mennonite Immigration from Russia," 149.
15. Paul Tschetter, hymn #6, stanza nine (1873). HHMA.

Neu Hutterthaler Church Record Book, Paul Tschetter indicates that in the midst of some confusion, "suddenly [in early December] Mr. Hiller came with the written reply to our petition."[16] There is no explanation about why it had taken so long to get the letter to Ukraine.

By the end of 1873, Paul Tschetter took the position that it was time to leave Russia even without Presidential guarantees. In his view, no agreements with "men" were, in any case, ever fully guaranteed.[17] In the Neu Hutterthaler Church Record Book Tschetter recalls that, at the time (late 1873), he believed that "we must migrate only with good hope."[18] He also wrote that "where there was no great ambition to migrate before," the letter from Grant did "made a great impression."[19] Tschetter said that he read the President's letter to the entire Neu Hutterthal community at a special meeting.[20]

With regard to the military exemption issue, the relatively unpopulated states and territories of the mid-western United States were at that time actively competing for settlers. They were thus quick to grant freedom from militia service to religious groups that requested it. Tschetter was likely aware of this phenomenon; Mennonite leaders certainly were and would have told him about it. In 1873 the United States had no national military draft or compulsory military service and this compared favorably to the situation in Russia.[21] It is also true that the United States Constitution guaranteed religious freedom, a condition Hutterites had never experienced in Russia except as a privileged minority group. All of these things were attractive to the prospective immigrants.

American railroad companies also played a major role in convincing Hutterians and Mennonites to immigrate to the United States. More important than the personal contacts made in summer 1873, were ongoing negotiations with two American Mennonite groups: the Mennonite Board of Guardians (headquartered in Summerfield, Illinois) and the Mennonite Executive Aid Committee of Pennsylvania (in Lancaster).[22] At the time many United States congressmen as well supported large

---

16. NHCRB, 16.
17. Ibid., 18.
18. Ibid., 17.
19. Ibid.
20. Ibid.
21. Ibid., 16.
22. Schmidt, "The Immigrants and the Railroads," 14.

scale immigration, hoping to develop the hundreds of thousands of acres taken directly or indirectly from the continent's indigenous peoples. They viewed western development as important for both military and economic reasons. Corporate donors to American political parties often had a vested economic interest in immigrant settlement issues.

American railroad companies needed farmers who would pay freight rates to subsidize the laying of track and to ensure future profits. The United States Government gave the railroads free strips of land, twenty miles wide, in alternating sections of 640 acres along each side of track that was laid.[23] 50% of the land remained in U.S. Government hands. The Homestead Act of 1862 priced quarter sections of the government land (160 acres) at $1.25 per acre. The railroads usually sold their land at higher prices, from $2.50 to $7.50 per acre.

The primary Hutterite and Mennonite problem with homesteading arrangements was their interest in "obtain[ing] possession of lands in a compact body."[24] Since much of the land was divided into alternating arrangements of government and railroad owned land, a bill was introduced in the House of Representatives that explicitly authorized a revision of the Homestead Act. The bill would have allowed government-owned sections to be joined together with railroad land with the stipulation that the Anabaptist settlers pay higher prices for this opportunity. Assuming that they would be granted large contiguous acreages, seven of the twelve delegates (not including the Tschetters) had signed a tentative contract with the Northern Pacific Railroad in August, 1873, for the purchase of Red River valley land. The properties "adjoin[ed] the railroad in Dakota Territory" and were "within 50 miles of the Red River."[25] The contract was time-sensitive, however, requiring "that on or before the first day of March, 1874, the Mennonite committee will notify the company whether they will settle on their line."[26] The deal was contingent on the passage of legislation amending the Homestead Act.

A bill introduced in the House of Representatives went nowhere but in early 1874, the United States Senate debated similar Homestead legislation. The bill was presented by Pennsylvania Senator Simon

23. Ibid.
24. 43rd Congress, 1st Session, H.R. 2121, House of Representatives, February 24, 1874. John F. Funk collection, Box 51. AMC.
25. Correll, "President Grant and the Mennonite Immigration from Russia," 49.
26. Ibid.

Cameron, at the request of Pennsylvania Mennonite leader Amos Herr and John F. Funk. This bill would have made it possible for Mennonites and Hutterites to settle on 500,000 acres of combined government/railroad land in the Red River Valley, exactly where the Mennonites and Tschetter wanted to settle.[27] In President Grant's address to Congress on December 1, 1873, he advocated personally for this legislative "concession" that would bring to the United States "a large colony of citizens of Russia . . . to settle in a compact colony." He described the immigrants as "industrious, intelligent and wealthy," as well as "desirous of enjoying civil and religious liberty."[28] Apparently the Jansens, Tschetters and others had made a good impression on Grant.

Political timing was not good, however, since major proponents of the "Mennonite Bill" were associated with political corruption in the Grant Administration. This was one of the more tainted presidencies in United States history and a reputation for incompetence grew during Grant's second term in office. Secretary of State Hamilton Fish also opposed the Homestead Act amendment because he thought it might hurt United States relations with Russia. Fish was also concerned that decisions were being made about territories that had not yet been divided into states.[29] There were other opponents as well. Nativist politicians in the Republican Party feared unassimilated Eastern Europeans and many senators were concerned about the implications of pacifist religious beliefs. Michael Hiller later suggested that Mennonite leader John F. Funk hurt the Russian Mennonite case by sending a separate petition to Congress, "overpublicizing" the issue.[30]

Exacerbating these problems was the fact that competing railroad companies and their stockholders wanted immigrants to settle in areas other than northeastern Dakota Territory.[31] The fact that the Anabaptist colonists were associated with Jay Cooke was especially problematic. Many railroad companies had over-expanded into sparsely populated

---

27. "A Mennonite Request," *Dakota Territory Press and Dakotan*, December 4, 1873, in C. Hiebert, ed., *Brothers in Deed to Brothers in Need*, 91–92. See also Liebbrandt, "The Emigration of the German Mennonites," 13.

28. President Ulysses S. Grant, "Annual Message to Congress," in C. Hiebert, *Brothers in Deed to Brothers in Need*, 67. See also Correll, ed., "Mennonite Immigration into Manitoba."

29. Harder, "The Russian Mennonites and American Democracy under Grant," 56.

30. Ibid., 65.

31. This story is told in R. Janzen, *The Prairie People*, 27–28.

regions, contributing to investor wariness and helping precipitate the Panic of 1873, a national economic depression. Jay Cooke's Northern Pacific Railroad declared bankruptcy on September 18, not long after the Tschetters returned to Europe. This caused the stock market to close for ten days and precipitated an economic downturn that continued until 1879.[32] The connection with Cooke, so advantageous during the summer of 1873, turned out to be a liability. Tschetter himself was probably unaware of the complexity of these various developments.

Immigration Fever

Back in south Ukraine, immigration fever spread, especially in the Hutterite community. Paul Tschetter's reports were instrumental and motivational.[33] One theme that runs through Tschetter's diary and his later reflection, "Report on Why We Had to Leave Russia," was the importance of preserving Hutterite Christianity from the influence of Mennonites, from what he described as "a Mennonite fog." It was Tschetter's hope that by moving away from the large and influential Russian Mennonite community in Ukraine that the Hutterite people would be better able to preserve their unique beliefs and practices. Tschetter wrote that the 1870 *ukase* could even be interpreted as a spiritual opportunity, a God-given effort to "humble" the Hutterite people and "to rouse us from our sleep."[34] Emigration might revitalize the spiritual life of the Hutterite people and Tschetter anticipated a religious "awakening" in the new world.[35] Russian Government policies were viewed as a type of persecution.

In Paul Tschetter's opinion the Russian Mennonites had become "proud" and "presumptuous." They "crowded themselves into holding any office they possibly could" and they exerted a negative and contaminating influence on the Hutterites.[36] In his "Report on Why We Had to Leave Russia," Tschetter wrote about economic inequality and material differences between individual Russian Mennonites; about the wealth of some and the poverty of others. Tschetter noted land owner-

---

32. Tindall, *America: A Narrative History*, 700–701.
33. Hofer, ed., "The Diary of Paul Tschetter," 110.
34. NHCRB, 8.
35. Ibid., 7–8.
36. Paul Tschetter, "Report of Why We Had to Leave Russia," NHCRB, 7.

ship restrictions and pointed out that native Russians often resented the Mennonites.[37] In his writing Tschetter asks, "Why are the German people enjoying so many privileges? That is why they are getting rich," amplifying opinions held by disgruntled Russian peasants. According to Tschetter, "Their [the Mennonites] pride had risen to a point where it could not rise any higher, and at its highest point became an abomination before God."[38]

In the Russian Empire, the serfs were freed in 1861 but like liberated slaves in the United States, most of them remained poor and did not have the financial resources to purchase land. Nor was Russia undergoing a major industrial revolution that provided jobs in a growing manufacturing sector. Many freed serfs thus came to work for Mennonites (and Hutterites) after their previous employers could not afford to support them. Without free labor some Ukrainian noblemen sold their estates and properties to wealthy Mennonites causing the Russian upper class as well to harbor resentment against the Anabaptists.

Paul Tschetter appears to have been very aware of all of these developments. He notes that Hutterites, like Mennonites, were beginning to hire Russian peasants to do farm work and other chores. As Arnold M. Hofer later described it, "Most, if not all, families hired Russians for the work that was least desirable."[39] These laborers lived in substandard housing, often sleeping in Hutterite barns and they worked for wages lower than those paid to Hutterites. Hofer said that his Prairieleut grandmother often expressed remorse that the family's Russian servants had not been treated very well.[40] After 1917, all of this came back to haunt those people that remained in Russia. Paul Tschetter's fears were confirmed during the Russian Revolution and the Civil War that followed.

Paul Tschetter wrote that in southern Ukraine his people had "departed far from the path of our forefathers."[41] He lamented the rampant materialism affecting Hutterite culture. He noted a lack of commitment to the peace position, which he believed was being compromised; that his people had "failed in our defenselessness" when they performed

---

37. Ibid.
38. Ibid.
39. HMCC, eds., *Hutterite Roots*, 111.
40. Arnold Hofer, interview, July, 2000.
41. NHCRB, 8.

non-combatant military service during the 1853 Crimean War.⁴² On both issues, materialism and a compromised peace position, Tschetter blamed the influence of the Mennonites.

Tschetter also disliked the growing acceptance of "worldly" practices such as the production and smoking of tobacco as well as the use of snuff. Tschetter and other Hutterites were also concerned about the placement of young Hutterite males and females in Mennonite factories, shops, houses and farms in the Mennonite villages. Mennonite businessmen marketed their products throughout the Russian Empire opening the Mennonite (and Hutterite) community to secular influences. Tschetter held Mennonites accountable in a variety of ways for helping to corrupt the historic Hutterite understanding of the Christian faith. Unlike his communal Hutterite brothers and sisters, his vision of Hutterite spiritual revitalization did not ascribe special importance to community of goods. But it was time, he thought, to move elsewhere, away from Mennonites.

The Grant Administration's response to Tschetter was slow to arrive and it did not grant all of his requests. But he was ready to immigrate nonetheless. Still he worried that not all of the Hutterites would follow him. In his November 29, 1873, letter to John Funk, Tschetter said that internal dissension within the Hutterite community had led to "much evil spoken about America."⁴³ Tschetter predicted a much lower immigration rate than what eventually materialized. "I believe that the emigration will not be larger because faith is weak," he noted.⁴⁴ But Tschetter was wrong. Immigration fervor quickly stifled lingering dissent. In contrast to the Mennonites, two-thirds of whom remained in Russia, the Hutterites acted with uniformity in the immigration endeavor. Almost the entire Hutterite population decided to leave even though the community was split into a variety of communal and non-communal factions.

By the end of 1873, Hutterite villagers were actively seeking buyers for personal and communal property and arranging for travel across the Atlantic. They were securing passports and necessary medical certificates. It often took months to get these documents, which required

42. Ibid.
43. Paul Tschetter, correspondence with John F. Funk, November 19, 1873. AMC. A. M. Hofer, ed., *History of the Hutterite Mennonites*, 5.
44. HMCC, eds., *History of the Hutterite Mennonites*, 61.

the payment of special fees and bribes. The total cost often amounted to fifty dollars per family.[45] Many Hutterites sold their properties at a great loss in order to leave quickly before the full enforcement of the *ukase*.

The Hutterites Prepare to Leave Ukraine

At Neu Hutterthal village the decision to immigrate was ridden with special emotion. The village was only seven years old at the time the properties were sold. Very recent effort had been put into residential construction and land development. Tschetter had not received confirmation of requested privileges from the United States Government. But ideological arguments prevailed in this small twenty-family community and preliminary real estate negotiations began as early as September 1873!

Almost immediately a local nobleman offered to purchase all of the Neu Hutterthal properties for 150,000 rubles. The sale was made verbally but the deal was not completed by the agreed-upon closing date of November 1, 1873. Perhaps trying to improve on the terms of the sale, the buyer made many "excuses" so that even "165 days later" (mid-March, 1874), there was no signed contract.[46] Hundreds of Hutterite and Mennonite sellers were driving down land prices.

Paul Tschetter was greatly distressed by the delay of the sale because, as he noted, "all our cattle, horses, and agricultural implements the nobleman had already taken possession of and sold at public auction."[47] Some Neu Hutterthal residents had to buy back their own horses in order to complete the spring (1874) plowing, not knowing when they would be able to leave. Two other Hutterite villages (Hutterthal and Johannesruh) had an even more difficult situation since they had contracted for Crown land via Johann Cornies. Due to the slowness of government bureaucracy and the legal terms of the leases, some land transfers and payments took three years to complete.[48]

Unlike others at Neu Hutterthal, Paul Tschetter refused to plant crops in the spring of 1874. He did not "have ambition to start plowing again because I thought that if I would begin to farm again, we would

---

45. Ibid, 50. The fifty dollar figure is based on 1974 calculations.
46. NHCRB, 16.
47. Ibid.
48. HMCC, eds., *A History of the Hutterite Mennonites*, 50. 61.

all remain in Russia and our young men would be drafted."[49] Instead the impatient Tschetter left for North America before the sale of the village was completed. He requested and received a "pass to migrate" from the government and convinced five families to join him. They left the remaining Neu Hutterthal families to continue farming while negotiations with the buyer were finalized.

Two Hutterite villages were successful in selling land and leaving even earlier than Tschetter. The first Hutterites to leave Ukraine were members of communal groups from the villages of Scheromet and Hutterdorf as well as a noncommunal Hutterdorf faction. All of the Scheromet properties were sold to a single Mennonite buyer: Peter Epp.[50] Interestingly, the sense of urgency to leave for North America was just as high in the communal factions as it was in the noncommunal group, even though communalists had not been personally represented in the summer 1873 delegation.

The first immigrant group of 384 people was one of the largest and was led by Michael Waldner, Darius Walter, William Tschetter, and David Waldner.[51] The group divided in half for the journey between Ukraine and Germany (between June 6 and June 9, 1874) and re-united in Hamburg before continuing across the ocean.[52] The immigrants arrived in New York City on July 5, after sailing for sixteen days on the *Hammonia*. Here they were met by Northern Pacific Railroad representative Michael Hiller, who was once again "helpful in all things."[53]

En route to America a member of the Darius Walter group drafted diary comments that are reminiscent of Paul Tschetter. He too disliked being in such close quarters with people who lived a different lifestyle. "It was hard to take it all in love," he noted.[54] Most of the Hutterite immigrants purchased boarding tickets in the most economical class. In his review of ship list records Arnold M. Hofer discovered a bit of subterfuge as well; in order to secure the best travel rates the Hutterites

---

49. NHCRB, 16.

50. Janzen, "Reise nach Amerika," in Frances Janzen Voth, *The House of Jacob: The Story of Jacob Janzen and his Descendents* (Tucson, AZ: self-published, 1984), 64–65.

51. HMCC, eds., *A History of the Hutterite-Mennonites*, 66.

52. HMCC, eds., *Hutterite Roots*, 97.

53. HMCC eds., *History of the Hutterite Mennonites*, 66.

54. HMCC, eds., *Hutterite Roots*, 97.

Great Plains Railroad Lines and Laid Track, 1874

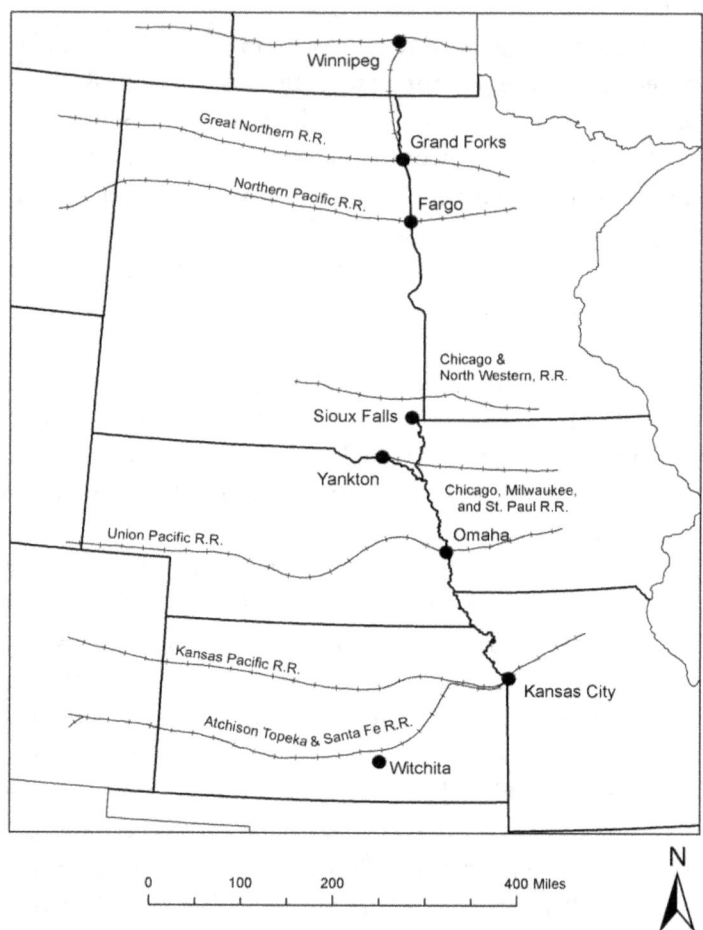

Map 5.1 Great Plains Railroad Lines and Laid Track, 1874.
Map courtesy of Stuart McFeeters.

listed an overabundance of children under the age of one as compared to those who were between the ages of two and three.[55]

The contact with Michael Hiller in New York City leads one to assume that the first Hutterite group was following Paul Tschetter's recommendation and expected to settle in the Red River valley, north of Fargo: in Tschetter's "New Jerusalem." Hiller's Northern Pacific Railroad had tracks in that area and had no interest in Hutterites settling anywhere else. The Northern Pacific was one of four railroad companies that had been granted sections of free government land with the promise that track would eventually be laid across the North American continent.[56] In total, this represented 88 million acres of land, including 200 feet on each side of laid track as well as alternating quarter sections.[57] The Northern Pacific line ran from Duluth, Minnesota through Minneapolis, Brainerd and Moorhead, to Bismarck, in Dakota Territory.[58]

In early 1874, Hiller made a personal visit to the Mennonite colony areas in Russia on behalf of the economically struggling Northern Pacific in an attempt to increase the total number of immigrants. While there he visited Paul Tschetter at his home in Neu Hutterthal.[59] But the first Hutterite immigrants did not sign a contract with Hiller and the Northern Pacific. A competing railroad, the Chicago, Milwaukee and St. Paul, was simultaneously laying track from east to west across the southern part of Dakota Territory, in what later became the state of South Dakota. This company, through a subsidiary (the Dakota Southern Railway) started providing service between Sioux City, Iowa, and Yankton, Dakota Territory, in February, 1873, increasing agricultural marketing possibilities and leading to the establishment of lumber yards and implement stores on the far southern edge of the Territory.[60] Although most railroads suspended construction activities after the Panic of 1873, lines already established continued to operate.

---

55. R. Janzen, *The Prairie People*, 31.

56. The other companies involved were the Union Pacific, Southern Pacific and Santa Fe railroad companies.

57. Hasselstrom, *Roadside History of South Dakota*, 19.

58. *Travelers' Official Guide of the Railway and Steam Navigation Lines*. Schmidt, "The Immigrants and the Railroads."

59. NHCRB, 15.

60. Schell, *A History of South Dakota*, 14.

We will never know what the Northern Pacific's Hiller told the immigrants when they arrived or why the Red River Valley settlement did not materialize. There was indeed a frenetic competition for immigrants between railroad companies and the Hutterites had no centrally coordinated leadership structure. Dozens of Hutterite groups from different Russian villages, and from both communal and noncommunal groups, journeyed across the Atlantic at different times over a five year period (from 1874–1879). Railroad companies competing with the financially stressed Northern Pacific were somehow successful in creatively altering Tschetter's (and Hiller's) original plan.

Companies such as the Missouri and Burlington Railroad (which had tracks directed toward Nebraska), and the aforementioned Chicago, Milwaukee and St. Paul, wanted the Hutterites to settle hundreds of miles south of the Red River valley.[61] Most railroad agents spoke German fluently and they were effective promoters. New settlers meant new customers.

In reviewing railroad land company records and government files, Ernst Correll confirmed that the railroads were extremely influential in deciding who would settle where. According to Correll, "The keen competition between the land departments of the various railroad companies resulted in rapid contractual arrangements with the Mennonite pioneers. As a result the original plans for compact settlements were more or less abandoned."[62] Correll was likely thinking of Hutterites as well as Mennonites. Evidently the inability to secure favorable legislation led to the complete abandonment of the Red River valley settlement idea by the American Mennonite Board of Guardians and the Mennonite Executive Aid Committee of Pennsylvania. Both were actively involved in negotiations with the railroads that pushed the Anabaptist immigrants in more southerly directions. These organizations eventually encouraged the Hutterites to settle in southeastern Dakota Territory where a group of about 100 Crimean Mennonites had established a community in October, 1873. This group, led by Daniel Unruh, arrived at John F. Funk's home in August, 1873, shortly after the Tschetters returned to Russia. At least four of the Mennonite delegates

---

61. *Travelers' Official Guide of the Railway and Steam Navigation Lines.*
62. Correll, "President Grant and the Mennonites," 151.

ran into members of the arriving Unruh group as they were about to board the *Hammonia* to cross the Atlantic Ocean.[63]

John J. Gering later wrote that the Anabaptist delegates "were just packing their trunks at Castle Garden when they met with the agreeable and unexpected surprise of the entire trip," i.e. with the Daniel Unruh group.[64] Boese and Gering suggest that this meeting was the basis for Swiss and Low German Volyhnian Mennonite settlement in Dakota Territory; that it made a "deep impression on the delegates later."[65] According to Gering, "They only had a few hours together but this short visit established a friendship between Mr. Schrag and Mr. Unruh that continued throughout that period of their lives."

The Gering account conflicts, however, with delegate Andreas Schrag's personal diary where he states that he did not have "time" to talk to Unruh.[66] J. A. Boese's 1967 narrative goes further and suggests that the Tschetters and Tobias Unruh were also there to meet Daniel Unruh.[67] Boese wrote that Unruh spent a "few hours" with Paul and Lohrentz Tschetter and Tobias Unruh and that the meeting came to an end when Paul Tschetter and Daniel Unruh "knelt down in prayer together." Newspaper publisher Jacob J. Mendel later repeated this story, which was likely corroborated by oral accounts.[68] The Daniel Unruh group was the first large assemblage of Russian Anabaptists to immigrate to the United States but on arrival they had not yet decided where to settle. Most of the members stayed in Elkhart for a couple of months, while Daniel Unruh and John F. Funk traveled through some of the same country that the twelve Russian delegates had just visited. Unruh and Funk added a visit to southeastern Dakota Territory and this region (according to John D. Unruh) left "the most favorable impression."[69] In

63. Swiss-German Centennial Committee, eds., *The Swiss Germans in South Dakota*, 13.

64. Gering, *After Fifty Years*, 20.

65. Boese, *The Prussian Polish Mennonites*, 63.

66. Swiss-German Centennial Committee, ed., *The Swiss Germans in South Dakota*, 13. Andreas Schrag, who later brought his Swiss Volynian group to southeastern Dakota Territory, notes "I did not have time to speak to these people, since our ship was ready to leave."

67. Boese, *The Prussian Polish Mennonites*, 63.

68. Mendel, *A History of the People of East Freeman, Silver Lake and West Freeman*, 13.

69. Unruh, *A Century of Mennonites in Dakota*, 26.

October, 1873, the entire Unruh group traveled to what is now Turner County and settled on Turkey Ridge, near Swan Lake, where they saw "a good stand of grass."[70]

The following summer (1874) the Pennsylvania Mennonite Executive Committee sent a five man delegation, including Amos Herr, to visit the Unruh settlement, stopping first to see John F. Funk. This committee provided financial and organizational assistance to the Unruh group and they were pleased with what they saw on Turkey Ridge.

The Dakota Territorial Immigration Commission, under the leadership of Jacob Brauch, also played a role in the Hutterite decision to settle in southeast Dakota Territory. As John D. Unruh puts it, "Brauch was instrumental in bringing many Mennonites [he includes Hutterites in this designation] to Dakota who would not have come otherwise."[71] Brauch actively promoted Germans-from-Russia settlement in the region. He kept careful watch on the Unruh settlement and knew that Pennsylvania Mennonites had visited Unruh. According to Territorial Immigration Commission records, the Pennyslvania delegation liked the soil, climate, water supply, and crops that they saw when visiting Unruh.[72] In May, 1875, Jacob Brauch visited members of the Mennonite Executive Committee delegation in their homes in Pennsylvania and wrote that they were actively promoting settlement in southeastern Dakota Territory. The Dakota Immigration Bureau, established in December 1875, sent representatives to meet immigrant trains in Chicago as well as steamboats in New York City and Philadelphia to advocate settlement in the Territory.[73] Federal funding for this project continued until 1877.

There are thus many reasons why the Hutterites did not go directly to the Red River valley as planned. Railroad company competition, Territorial advocacy, government regulations, the active lobbying of Daniel Unruh and Mennonite organization preferences led the way. But none of these developments were coordinated and some were not in place by the summer of 1874. The first Hutterian immigrants thus had a hard time making a decision about where to put down roots.

70. Boese, *The Prussian Polish Mennonites*, 65, 108.
71. Unruh, *A Century of Mennonites in Dakota*, 26.
72. Ibid., 27.
73. Schell, *A History of South Dakota*, 118.

Records indicate that a German-speaking land agent intercepted the first Hutterite group when they were in the city of Chicago. He offered them free passage to what he suggested was better land than Dakota Territory, near Burlington, Iowa. The inexperienced 384-person Hutterite group trusted him and accepted his offer. John Hostetler described the agent as "a smooth, German-speaking man, apparently passing as an agent of the Burlington Railway."[74] John D. Unruh reminds that railroad agents used "unethical means to discourage Dakota-bound immigrants."[75]

Language differences, miscommunication and geographical illiteracy complicated all decision-making processes. The fact that Paul and Lohrentz Tschetter, the only Hutterites who had seen the Red River Valley, were not in the first Hutterite immigrant group probably had significant impact on decisions that were made. Would Tschetter have so easily been taken in by fast-talking entrepreneurs?

After leaving Chicago, nothing seemed to go right for the first Hutterite immigrant group. A serious epidemic disrupted the Iowa plans, for example, causing the railroad to take the group to Lincoln, Nebraska instead.[76] Here most of the immigrants were lodged at a reception house, while a small group of men looked for land in an area that had been rejected by Paul Tschetter the previous year. Railroad companies not only provided travel at low rates but typically covered lodging along the way and at the point of destination, while land purchases were arranged and houses constructed. The railroads promised additional land for churches and schools and reduced rates for the hauling of freight and coal.

But in Nebraska things went from bad to worse for the first Hutterite immigrants. In July, 1874, while the exploratory group was looking for land, dysentery broke out in the immigrant house killing thirty-six Hutterite children and one seventy-eight year-old man (Darius Stahl).[77] The Hutterites viewed this as a bad sign especially since they had not been successful in finding acceptable land. Members of one of the communal groups traveled north to Yankton on the Missouri River where

---

74. Hostetler, *Hutterite Society*.
75. Unruh, *A Century of Mennonites in Dakota*, 25.
76. Towne, *Jacob Hutter's Friends*, 213.
77. Krause, *Tschetter-Waldner Families*, 3.

Figure 5.1 Bon Homme Colony, 1875.
Photograph courtesy of Tony Waldner.

they resided temporarily in a large rented house.[78] Here they made contact with Daniel Unruh, who strongly encouraged them to buy land near his settlement thirty-five miles north.

Some of the Hutterites followed Unruh's advice; others did not.[79] For example, the communal Hutterite group led by Michael Waldner decided instead to purchase 2,500 acres of land on the bluffs of the Missouri River, ten miles directly west of Yankton. They called their commune the Bon Homme Colony. In order to avoid Homestead Act land restrictions the group purchased the property privately from American Indian agent Walter A. Burleigh.

The other communal group (led by Darius Walter) constructed a communal village near the Wolf Creek (the Wolf Creek Colony). It was situated thirty miles north of Bon Homme and about twenty miles west of the Daniel Unruh settlement. Before building the colony this group spent a difficult first winter living in "dugouts" on government land near Silver Lake, seven miles north of what became the town of Freeman.[80]

---

78. *CHB II*, 748.
79. Marion Kleinsasser Towne, *Jacob Hutter's Friends*, 213.
80. *CHB II*, 749.

The third faction of Hutterite settlers in the first immigrant group, the noncommunalists from Hutterdorf village, homesteaded in Hutchinson County near the Wolf Creek Colony. Ministers in this group included David Waldner, Wilhelm Tschetter and Johannes Hofer.

The Tschetters Leave Ukraine

Paul and Maria Tschetter's family and the five families that joined them left Neu Hutterthal the next fall, on September 22, 1874. They were the second, and smallest, Hutterite group to leave Russia. Accompanying Paul and Maria were their children, Susanna (13), Paul (9), Maria (4), Barbara (3), and Jacob W. (5 months). The other families were headed by Joshua and Susanna Hofer, two sons of Lohrentz Tschetter (Lohrentz Jr. and Paul), Joseph and Maria Tschetter (Joseph was Paul Tschetter's brother), Joseph and Susanna Hofer (Paul Tschetter's sister), and Jacob and Marie Tschetter (Jacob was also a brother of Paul Tschetter), plus two sons of George Gross (George and William).[81]

The Paul Tschetter group embarked on a six-week journey from Ukraine to Dakota Territory, in what Tschetter described as "a long and hard journey into the unknown."[82] They went by train across Eastern Europe and through the city of Hamburg, Germany following Tschetter's earlier route and they arrived in New York City on November 6, 1874. Along the way they held daily prayer services and often dined on dried fruit and hard biscuits.[83]

The group then journeyed to Elkhart, Indiana, where they spent the winter, arriving on November 11. As John F. Funk notes in his leather-bound diary: "Bro. Paul Tschetter from Russia with five families arrived unexpectedly."[84] Funk was evidently caught off-guard by the group's arrival. Newsmen who covered the Hutterite immigration did not always understand the people about whom they were writing. An article published in the *New York Herald* on November 12, 1874, one day after the Tschetters arrived in Elkhart, for example, is titled, "Russian Mennonites," and it notes the arrival of many Anabaptist

---

81. HMCC, eds., *A History of the Hutterite Mennonites*, 71.
82. Paul G. Tschetter, "Anecdotes ..."
83. Towne, *Jacob Hutter's Friends*, 218.
84. John F. Funk, "1874–1875 Diary," Wednesday, November 11, 1874 entry. AMC.

immigrants. The writer insists, "They are not afraid of the Indians, and will fight sufficiently, if necessary, to save their scalps."[85]

The Neu Hutterthal emigrants sailed across the Atlantic on the *Suevia*. The Tschetter family, like many others, brought along a large cedar chest filled with family keepsakes.[86] One scary moment occurred while they were in New York City. According to Hutterite records, a "gypsy" nearly succeeded in kidnapping eleven-month-old Jacob S. G. Hofer, a nephew of Paul Tschetter.[87] But the abductors were "pursued" and Jacob was brought back safe and sound.[88]

In Elkhart, the immigrants rented a large house on Prairie Street through the efforts of John F. Funk but living quarters were close with only one private room for each family grouping.[89] Funk did not find it easy to secure temporary lodging for the Hutterites and he admitted frustration with his fellow Mennonites. In his diary Funk notes that on one occasion "he sought all day for a house for the Russian Brethren and did not succeed in getting one." He was "completely disgusted and tired of such a set of nonsensical fools as we have here in the city of Elkhart."[90] "100 houses are said to stand idle and empty," Funk writes, but the owners appeared to "be afraid of these [Hutterite] people." Funk's journal entry for November 13, 1874, closes with the comment, "I must think our people are a very narrow minded unfeeling people." Elkhart-area Mennonites were reluctant to host the Neu Hutterthal group for an entire winter, fearing that they would not be adequately compensated.

Two days later, on Sunday, November 15, Paul Tschetter was asked to preach a sermon at a local Mennonite church. He also spoke on at least one other occasion, at a service on Christmas Day, where the evangelical-leaning Funk noted that the attendance was "good" and that Tschetter's sermon had been "very good" but "not so spiritual as it should have been."[91]

---

85. "Russian Mennonites: Our Guests From the Black Sea—How They Look and What They Bring," *New York Herald* (November 12, 1874). Box 2, MLA. John F. Funk Collection. AMC.

86. Paul G. Tschetter, "Anecdotes..."

87. Peterson, ed., *People of the Old Missury*, 96.

88. HMCC, eds., *A History of the Hutterite Mennonites*, 72.

89. NHCRB, 18.

90. John F. Funk, November 13, 1874 diary entry. AMC.

91. John F. Funk, December 25, 1874, diary entry. AMC.

After staying in Elkhart for four months the Neu Hutterthal group bade farewell in March, 1875 and traveled west to Chicago, where Tschetter had written his critical hymn two years earlier. There they boarded the Chicago-Milwaukee Railroad line en route to Yankton. The unanswered question is why Tschetter took this route west. Why not go further north on the Northern Pacific line toward St. Paul, Minnesota, then across to Fargo, as he had presumably always planned to do?

Before leaving Russia Tschetter was likely informed about where the first Hutterite immigrant group had settled. There is no documentation but perhaps this is why Tschetter decided to head straight to Yankton. In Elkhart John F. Funk would likely have confirmed this information and promoted settlement in southeastern Dakota Territory. Old traveling partner Tobias Unruh made the same choice.

Yet in 1998, grandson Paul G. Tschetter told the author that his grandfather often said that the railroads had misled him while he was in Chicago; that he expected to end up further north.[92] According to Paul G. (who died in 2000), when his grandfather arrived in Yankton he "grabbed the arm of the Chicago, Milwaukee, and St. Paul Railway land agent and asked, 'Where are we? I've never been here before.'"[93] Tschetter wanted to know how far it was to the town of Fargo. "And where is the Red River Valley? That's where we were to go!" he exclaimed.[94] The railroad agent's honest answer: "Two or three hundred miles north of here."[95] In this version of events Paul Tschetter was told that if he wanted to settle in the Red River valley he would have to return to Chicago and start that part of the trip all over again.[96]

The notion that Paul Tschetter and his entourage could have been so misled makes Paul G. Tschetter's account difficult to believe. Yet this story is partially confirmed in Paul Tschetter's own "Why We Had to Leave Russia," where he is emphatic that when he arrived in the United States he believed that the Northern Pacific Railroad would make it possible for his group to purchase land in the Red River Valley in northeastern Dakota Territory, near Grand Forks, not in the southeastern

---

92. Paul G. Tschetter, interview, July 1998.
93. Paul G. Tschetter, "Monologue."
94. Ibid.
95. Paul G. Tschetter, "Anecdotes."
96. Paul G. Tschetter, interview, June 1998.

part of the Territory.⁹⁷ Did John F. Funk and others cause him to change his mind by the time he left Elkhart? Not according to Nancy Peterson, who refers to what happened as a "deception."⁹⁸

In spring 1875 Paul Tschetter really did not have much of a choice, however, if he wanted to keep all of the Hutterite people together in one place, even in a loosely contiguous settlement, and this was one of his major immigration goals. Since the first group of Hutterians had already purchased land west and north of Yankton, what other settlement choice did Tschetter really have? Members of the noncommunal Hutterdorf village were already breaking up the prairie sod and building homes. Perhaps Tschetter's later reflections represent wishful thinking. In any case, it is ironic that Tschetter was settling in an area where there was once again a large contingent of Mennonites, the very people from whom he was trying to escape.

After disembarking with all of his earthly possessions, Paul Tschetter and the others found themselves in Yankton, a town located on the banks of the Missouri River on the border between Nebraska and Dakota Territory. The Neu Hutterthal village immigrants stayed here for a month, some of them housed temporarily in tents. Yankton at the time was the capitol of Dakota Territory and the site of the government land office which assisted settlers who were moving north and west up the James River.⁹⁹ Yankton was also a rough river town with many saloons that were frequented by gamblers, soldiers, steamboat workers and prostitutes. In 1876, the territorial court tried Jack McCall there for the murder of Wild Bill Hickok. Yankton was not the kind of place that Paul Tschetter would have liked.

Leaving most of the Neu Hutterthal contingent in town, the Rev. Tschetter and a few Hutterite men, accompanied by a land agent, viewed land about forty-five miles northwest of Yankton. They traveled the first twenty miles on roads that consisted of ruts left by previous wagons, eating toasted bread and dried apples to keep them going and stopping briefly at a trading and supply store. From this point they traveled on completely unmarked and un-rutted trails onto the open prairie. There was plenty of tall grass, "taller than their ten-year-old boys" and

---

97. NHCRB, 18.

98. Nancy Peterson, interview with Paul G. Tschetter, 1987. Handwritten notes in the possession of Nancy Peterson.

99. Schell, *A History of South Dakota*, 110.

they considered this to be a good sign.[100] Nancy Peterson describes Paul Tschetter's exploratory trip in the following manner:

> For the first 20 miles there was a road of sorts, at least wagon ruts led them to the ford of the James River and cut the prairie north of the river as far as a trading post, where they spent the night. Then they left all signs of settlement behind and moved on north and west through a sweep of land that rolled gently as far as they could see . . . For miles and miles there were no trees . . ."[101]

There is no written record of what happened when they arrived in the Bridgewater area but Tschetter and his entourage must have visited Hutterites who were already settled there. Perhaps the Tschetter group stayed overnight with friends and/or relatives from Hutterdorf village or with the communal Darius Walter group. Before returning to Yankton a surveyor accompanying the group paced off the land that Tschetter selected and put up a pole with a piece of shirttail attached. The group then returned to Yankton and made preparations to bring the Neu Hutterthal assembly north.

In Yankton, Paul Tschetter purchased material necessities including two wagons, two yoke of oxen, a plow and lumber. Then the immigrants headed north putting down roots on land about ten to fifteen miles from where the noncommunal Hutterdorf villagers had settled. The Wolf Creek Colony was also in the vicinity. Noncommunal Hutterites who arrived in the following months and years continued to purchase land in what is now Hutchinson County or in nearby McCook County.

The Paul Tschetter homestead was located six miles west and six and one-half miles north of what is now the town of Freeman. The house that was constructed followed Eastern European patterns and was positioned in a northwest to southeast direction. As Clifford Walters notes, barns face northwest "for protection against the cold northwesterly winds."[102]

Figure 6.1 below shows a copy of the General Land Office deed that was issued a couple of years later. It is dated April 5, 1877 and includes the signature of President Rutherford B. Hayes. It stipulates that the land grant consists of "the North half of the South East quarter of Section twenty six and the North half of the South West quarter of

---

100. Paul G. Tschetter, "Anecdotes . . ."
101. Peterson, ed., *People of the Old Missury*, 96.
102. Clifford Walters, correspondence, May 2003.

Section twenty five, in township one hundred, of Range fifty seven, in the district of Lands subject to sale at Yankton Dakota Territory containing one hundred and sixty acres."[103]

The Neu Hutterthal immigrants filed claims for five individual homesteads. One of these was set aside for Paul Tschetter's parents, Jacob and Barbara Kleinsasser Tschetter, who arrived the following year along with most of the remaining residents of Neu Hutterthal village, a total of 122 people. This second Neu Hutterthal group arrived in New York City on the *Main* on September 4, 1875. It included Paul's brothers, David and Joseph and their families, as well as his youngest brother, John and his sister Barbara.[104] Most of the Neu Hutterthal immigrants homesteaded near the Paul Tschetter group, or close to the town of Olivet along the James River about ten miles south. It was there on a hill overlooking the James River that Paul Tschetter's uncle, Lohrentz was buried in December 1878 at age fifty-nine.[105]

In 1877, thirteen communal families from the Johannesruh village arrived and they established the Elmspring Colony also on the James River. The leaders of this group were Jacob Wipf and Peter Hofer. Since Wipf was a teacher (*Lehrer*) who had attended the Mennonite high school at Halbstadt, his group came to be known as the *Lehrerleut*.

North American communal Hutterites were now divided into three groups. In addition to the *Lehrerleut* at Elmspring, there were the *Schmiedeleut*, named after Michael Waldner (a blacksmith or *Schmied*) at Bon Homme, and the *Dariusleut* (named after Darius Walter) at Wolf Creek. The communalists referred to noncommunal Hutterian friends and relatives as *Prairieleut* or "people of the prairies," since the latter usually homesteaded on the open prairies instead of buying property that was near a body of water.

Although this was not part of the original plan, the communal Hutterites were never able to agree on the creation of a single church organization even though all three groups adhered to the same beliefs and practices. The three colonies and their many daughter communes that were established in the decades that followed became separate, permanent and endogamous factions. Differences of opinion between the

---

103. United States General Land Office document, April 5, 1877. WTC. The original homestead papers are in the possession of Donald Hofman, Omaha, Nebraska.

104. Waldner, ed., *Russian Record*, 41.

105. Ibid., 43.

first three Dakota Territory communal leaders were basic to this fractious development. Attempts to bring together two of the groups nearly succeeded in 1876 when Michael Waldner was "elected" and "ordained" as a Hutterite "elder" but the "election" was later contested.[106] A description of these events is found in the diary of communal Hutterite-turned Prairieleut minister, Joseph "Yos" Hofer.[107]

A fourth group of noncommunal Hutterites (from Hutterthal village) arrived in Dakota Territory in the fall of 1875. They were led by Elder Michael Stahl and Martin Waldner. Two additional groups from Hutterthal arrived in the years 1877 and 1878. Paul Tschetter's eighty-year-old grandmother, Anna Tschetter, was in the latter group.[108] But the largest group of noncommunal Hutterites did not arrive in the Dakotas until the summer of 1879, when 334 people from the Johannesruh and Hutterthal villages were finally able to complete the sale of their properties. It was also in 1879 that the last residents of Neu Hutterthal village arrived in North America. Hutterite folk tradition suggests that some of the 1879 immigrants could have left earlier. They hedged their bets, however, just in case reported conditions in the Dakotas were not to their liking.[109]

By the end of 1879, most Hutterites living in south Ukraine had immigrated to North America. Only thirty-five people with Hutterian background remained in Russia. Most of them had married Mennonites and joined the Mennonite Church. These included Paul Tschetter's aunt, Barbara, who married a Mennonite named Daniel Unger. Lenhart Tschetter (Paul Tschetter's first cousin, once removed) also married a Mennonite and stayed behind. Both of these families suffered the horrors of World War I and its aftermath, including the Communist Revolution, the Russian Civil War and the great famine that followed. Lenhart and his wife Anna immigrated to Canada in 1926.

In North America the noncommunalists comprised about two-thirds of the total Hutterite population and they immediately formed three large

---

106. A. M. Hofer, ed., *The Diary of Joseph "Yos" Hofer*, February 27, 1876 and July 31, 1876 entries.

107. Ibid. Further description of the attempt to merge the three groups is found in R. Janzen, *The Prairie People*, 70–74.

108. Wesley Tschetter, "Reflections on the Life of Paul Tschetter."

109. Wesley Tschetter, correspondence, December, 2008. Tschetter heard this story from older Prairieleut relatives.

churches as well as a number of associated house congregations. By the time of the 1880 census, the noncommunal/communal breakdown stood at 443 Hutterians residing in colonies; 822 on private land.

Financial Assistance

During the first years of settlement many immigrants lacked sufficient funds to purchase farm implements, draft animals, seed and other necessities, for example, lumber for the construction of homes and barns. During the 1870s and 1880s credit was tight for farmers in the Midwest and Plains states. Organizations like the Southern and Northern Alliances later proposed an inflation of the currency based on silver to make it easier for farmers to borrow money. This was the position of the Populist and Democratic Parties in the late nineteenth and early twentieth century but mid-western farm interests were not represented in the White House until Woodrow Wilson became President in 1912.

The colony Hutterites advantageously obtained special funding from two Christian communal groups: the Harmony Society in Pennsylvania and the Amana Society in Iowa. The Harmonists were a communal Radical Pietist group founded by George Rapp in Germany that had immigrated to Pennsylvania in 1805.[110] At one time reaching a membership of 1,000 people, the Harmonists practiced celibacy and, by the 1870s, had decreased to a few dozen members. The society held significant financial assets, however, some of which were offered to the communal Hutterites. In the late 1870s, for example, the Harmonists granted 4000 dollars to the Bon Homme Colony "to help with start-up costs."[111] According to Harmony Society archivist Raymond Shepard, the group also provided thousands of dollars in loans, some of which were never re-paid.[112]

There were other relationships with the Harmonists. In 1880, for example, four single noncommunal Hutterite men took jobs with the society at their Tidioute, Pennsylvania location. All of these men later returned to Dakota Territory and one of them, Paul Gross became a

---

110. Bestor, *Backwoods Utopias*, 34–36.

111. Mendel, *A History of the People of East Freeman, Silver Lake and West Freeman*, 106.

112. Raymond Shepherd, interview, October 2005. The Old Economy (Pennsylvania) Archives possesses a financial statement that confirms this information.

Prairieleut minister.[113] Four years later, however (in 1884), when economic hard times hit the Bon Homme's daughter colony, Tripp, nineteen families there, including leader Michael Waldner, relocated to the same Tidioute, Pennsylvania area. They lived there until 1886, while the Harmonists and Hutterites seriously contemplated a permanent merger. There were major disagreements over theology, however, and the Hutterites did not like the fact that the central Harmonist site (at Economy) was very close to the city of Pittsburgh.[114]

The other group that offered assistance to the communal Hutterites was the Amana Society or Inspirationists. This was another group of radical German Pietists who had fled to the United States earlier in the nineteenth century. Established by Johann Rock and Eberhard Gruber as the "Community of True Inspiration" in the early 1700s, the group moved to southeastern Iowa in the 1840s, where they established a number of communal villages west of Cedar Rapids. Amana provided thousands of dollars in financial support to Bon Homme Colony as well as expertise in the construction of a mill.

Financial aid from kindred communalists was not available to the noncommunal Hutterites. They received support instead from special relief committees established by American Mennonite groups. This included, on one occasion, 2,000 sacks of flour and other supplies.[115] The Mennonite Church Board of Guardians was especially helpful through the advocacy of old friend John F. Funk. The Board not only made arrangements with steamship and railroad lines but provided financial support for start-up costs. Some of this aid was in the form of grants; much of it was loaned. A Board of Guardians circular dated December, 1873, assured Russian Mennonites of financial assistance in terms of gifts and loans and said that German-speaking agents would meet them at the Castle Garden immigration center in New York City.[116] These agents ensured that railroad tickets were purchased correctly but, as noted, they also pushed the interests of particular companies. In this regard it is interesting to note that John F. Funk's brother, Francis Funk, was one of these agents, although we do not know whether he played a role in any settlement decisions.

113. R. Janzen, *The Prairie People*, 68.
114. Raymond Shepherd, interview, October 2005.
115. Boese, *The Prussian Polish Mennonites in South Dakota*, 65.
116. Schell, *A History of South Dakota*, 78.

John Ruth's history of Lancaster County (Pennsylvania) Mennonites, *The Earth is the Lord's*, includes many references to financial donations made to the immigrants by Lancaster County Mennonites.[117] New arrivals were also provided temporary housing in southeastern Pennsylvania and Indiana, sometimes for months at a time. Assistance was also extended from General Conference Mennonites via Christian Krehbiel, who served with John F. Funk on the Mennonite Board of Guardians, and who in 1879 moved to Kansas where he lived beside many of the Russian immigrants.[118]

Paul Tschetter's own emigrant group, members of the Neu Hutterthal village in Ukraine, was better off financially than many other Hutterites. A compilation of extracts from John F. Funk's *Herald of Truth*, contains a letter confirming this from Prussian Mennonite delegate Wilhelm Ewert, dated October 30, 1873. Ewert writes that the "colony [sic] represented by Tschetter [Paul Tschetter] did not require any emergency financial help," noting that the Tschetter was "fortunate in being able to sell at fair prices [in Ukraine]."[119]

But financial issues were a constant concern for most Prairieleut settlers and it was often difficult to meet loan re-payment schedules. In January 1889, Paul Tschetter drafted a letter to John F. Funk on behalf of many of his congregants. He asked him to consider forestalling interest payments on loans or even forgiving them entirely.[120] Funk in turn filled *Herald of Truth* issues with constant appeals for financial assistance for the Anabaptist immigrants.

---

117. Ruth, *The Earth is the Lord's*.

118. Jansen, *Memoirs of Peter Jansen*, 38.

119. "Russian Immigration in Early Seventies," Letter from Wilhelm Ewert (Thorn, West Prussia) to John F. Funk. AMC.

120. Paul Tschetter to John F. Funk, January 12, 1889. John F. Funk collection, Box 16. AMC. An earlier letter, dated October 8, 1888, mentioned a Prairieleut individual who had borrowed 100 dollars.

6

A New Life in Dakota Territory

> It has been said that around Freeman and Bridgewater the woods are full of Tschetters ... More than forty families of Tschetters are recorded, so many in fact, that they are distinguished from each other by numbers.[1]
>
> —Works Progress Administration Guidebook, 1938

UNTIL THE 1870S, DAKOTA TERRITORY WAS A NATIVE AMERICAN FRONTier inhabited by a number of different tribes and bands. The Appropriations Act of 1871, however, stripped indigenous tribes of their official status as independently governing entities. After 1871, they were restricted to the government-determined boundaries or "reservations" and the United States no longer negotiated treaties with them. The 1871 Act opened the eastern half of Dakota Territory to settlement by anyone that wanted to live there. This made Hutterite immigration to the region possible.

Even with restrictions on movement, the Lakota people continued to cross the Dakota Territory, hunting buffalo and other game; the large buffalo herds were not depleted until the 1880s. Many Hutterians discovered American Indian remains on their property, for example, rock circles. Lakota Indians living in teepees continued to be found outside reservation boundaries in many parts of southeastern Dakota Territory.[2]

When Peter Jansen traveled through the region in the early 1870s, he said that "wild game abounded, and we saw large herds of antelope.[3] Jansen sighted many buffalo "carcasses," which had been "left to rot."

1. Hasselstrom, *Roadside History of South Dakota*, 120.
2. Beadle, *Autobiography*, 13, 22.
3. Jansen, *The Memoirs of Peter Jansen*, 39.

There were prairie chickens and ducks in abundance and almost no settlers. Overnight lodging meant bedding down in sod stables or haystacks. Dakota Territory Surveyor General William Beadle wrote that in the 1870s, Sioux Falls, now the largest city in South Dakota, consisted of a military barracks and one small store.[4] Beadle wrote that when traveling between Sioux City, Iowa and Yankton he "had to stop and cut the gumbo, mud and grass from the wheels" of the wagons to keep going.[5] The Prairieleut Hutterthal Church history book describes "a vast expanse of ever waving wind-driven prairie grasses" and no forest.[6] Linda Hasselstrom refers to the region as "tall grass country."[7]

In the early 1800s members of the Lewis and Clark expedition crossed the Dakota Territory but not until 1883 did a constitutional convention designate the 46th parallel as the boundary between what became South and North Dakota. Statehood arrived six years later (in 1889) with South Dakota becoming the 40th state in the union. Sparsely populated at the time the Tschetters arrived, the Territory's population increased rapidly from 81,781 people in 1880 and to an amazing 248,569 by 1885.[8]

Unfortunately Hutterite settlement was undertaken during the economic depression years of 1873–1877, which made life difficult. Many of the noncommunal Hutterites initially lived in quickly constructed sod houses with dirt floors. These were later replaced by house/barn structures built of wood and stone. Frame houses were constructed out of pine boards and covered with tar paper to protect the residences from rain, wind and snow. Each house had a Russian-style kitchen that included a stove made of earthen bricks connected to a central chimney. Meat was cured in the chimney and bricks attached to the oven were laid throughout the house to provide a central heating system.

In the United States the Hutterite immigrants had to learn a new language and become acquainted with an unfamiliar system of weights and measures, new forms of currency and a democratic form of govern-

---

4. Beadle, *Autobiography*, 13.
5. Ibid., 8.
6. A. Kleinsasser, ed., *Our Journey of Faith*, 1.
7. Hasselstrom, *Roadside History of South Dakota*, 3.
8. H. Schell, *History of South Dakota*, 159. Other sources for South Dakota history include Milton, *South Dakota: A History*; Karolevitz, *Yankton*; and Dakota Territory Centennial Committee, eds., *Dakota Panorama*.

ment. They had to get used to extremely hot summers and bitterly cold winters. Heavy winds brought clean air but also dangerous accentuations of weather conditions that were harmful to crops and livestock. Fences had to be constructed to protect crops from ranging animal life. In an era that preceded modern medicine, serious illnesses were a common experience and a concern for every Hutterian family. Some Prairieleut responded with great frustration and many complained that they should have never left Russia.

Feelings of social isolation were accentuated by the fact that the Homestead Act made it impossible for the Prairieleut to construct Eastern European-style villages since each family was required to reside on its own quarter section of land. Unlike the situation in Ukraine all Hutterites in the Dakotas lived in the countryside at great distances from one another. Neighbors were not seen as often; farm work was done with greater independence. All of this led to significant social and psychological discontent.

The only way that Prairieleut Hutterites could in part duplicate the European village social structure was for families on adjoining sections of land to construct houses in shared corners. This led to the construction of a number of four-family mini-communities. According to Paul Tschetter's brother, Jacob, "It was meant to be something like life in the colony. Each had their private living quarters but ate together."[9] This was not quite the way things usually worked but families did sometimes share meals. The homes in these creative residential plans were also usually located on a main road so that guests could get to them easily. Maps indicate that a number of families followed a quadruple (or at least double) residential construction plan, allowing the isolated settlers to re-create, in a small way, the village life that had been left behind in Ukraine.

O. E. Rolvaag wrote that the rolling hills of the prairies awakened memories of waves on the ocean.[10] Hutterites made similar comments. In terms of terrain, the prairies also reminded Hutterites of the Ukrainian steppes. But there was not the same sense of "closeness" that was found in Eastern European village life.[11] Never before had any Hutterian felt as lonely and isolated as he and she did in Dakota Territory. Compared

9. Jacob A. Tschetter, "Family History."
10. Zempel, ed., *When the Wind is in the South and Other Stories*, 14.
11. Paul G. Tschetter, "Anecdotes."

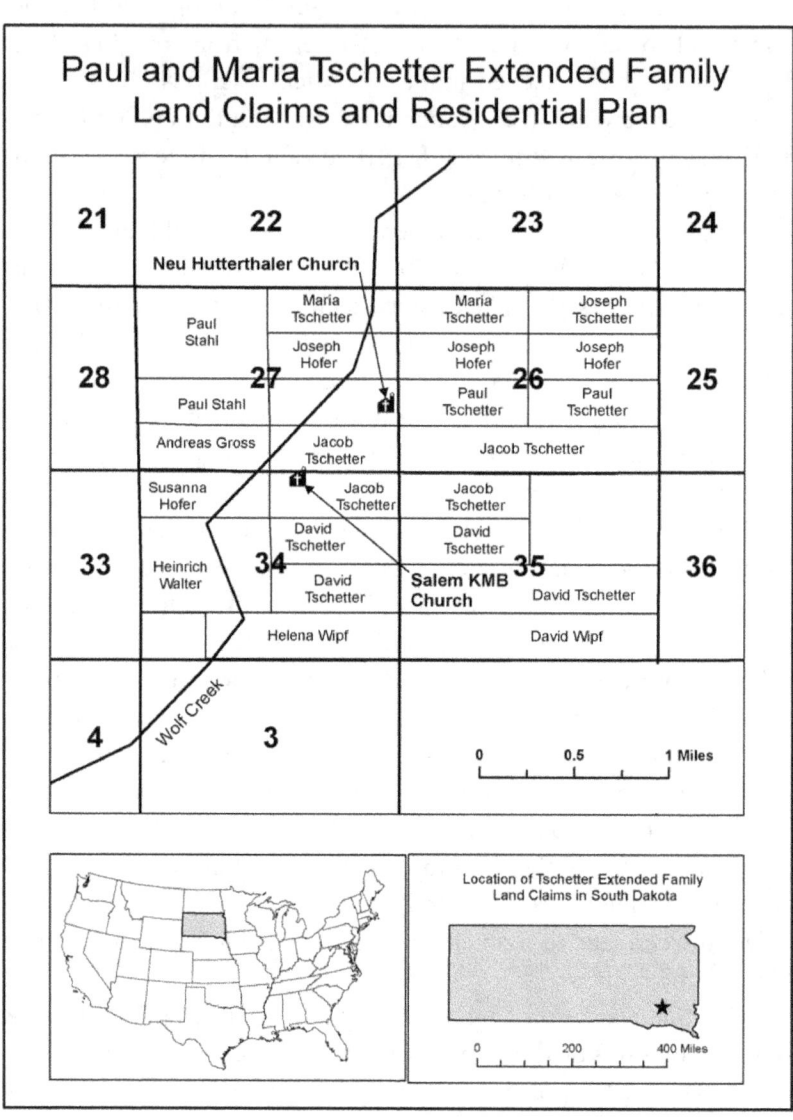

Map 6.1 Paul and Maria Tschetter Extended Family Land Claims and Residential Plan. Map courtesy of Stuart McFeeters.

to the 1842–1879 experience in south Ukraine, there was no developed Mennonite or non-Mennonite agriculture, educational system or light industry.

In the Wolf Creek Colony area Paul Tschetter and his siblings Joseph, Jacob, David and Susanna, all qualified for 160-acre Homestead land allotments. After paying an eighteen dollar filing fee, they positioned their houses according to the quadruple plan described above and shown below.

The Tschetter clan purchased land allotments that had a distinctive and unusual shape. In order for each family to have land that lay against the Wolf Creek, they homesteaded property that was divided into 80 acre-wide rectangular strips, two farms on each side of the road (west and east) and each homestead with access to the creek. This ensured that each landholder had direct access to water for stock as well as berries, plums, chokecherries, fish and small lumber. Today one sees the winding indentation of the Wolf Creek running through land that is still owned by Hutterians but their crops are now planted right up to the water's edge. The water level is much lower than it was in the late nineteenth century and there are very few bushes and trees.

In accordance with the 1862 Homestead Act the Tschetters paid $1.25 per acre for their land. When Paul's parents Jacob and Barbara arrived in the fall of 1875, they filed a claim for a separate but adjacent quarter-section of land that had been pre-selected by Paul Tschetter. Most Hutterian settlers secured an additional 160 acres through the 1873 Timber and Culture Act, which provided a second quarter section of land if at least 10 acres of it was planted in trees. Property owners were also required to establish residence on any land that was homesteaded. In the Freeman *Courier* Prairieleut Jacob J. Mendel described ways that some Hutterians avoided the residence requirement through deceitful arrangements, like putting up a shack that was actually never lived in. But these were rare occurrences.[12] More problematic was the issue of boundary determinations. Jacob A. Tschetter wrote that many Hutterites used "numbered rods stuck in a pile of dirt at the corners" to establish borders.[13]

---

12. Mendel, *History of the People of East Freeman, Silver Lake and West Freeman*, 15.
13. Jacob A. Tschetter, "Family History," 97.

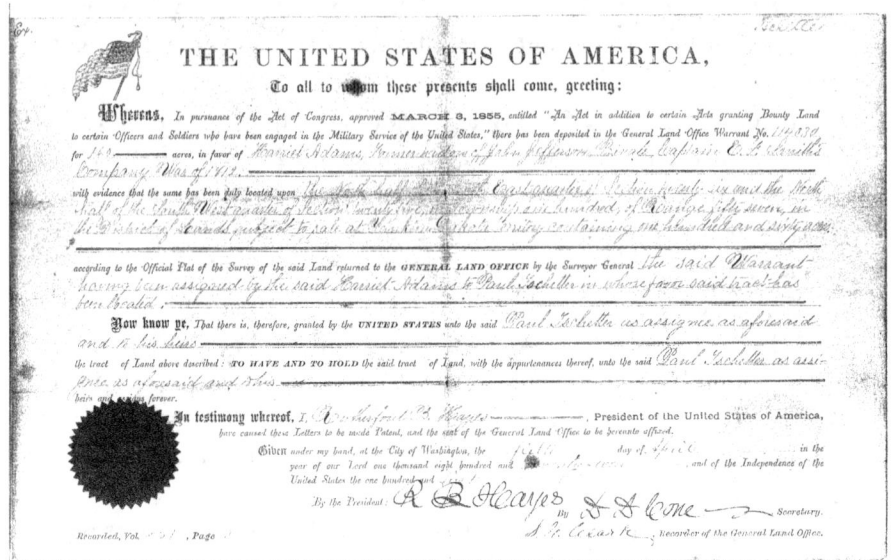

Figure 6.1 United States General Land Office Deed with Paul Tschetter's Signature. Document courtesy of Donald Hofman.

Farming in the Dakotas

Most Prairieleut families planted large gardens and had at least one milk cow to provide milk, cheese, butter and other dairy products. Common garden crops included watermelons, grapes and pumpkins. There were also potatoes and a variety of vegetables. One person planted sugar cane.[14]

Most of the farmland, however, was planted in flax and ("Turkey Red") hard winter wheat both of which became important commodities. In a 1991 article in *Scientific American* James Young also credits the Hutterites and Mennonites for introducing the tumbleweed to the Great Plains suggesting that the Russian thistle seed or knapweed was unintentionally mixed in with wheat and flax seed brought from Russia.[15] He notes that the seed first appeared in 1877 "on a farm in Bon Homme County" and that many people later "believed that Russian Mennonites had deliberately introduced the weed" as "retaliation for the derision of other immigrants."[16]

14. A. M. Hofer, ed., *The Diaries of Joseph "Yos" Hofer*, July, 1873 to November 1873 entries.

15. J. A. Young, "Tumbleweed," 84.

16. Ibid.

In any case, most noncommunal Hutterite families also had livestock, including ducks, geese, chickens, sheep and hogs. Chickens were particularly important because of the constant supply of eggs, which were eaten in various forms and used to make noodles. Nearby there were wild prairie chickens, turkeys and antelope living in the open fields. Meat and dairy products (milk, cheese and butter) were eventually marketed but early on were used primarily to meet each family's basic dietary needs. The average Hutterite fare also included wild fruit gathered from creek beds. Hutterian specialties included special breads, home-made sausage, stewed beef, sauerkraut, *Kuchen*, a special *Gashtel* (crumb soup made from graded dough), *Moos* (various kinds of fruit puddings), and *Zitala* (jellied pigs feet).

Immigrant life was filled with a constant series of chores and these involved all age groups. For men and women this included twice daily milking responsibilities. Men took primary responsibility for the care and feeding of livestock as well as planting, tilling and harvesting crops although Hutterite women frequently assisted in all of these endeavors. Women cleaned family residences and they also worked in the garden, prepared meals, made, ironed and washed clothes and kept stove fires going with corn cobs, small pieces of wood, buffalo chips and other dried manure as well as straw and hay that were twisted into knots. Straw also provided bedding material. Children helped their parents wherever they were needed.

The banks of the Wolf Creek were bordered by willows and cottonwoods, which were used as building material. Meadows along the creek provided hay for cattle. The creek itself provided water for stock as well as fish and crabs. Wild fruit growing along the creek was preserved by drying.[17]

In the 1870s the Wolf Creek bottom was a virtual freeway that generally ran north and south. It was a common route for American Indians traveling through the area in the fall and spring, which brought "fear" to some early settlers.[18] Herbert Schell's *History of South Dakota* derogatorily describes the tribes as "pacified" by 1868.[19] But Paul Tschetter's

---

17. Jacob A. Tschetter, "Family History," 96

18. Mendel, *History of the People of East Freeman Silver Lake and West Freeman,* 21.

19. H. Schell, *History of South Dakota,* 109.

Figure 6.2 Loading Manure with a pitchfork.
Photograph courtesy of Donald Hofman.

son, Jacob W., recalled seeing a small group of Indians camped overnight west of the Paul Tschetter property on the Wolf Creek.[20] And Paul Tschetter told his granddaughter, Anna Fisher, that he once saw a group of Indians skinning a horse along the same creek.[21] As a result he had followed a different route home. Edna Wurtz and Catherine Masuk tell the story of American Indians "who painted their faces and howled and danced into the night."[22]

According to Wesley Tschetter, if American Indians traveled north along the Wolf Creek, then turned west and cut across the prairie to Firesteel Creek northwest of Mitchell, they could reach their homes along the Missouri River (later designated the Crow Creek Reservation) by following a sequence of creek and river valleys.[23] The river bottoms of the Wolf Creek and the James River (located nearby) also served as

---

20. Jacob W. Tschetter, interview with Wesley Tschetter (n.d.). WTC.

21. Anna Hofman Fisher, interview, May 2004. A similar story is told in Guericke, *Precious Memories*, 41.

22. Wurtz and Masuk, *Rooted and Grounded in Love*.

23. Wesley Tschetter, interview, May 2004.

convenient travel routes for the Rev. Paul Tschetter as he visited church families and conducted worship services in private residences.[24]

In addition to wheat and oats, the immigrants also marketed corn and rye. In the early years some of the grain, especially oats, was stored in the attics of private residences to provide extra insulation. Many of the crop yields were low. Much depended on weather conditions and especially rainfall amounts, which in southeastern Dakota Territory averaged about twenty to twenty-two inches per year. The quality of the rich virgin soil was good but the unbroken sod had to be plowed on foot with oxen or horses.

The early settlers relied on ox-drawn carts as a primary mode of transportation. This is the way they got to church, to town and to visit friends and relatives. But this was an extremely slow form of transport. Not only did the oxen walk slowly. When they discovered watering holes en route the oxen customarily insisted on getting a drink and cooling off before proceeding.[25]

Some farm chores were done with assistance from neighbors. These included harvesting, quilting, corn husking and hog butchering. Threshing machines were too expensive for most people but eventually every Hutterite family had its own grass mower, rake and harvester for cutting grain.[26] As the years moved on each Prairieleut farmer began to take care of more and more of his/her own sowing, plowing, harrowing and cultivating as well as hay-making. After teams of horses replaced oxen much human labor was still required. Paul Tschetter's niece, Justina S. W. Glanzer reminisced, "I plowed at home with two horses and a hand plow. It seemed to me I was alone in the world."[27]

Most farm families had many children and they provided an important labor force.[28] Paul Tschetter's granddaughter, Justina Guericke, recalled that she cooked her first supper at age nine for a minister who had come to visit the Rev. Tschetter, who was at the time living with

---

24. Ibid. Wesley Tschetter gathered much information from interviews with Jacob W. Tschetter, one of Paul Tschetter's children. Jacob spent his last years living in Wesley's home (the home of Emil and Barbara Tschetter). Jacob W. Tschetter died in 1960, at age eighty-five.

25. J. S. W. Glanzer, *Life Story of S. W. Glanzer and Justina W. Glanzer*, 1.

26. K. J. Walter, *Matthias M. Hofer Family Record*, 5.

27. J. S. W. Glanzer, *Life Story of S. W. Glanzer and Justina W. Glanzer*, 2.

28. George Rath, *The Black Sea Germans in the Dakotas*.

Figure 6.3 Emil Tschetter (Paul Tschetter's grandson) with a team of horses. Photograph courtesy of Wesley Tschetter.

them. "I boiled potatoes with jackets," wrote Justina, "opened a can of sardines and a jar of fruit and made some tea."[29] She also wrote, "I milked my first cow by hand at the age of 8 years. When our first big horse barn was built, I helped dad haul home all the lumber for the barn."[30] Justina also helped seed, weed and harvest crops.

Although most of the settler's first homes were made of sod, Paul Tschetter had enough money to purchase lumber from Yankton.[31] He set aside $600 for start-up costs and spent most of this money during the first few months for the purchase of wagons, oxen, a plow, and lumber.[32] Those who lived in sod houses liked the fact that their homes were well insulated, something that was beneficial in both cold and hot weather. But they also had to deal with slowly crumbling walls since the sod could not withstand wet conditions for a long period of time. Walls were also quickly infested with insects and sometimes mice. Paul and Maria Tschetter never experienced these inconveniences.

29. Justina Guericke, *Precious Memories of a Historical House*, 26.
30. Ibid.
31. J. E. Hofer, "A History of the Neu Hutterthaler Church, 10.
32. Peterson, *People of the Old Missury*, 98.

To build his house with wood Tschetter made thirteen separate trips to Yankton for loads of lumber and other supplies.[33] On at least one occasion Paul took two wagons, driving one while the other was driven, in turn, by his thirteen-year old daughter, Susanna and ten-year-old son "Big Paul."[34] In order to find their way back and forth across the last fifteen miles of open prairie they tied white pieces of cloth to the tall grasses.

Prairieleut farm and house structures were typically built using square-headed nails. Lime stones gathered from creek and river hillsides solidified foundations and walls and provided each home with thick insulation. These stones were oven-fired for at least ten days before they were used for building. One assumes that this was the construction method used by Paul and Maria Tschetter.

Paul Tschetter's house was forty feet long and had a high roof and large attic. There were three bedrooms on the first floor, plus a living area.[35] Unlike other settlers Paul Tschetter did not construct a traditional house-barn combination. There is little additional information about the Paul and Maria Tschetter home place and no photograph has been located. But the home of Paul Tschetter's brother, Jacob, is described in detail in granddaughter, Justina Guericke's *Precious Memories of a Historical House*. Paul Tschetter's house probably had a similar design.[36]

The Jacob Tschetter house was constructed of "thick stone" for insulation and had shuttered windows. In the main living area there was a coal-burning stove and a fireplace built between the walls, with utensil shelves lined up inside the chimney. This Russian stove was important not only for cooking but for providing heat. The house also had a root cellar, which protected fruit, vegetables, meat and dairy products from extreme heat and frost. Guericke remembered that there was also a potato bin in the cellar as well as tubs of sauerkraut and pickled watermelons.[37] The Tschetters also built a smoke house for curing meat and a summer kitchen. To ensure a regular supply of water, they dug a well and also constructed cisterns.

33. Paul G. Tschetter, taped interview with Nancy Peterson (n.d.). Wesley Tschetter, interview, April 2005.
34. Wesley Tschetter, interview, April 2005.
35. Peterson, *People of the Old Missury*, 98.
36. Guericke, *Precious Memories of a Historical House*.
37. Ibid., 3.

Guericke recalled a large number of doors in the Jacob Tschetter house. As she put it,

> The biggest bed room had double doors. Those doors were opened when they had church services in the front room. West of the bedroom was another front room. This room had many doors; one to the south connected to the hallway. To the west was a door that led to a big storage pantry. To the north, it led to the kitchen and dining room.[38]

Each immigrant family built almost all of its own furniture, including chests, tables, cradles and chairs. This was another responsibility taken on by Paul and Maria Tschetter and their children. There was no indoor plumbing so water had to be carried up to the house daily in heavy buckets from a well. Much time was spent on one's feet; walking was the primary method of transportation. Lighting inside houses was provided by homemade candles and tallow dips that required constant care.

Prairieleut women made most of the family's clothing, with an emphasis on simplicity, practicality and modesty. Older children handed down shirts, pants and shoes to younger brothers and sisters. Clothes were often made from remnant scraps of whatever materials were available. Perhaps this explains why local newsmen sometimes had negative impressions about the way that the new settlers looked. An article in the Yankton *Press and Dakotan* in May 1875 described "Mennonites" who settled in the area as "ungainly in figure, and the women are crossgrained and ugly." The writer admits that "possibly, a portion of this ugliness might be attributed to their painful plainness of dress."[39]

Turn of the Century Recreation

Forms of recreation were limited for a people trying to survive on the open prairie. But children always find ways to entertain themselves. Pieces of wood were turned into toys, as were rolling pins and broken dishes. Mothers made dolls for their daughters. There were races, ball games and other outdoor sports, sometimes in the ice and snow. Jacob A. Tschetter wrote that in the early 1900s, his family built a pond,

---

38. Ibid.

39. *Yankton Press and Dakotan,* May 9, 1875, in C. Hiebert, *Brothers in Deed to Brothers in Need,* 237.

Figure 6.4 Jacob W. and Susanna Tschetter Farm House.
Photograph courtesy of Wesley Tschetter.

where children ice-skated in the winter and went swimming in the summer.[40] Many Prairieleut fished in local streams and rivers with spears as well as poles. They caught carp, bullheads and catfish. In the evening older Hutterians entertained boys and girls with scary ghost and wolf stories.

Of special importance were the social occasions that accompanied weddings and funerals. Hutterite weddings, for example, were three to four day affairs, usually held at the home of the bride's parents. This meant extensive preparation for meals eaten by a hundred or more guests. On these occasions strong alcoholic beverages were always available. In 1905, a wedding reception for Christ Hofman and Paul and Maria Tschetter's daughter, Justina, was held at the Paul and Maria Tschetter family home. The menu consisted of noodle soup, beef stew, pork sausage, fried potatoes, sauerkraut and zwiebach.[41] The newlyweds received a number of very practical gifts, including dishes, cutlery and even poultry.

40. Jacob A. Tschetter, "Family History," 92.
41. Guericke, *Precious Memories*, 6.

Natural Disasters, Accidents and Disease

Pioneer life was not easy. As Herbert Schell notes, "While the story of pioneering on the Dakota prairie has many variables, pioneering essentially is a process of adjustment and adaptation."[42] A major problem was the threat of uncontrolled prairie fires. On the open prairie grasses grew so tall that livestock could lie down and "disappear" in them.[43] This was hot fodder for lightning whenever it struck the ground. Fires were especially difficult to contain in fields that had not been cultivated. All farmers had to dig fire lines to impede the potential progress of these fires. Lohrentz Tschetter's son, Lohrentz Jr., became mentally incapacitated and was institutionalized after inhaling too much smoke from one conflagration. In his diary, Joseph "Yos' Hofer first wrote that the fire was in fact "started" by Lohrentz Jr.[44] A few weeks later he corrected himself noting, "Tschetter [was] declared innocent."[45]

After too much rainfall there were also problems with flooding. But the most serious impediment to crop production was the various infestations of grasshoppers and locusts as well as dramatic changes in climate. The latter included dust storms, hail and blizzards. Grasshoppers were sometimes so thick on the prairies that they blocked the sun and ate the bark from trees and logs. Crops were often completely destroyed as were garden vegetables such as corn and potatoes. William Beadle described an August 1874 attack in the following manner: "They would eat almost anything vegetable, would cut off the heads of wheat ... would strip the succulent corn of foliage and ears, and would eat onions down below the surface of the ground."[46] On May 4, 1877, Dakota Territory declared a "Day of Fasting" due to an especially bad infestation of grasshoppers.[47]

A particularly devastating blizzard struck southeastern Dakota Territory on January 12, 1888.[48] That evening four of Paul and Maria Tschetter's children spent the night in a schoolhouse after a perceptive teacher (Paul Decker, Paul Tschetter's son-in-law) recognized the dan-

---

42. Schell, *A History of South Dakota*, 175.
43. Peterson, *People of the Old Missury*, 99.
44. R. Janzen, *The Prairie People*, 239–40.
45. A. M. Hofer, ed., *The Diary of Joseph "Yos" Hofer*, August 1880 entry.
46. Beadle, *Autobiography*, 51.
47. Schell, *A History of South Dakota*, 121.
48. For a detailed account of the 1888 blizzard, see Laskin, *The Children's Blizzard*.

ger of sending them home. The four who stayed in the school and survived were Jacob W., Joseph W., Barbara, and Justina.[49] Other children were not as fortunate. It was during the 1888 blizzard that a number of Swiss Mennonite children froze to death in a field east of the town of Freeman. Severe winters were especially dangerous for Hutterite immigrants who spent the first couple of winters in dugouts that were covered with thatched roofs. Unprotected livestock were always vulnerable.

Natural disasters, from tornadoes to lightning storms, claimed the lives of many Hutterian settlers. A tornado on August 28, 1884, took the life of seventy-three-year-old Elias Wipf as well as twenty-one-year-old Maria Hofer Wipf and five-year-old Joseph Wipf. As described by Reuben Goertz, the tornado lifted Elias and Maria into a ravine after first stripping Maria's scalp "almost completely off her head and ripping out Elias' eyes and nose."[50] These were all members of Paul Tschetter's congregation and the tornado struck down only two miles north of the Paul Tschetter farm.[51] Old acquaintance, John F. Funk was present at the viewing of the Wipf family victims.[52] In the Neu Hutterthaler Church Record Book one finds that in 1885 Susanna Glanzer was killed by lightning. Two years later lightning also struck and killed Peter Hofer while he was loading a wagon.[53]

Some deaths were the result of human frailty. On August 8, 1903, for example, 54 year-old Joseph Hofer (Paul Tschetter's brother-in-law) died in what was described officially as an "accident." According to the Neu Hutterthaler record book,

> He [Joseph Hofer] drove to town with a horse. While driving home one mile from town he fell from his seat and was hung up with the *puszne* (sic) and hung with his body with the head to the ground. So ran the horse for 1¾ miles before the horse was

---

49. Harold Stahl, interview with Wesley Tschetter, April 2004. Emil Tschetter, interview with Wesley Tschetter, January 1988.

50. Goertz, "The Legacy of the First American Tornado Ever Photographed in Dakota Territory, 1884."

51. NHCRB, 818, 819.

52. Schnell, "John F. Funk's Land Inspection Trips," 295–99. Funk's diary, dated June 3—July 26, 1873, is published in Clarence Hiebert, *Brothers in Deed to Brothers in Need*, 48–54.

53. NHCRB, 820.

stopped. He lived for 31 more hours but never regained consciousness. He was buried with great heartache at 54 years old.[54]

Older Prairieleut say that Joseph was drunk when the accident occurred.

The immigrants also had to deal with many illnesses. The Neu Hutterthaler record book contains handwritten notes in the margins that describe individual medical problems. These include kidney trouble, heart attacks, consumption (tuberculosis), strokes, dropsy, diabetes, palsy and asthma. William Beadle noted large-scale incidences of illness in Turner County, just east of the Hutterian settlements.[55] The year before his death Paul Tschetter watched as the community was devastated by the 1918 swine flu epidemic, which sometimes affected entire families.

There were also incidents involving wild animals. In 1880, Paul Tschetter's six-year-old son Jacob W. lay down by a bush near a creek while his parents were making hay and a snake bit him on the right index finger. Wesley Tschetter, who heard this story from his grandfather, notes, "The swollen finger soon became the size of an egg. Jacob was taken to Marion Junction . . . and a doctor lanced the figure whereby a tendon was cut and he lost the ability to bend his finger."[56] And there were also many farm accidents. A review of Prairieleut memoirs includes everything from a death by falling under a grass mower to fingers cut off.[57] In general injuries as well as illnesses were treated with tried-and-true folk remedies, like bloodletting with leeches. An infant suffering from paralysis was placed in a large pail of warm salty water for an hour every day until the symptoms abated. Doctors were consulted only if the sickness or injury was extremely serious or when major problems occurred. The most common response to illness was to request prayer.

Education and Folk Traditions

The Prairieleut frequently used nicknames to describe individual members of the community. These were based on physical, emotional, or other characteristics. The Neu Hutterthaler Church record book

---

54. Ibid., 826.
55. Beadle, *Autobiography*, 50.
56. Wesley Tschetter, interview May 2004.
57. R. Janzen, *The Prairie People*, 55, 56.

Figure 6.5 Tschetter School District Elementary School Building. Photograph courtesy of Wesley Tschetter.

is filled with these monikors, including the following: "Tractor John," "Tornado Wipf," "Krumpa Mike," "Turkey Yoppela," "Zonder David," "Ditscha Fritz," and "Floor Washer Wipf."[58] Another source lists "Butcher" Tschetter (who owned the Freeman meat market) as well as "Fox" Tschetter (he raised foxes).[59]

All Prairieleut children were required to attend public schools that were established by the Homestead Act. Tschetter's children attended these institutions but they usually were not in session for more than five months during the year because of farming obligations. For a number of years instruction was in the German language and the Bible was used regularly. There was much emphasis on memorizing historical and mathematical facts. Justina Guericke describes harsh pedagogical methods: "Those early teachers ruled with an iron rod. When a child wasn't too bright, instead of helping him, he would get black and blue stripes across his back."[60]

The school shown in Figure 6.5 was called the "Tschetter School District," following a common late nineteenth-century practice of nam-

58. NHCRB, 62, 74, 84, 87, 141, 142, 163.

59. HMCC, eds., *Hutterite Roots*, 11.

60. Guericke, *Precious Memories*, 5.

ing country schools after a local family. Jacob and Susanna Tschetter's farm was located about a half mile away, making it easy for their children to get to school in the morning. Many children had to walk a mile or two to the school building or drive a horse and buggy. For those who did the latter there was a small barn near the school building.

Although they never established their own private elementary schools, many Prairieleut helped found the Mennonite-affiliated Freeman College and Academy in 1900. John L. Wipf served as the first secretary of the college's board of directors and the institution's first building was constructed on land donated by Prairieleut John Gross.[61] Paul G. Tschetter suggested that his grandfather (Paul Tschetter) was not overly excited about the new college and secondary school, believing that it would be dominated by Mennonites and their concerns.[62] Tschetter's view of Christian education in general is shown, however, by his support for son David's attendance at a Lutheran academy in Canton, South Dakota, and son Joseph's enrollment at the short-lived Krimmer Mennonite Brethren Bethel College in Huron, South Dakota.

61. M. J. Waldner and M. D. Hofer, *Many Hands, Minds and Hearts*.
62. Paul G. Tschetter, interview, July, 1998.

7

Paul Tschetter and the Hutterite Colonies

> And all that believed were together, and not scattered here and there, divided, and in parts, one here and one there, everybody on his own, only concerned about his own; like all those Christian fellowships nowadays, who have withdrawn from the world, and are yet withdrawn from their brothers in the faith, and live in their own houses, just like the world.
>
> —Hutterite sermon on Acts 2:43–44[1]

DURING THE FIRST TWO DECADES IN DAKOTA TERRITORY MANY HUTTerites were pulled toward the communal traditions of their ancestors, which were based on the Hutterite reading of the book of Acts, chapters 2, 4, and 5. According to Acts 4:32: "The whole group of believers was united, heart and soul; no one claimed private ownership of any possessions, as everything they owned was held in common" (NJB). Historically, Hutterites referred to this way of life as *Gutergemeinschaft* or "full community of goods."

The Hutterites as a group gave up communal life from 1690–1757 and again from 1819–1859. Even after its resurrection in Russia in the late 1850s, less than a quarter of the members chose communal Christianity. The Hutterite majority accepted a more individualistic interpretation of the faith. But it was impossible to get away from the communal message. It was assumed, for example, in the Riedemann confession of faith, which all Hutterites, including Paul Tschetter, honored. Communalism was also an important theme in many of the *Lehren*, particularly the "Pentecost" sermon, which Paul Tschetter, like all Hutterite ministers, read every Pentecost Sunday. Hutterites revere Pentecost as the day when God sent the Holy Spirit to empower the

---

1. Peter Tschetter, ed., *Hutterite Sermon, Acts 2:43–44*.

early believers. Immediately thereafter they began to share all of their personal belongings.

Hutterites believe that Jesus himself lived communally with his disciples, as did the Apostle Paul with his own followers and associates, even though this is not clearly delineated in the New Testament. With regard to the epistles, Hutterites often cite 2 Corinthians 8:7–15, where Paul stresses the principle of equality; that no person should have abundance while another suffers want.

After Christianity became a state religion, forms of communalism continued in the evolving Roman Catholic and Orthodox Church organizations. Those who committed themselves to full-time religious service were commonly asked to live without private property, showing greater dedication to the church and limiting the possibility of corruption, since there was no personal wealth to pass on to descendents through inheritance. In the Catholic Church communal life was also associated with celibacy and a metaphorical "marriage" to the church. The introduction of monastic orders took the call to communal ministry a step further. In many of these communities it was believed that one could not show total dedication to God unless one lived communally as well as simply.

Hutterites assume that there will be no private ownership in heaven; that everything there will be organized communally under the guidance and leadership of God. Many noncommunal Christians take a similar stance or at least they do not anticipate class, ethnic, personality or property divisions in the afterlife. Hutterites ask noncommunal Christians why they are not willing to live now the way that they expect to live later in the afterlife.

The Hutterites believe the original Eden was also organized communally and that the introduction of private property was in fact a result of Adam and Eve's sin. In this regard the Hutterites believe that they are performing an important service to God as they help to bring to fruition his original communal vision: the equalitarian paradise in the Garden.

Yet Paul Tschetter, who considered himself a true Hutterite in every way, never lived communally. Tschetter grew up hearing heated debates about the communal/noncommunal issue. He observed various attempts to resurrect communal Hutterianism in three different villages in Ukraine. None of this made communal attractive to him. Tschetter revered and read the Hutterite sermons and hymns and he knew that the Hutterite fathers and mothers would have opposed noncommunal Christianity. But Tschetter refused to accept the communalist position as the one that God was calling contemporary Hutterites to live out. In his view God had a different plan for Hutterites in the late nineteenth century.

The reason for Tschetter's refusal to join a colony was grounded in his own experience. He saw how difficult it was to get people to share all of their material possessions and to thus evaluate the spiritual implications of social and economic decisions collectively on an almost daily basis. Communal life did not seem practical to Tschetter. The communal re-enactments of the 1850s, 1860s and 1870s were marked by factionalism, ill will and personality conflicts and Tschetter believed that God was calling him in a different direction.

Tschetter thought that Hutterite culture and belief could be preserved without community of goods. His central focus in Dakota Territory was to maintain a separate Hutterite identity outside of the colony context. Yet the quality of religious life in the noncommunal Hutterite churches and house congregations was questioned again and again by colony Hutterites as well as by neighboring Mennonites.

The colony Hutterites believed that the Prairieleut had strayed from the true communal pathway; from the holy order put into practice by Hutterian ancestors for three and a half centuries. They believed that the refusal to give everything to God, to practice true *Gelassenheit* by living communally, was a step away from true Christianity. The fact that the Prairieleut retained other Hutterian forms, traditional dress, the Hutterisch dialect, the *Lehren,* special hymns and various cultural traditions, was not enough. Colony members criticized noncommunal Hutterites for shallow spiritual commitments and self-centeredness. This position is substantiated clearly in the Acts 2 sermon, where the writer notes,

> Even so the great majority of today's Christians of this world can't adapt themselves, to live communally . . . For when one drives all the pigs from the meadow together and tries to feed them all out of one trough, we soon hear a lot of grunting and squealing and biting one another, getting into the trough with their feet, making much noise so that others dare not come near.

Therefore it's not possible for the godless people to live together and share in common.[2]

When communal Hutterites read the story of Ananias and Sapphira (in Acts 5), they attributed the quick death of both husband and wife to a similar kind of selfishness: the pair's refusal to give up all of the proceeds from the sale of their property. In the late nineteenth-century colony Hutterites used this reference to admonish the Prairieleut and they continue to do so in the twenty-first century. Communal Hutterites ask their noncommunal friends and relatives why they are not preparing while they are living on earth for the more important life that they eventually expect to live in heaven. Hutterite minister Hans Decker put it this way, "If there is no private property in heaven, there should be none either among God's people here on earth."[3] The Hutterite understanding of *Gelassenheit* is strongly affirmed in the *Lehren*. Christians are asked to turn their wills over to God *through* the community of believers. Without community of goods it is believed that the individual ego, under the subtle influence of Satan, takes control too much of the time.

In Hutterite history, as noted, community of goods was given up for two main reasons. In the first case (in the late seventeenth century) a major cause was extensive religious persecution with its many corollary effects. The second dissolution (in the early nineteenth century) was the result of economic problems and interpersonal conflicts, leading to new theological perspectives.[4] The Hutterite Chronicle names the Rev. Jacob Walter as the man who (in the early 1800s) "openly confessed his backsliding from the faith" and insisted on owning private property, ultimately "destroy[ing]" communal life.[5] Looking to the Chronicle for support Hutterites who joined one of the three Dakota colonies believed that noncommunal Hutterianism in its more recent manifestation was a corrupted form that had only been established during a time when spiritual conditions were at their weakest point.

It is thus not difficult to understand why one-third of the Hutterite immigrants decided to resurrect communal life in Dakota Territory or

2. Ibid., 1, 16.
3. Hans Decker, interview, August, 1988.
4. R. Janzen, *The Prairie People*, 20–21.
5. Waltner, ed., *Banished For Faith*, 99–101, 110. See also HMCC, eds., *Hutterite Roots*, 80, 83.

why many Prairieleut left their individual homesteads and joined them. Many noncommunalists felt a sense of personal guilt every time they heard stories about Jacob Hutter, Peter Walpot, and Andreas Ehrenpreis. The historic Hutterite narrative impacted the thinking of every person due to the abundant family ties and friendships that crossed communal/noncommunal lines. There were many visits and thus many opportunities to seek conversions. The Jacob W. Tschetter diary confirms many trips to the colonies to "play with cousins."[6] In his account, "Yos" Hofer also makes many references to colony visits throughout his life (he died in 1905). This is no surprise since "Yos's" mother-in-law, brother, and other relatives and friends lived there.

Interpersonal contacts caused much movement back and forth between the two groups and during the first decade a greater number moved in the colony direction. The communal Hutterites were in an advantageous position since most visits took place on the Colony grounds (members faced travel restrictions) and the early settlement years were financially difficult for individual farmers. By the 1890s, things turned around and there were just as many colony members leaving "for the prairie." There are many examples of the crossover phenomenon and as many as two hundred people moved back and forth before the turn of the century.[7] The following are some examples.

There were no "Tschetters" in the first group of 425 Hutterites who joined one of three colonies in the Dakota Territory.[8] But today there are hundreds. This is all because of Paul Tschetter's uncle, Peter Tschetter, who in 1877 "quit private ownership" after first homesteading with spouse, Sarah Hofer.[9] The Peter and Sara Tschetter property was located on the west side of the James River, ten miles from Paul Tschetter's home. A small lake nearby, the "Tschetter Slough," took on the family name.[10] But Peter and Sarah were attracted to communal life and they decided to join the Wolf Creek Colony. Thirteen years later (in 1890) they helped establish a daughter colony on their original homestead

---

6. L. Tschetter and E. Tschetter, eds., *Jacob W. Tschetter Family Record*, 5.

7. R. Janzen, *The Prairie People*, 69–70.

8. Kenneth Morgan and Mary T. Holmes, et. al., "Population Structure of a Religious Isolate: The Darisuleut Hutterites of Alberta."

9. J. K. Wipf and D. S. Wipf, eds., *Dariusleut Family Record List*, 164.

10. Anderson, "The Hutterites," 4.

property, which they ceded to the Dariusleut Hutterites.[11] This colony was called "Kutter," an archaic German word meaning a "small group."[12] Today Peter Tschetter's descendents are members of Dariusleut colonies in Alberta, Montana, Oregon, Washington, British Columbia, and Saskatchewan.

Another uncle of Paul Tschetter, Johannes, also homesteaded on land north of the James River, in Wittenburg Township. He and his wife eventually moved into the town of Bridgewater but their son, Johannes joined the Wolf Creek Colony and today also has many descendents among the Dariusleut Hutterites.[13] The Johannes and Anna Tschetter land was sold to Jacob and Fredericka Roth and it is described as "an outstanding purchase" in a local historical account because the sale included not only the land but "almost everything the Tschetters owned."[14] According to a history of Menno, South Dakota, "When they moved out they [the Tschetters] left most everything behind but their clothes. They even left their teenage son Peter Tschetter for some time to help the Roth's adjust to the new way of doing things on a farm in South Dakota."

Similarly, Prairieleut Fred Waldner originally homesteaded on land that later became the town of Freeman. He sold the land, but instead of living among the Prairieleut, Waldner joined the Bon Homme Colony. He did this after having a dream in which God told him that Jesus would only give him spiritual direction if he lived communally.[15]

There are many cases of Prairieleut turning communitarian. In 1867, at Hutterthal village in Ukraine, Paul Tschetter conducted the marriage of David Stahl and Justina Tschetter. Eight years later David and

---

11. "Jacob and Barbara Tschetter Genealogical Information," unpublished document. WTC. The Schmiedeleut "Tschetter Colony," established in 1942, took its name from the "Tschetter Slough," located ten miles northeast of the colony. The origin of the term "Kutter" is a mystery. John Hostetler wrote that the Kutter Colony was located in Kutter, South Dakota but the United States Geographical Survey has no record of a South Dakota town with that name. Some Hutterites suggest that the name "Kutter" was an old German or Hutterisch term that meant (to Hutterites) someone who lived noncommunally (like Peter Tschetter once had). Other Hutterites suggest that the term "Kutter" is a form of the word "Tschetter."

12. Tony Waldner, correspondence, July, 2007.

13. J. K. Wipf and D. S. Wipf, eds., *Dariusleut Family Record List*, 138. Genealogist, Alan Peters provided significant assistance in the analysis of Hutterite family records.

14. Historical Committee, eds., *Menno*, 546.

15. R. Janzen, *The Prairie People*, 198.

Justina joined the Bon Homme Colony.[16] More significantly, Hutterite Elder Michael Stahl, a noncommunal leader in Ukraine, joined the Wolf Creek Colony in 1876, after also first homesteading on the prairie. Life-transforming visions from God convinced Stahl that communal life was the path to heaven. In one vision, an angel told him that noncommunal Hutterites were "all corrupt—even the ministers," and that they "will not last."[17] After another vision, he went home, told his wife to pack up their belongings and proceeded to join Wolf Creek, where his ministerial status was immediately recognized.[18] This conversion must have had a particularly unsettling impact on Paul Tschetter since Stahl was a leading figure in Russian Hutterite life and had never supported community of goods.

Two other noncommunal ministers followed suit. Soon after arriving in North America, John Kleinsasser, one of the ministers in the Prairieleut Hutterthal Church, sold his farm and joined the *Lehrerleut* Elmspring colony. Then amazingly Kleinsasser's fellow minister at Hutterthal, John Waldner, did the same, although he joined the *Dariusleut* Jamesville Colony. Two Prairieleut ministers thus joined communal groups that never united as one religious body.

On at least one occasion the decision to join a colony was made at the very end of a man's life. The Neu Hutterthaler Church record book notes that one Paul Mendel joined a "colony" right before his death; at age 99½, on April 8, 1917.[19] A common entry in Prairieleut publisher Jacob J. Mendel's *History of the People of East Freeman, Silver Lake and West Freeman* announces the marriage of a Prairieleut woman to a colony man. In 1890, for example, "Mary Glanzer joined the Bon Homme Colony and married Andrew Kleinsasser."[20] After Prairieleut Jakob Entz died in 1880 by drowning in the James River, his widow moved into a colony.[21] In his diary, "Yos" Hofer lists many occasions when people

---

16. Krause, *Tschetter-Waldner Families*, 241.
17. R. Janzen, *The Prairie People*, 198.
18. A. M. Hofer, ed., *The Diary of Joseph "Yos" Hofer*, July 1876 entry.
19. NHCRB, 831
20. Mendel, *History of the People of East Freeman, Silver Lake and West Freeman*, 106.
21. E. J. Waldner, ed., *Banished for Faith*, 55.

"came to the congregation" (i.e. joined the colony). In all of these cases previous baptisms and Christian commitments were recognized.[22]

But there was also movement in the noncommunal direction. The aforementioned ex-Prairieleut minister John Waldner, for example, did not stay at the Jamesville Colony very long. After a few years of residence there he purchased private land near Freeman and re-joined the Hutterthal Church![23] Johann Hofer, the son of Wolf Creek Colony minister George Hofer left the Dariusleut and became a minister at the Hutterdorf Prairieleut church.[24] In Jacob J. Mendel's regional history, one finds many entries that announce movement in a noncommunal direction, such as the following (dated 1894): "The Joseph Waldner family left the Milltown Colony."[25] Many family splits resulted from these decisions. For example, after her husband John Wurtz died, Prairieleut Katherina Wurtz married Andrew Wurtz and joined the Elmspring Colony, bringing along her sons. But her three daughters all "married on the prairies."[26]

Crossover occurrences in a communal direction decreased substantially in the early 1900s, while Hutterite defection continued (although at a slow pace) until the 1920s and 1930s. By this time most Hutterite colonies in South Dakota had relocated to Canada as a result of World War I era mistreatment. Even as the crossover tide ebbed, however, contacts between friends and relatives continued. As late as 1918 Prairieleut Jacob J. Hofer wrote (in his diary) about many visits to colony friends and relatives.[27] Close relationships between prairie and colony were maintained throughout Paul Tschetter's lifetime.

Paul Tschetter's daughter-in-law, Katherina Tschetter, notes that when she was young her parents took her to a colony man who had the gift of healing. Katherina had eye problems which made it difficult to deal with bright light. In her 1945 autobiography she asserts that the

---

22. A. M. Hofer, ed., *The Diary of Joseph "Yos" Hofer*, August 27, 1876 entry.

23. Mendel, *History of the People of East Freeman, Silver Lake and West Freeman*, 16.

24. Emma Hofer, trans., "Excerpts from the Autobiography of D. J. Mendel," in HMCC, eds., *A History of the Hutterite Mennonites*, 71.

25. Jacob J. Mendel, *History of the People of East Freeman, Silver Lake and West Freeman*, 107.

26. HMCC, eds., *Hutterite Roots*, 11.

27. A. M. Hofer, ed., *Diary of Jacob J. Hofer, 1900–1920*, 40. HMCC.

"colony man" "cured" her and exclaims, "The Lord Bless them" (referring to the Hutterites).²⁸

During World War I many Prairieleut commiserated with colony Hutterites when two young men, Joseph and Michael Hofer, died while in custody at Fort Leavenworth. This experience is discussed in chapter ten. Prairieleut minister Jacob J. Hofer and many noncommunal Hutterians attended the funeral service at the Rockport Colony. As Hofer put it, "Because of their faith they were mistreated following which they became sick and died."²⁹

Paul Tschetter himself never expressed interest in joining one of the colonies.³⁰ But he held communal Hutterites in high regard and they reciprocated. In the Hutterite Chronicle, for example, Tschetter is referred to as "Brother Paul Tschetter."³¹ Tschetter visited the colonies often and when he referred to "the larger brotherhood" he always included the colony Hutterites.³² In a six paragraph biography of his father, Joseph W. Tschetter put it this way, "My father never lived in a Bruderhof [colony] nor did I ever hear him advocate joining the Bruderhof, although he was in a good standing with the brethren in the Bruderhof."³³ The Neu Hutterthaler Church once took a special offering to help relieve "suffering" as a result of a colony fire.³⁴

The Neu Hutterthaler Church's "record of ministers" includes colony leaders such as Peter Hofer (Elmspring Colony), Darius Walter (Wolf Creek Colony), Michael Stahl (Wolf Creek Colony) and Michael Waldner (Bon Homme Colony). In August 1901, Wolf Creek minister Michael Stahl, preached a funeral sermon for Prairieleut Peter Hofer. The Prairieleut minister Jacob J. Hofer's diary includes numerous references to attendance at Wolf Creek Colony church services.³⁵

---

28. Mrs. Joseph W. Tschetter, *My Life Story*, 4.
29. Arnold M. Hofer, ed., *Diary of Jacob J. Hofer, 1900–1920*, 79.
30. Mrs. Joseph W. Tschetter, *My Life Story*, 113.
31. *CHB II*, 706.
32. NHCRB, 821. J. E. Hofer, "A History of the Neu Hutterthaler Mennonite Church," 45.
33. Mrs. Joseph W. Tschetter, *My Life Story*, 113.
34. Paul G. Tschetter, "Monologue." Frances Janzen Voth, ed., *The House of Jacob*, 13.
35. A. M. Hofer, ed., *Diary of Jacob J. Hofer, 1900–1929*.

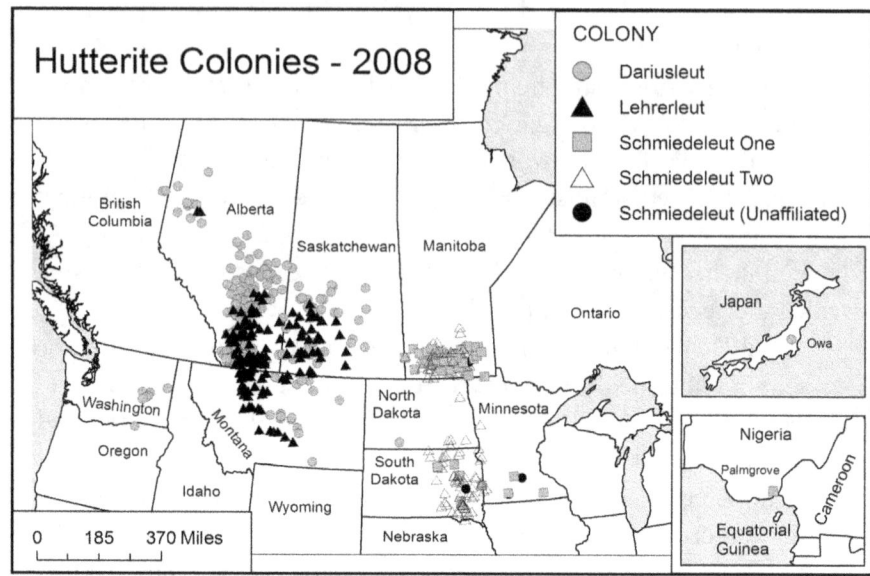

Map 7.1. Hutterite Colonies, 2008.
Map courtesy of Stuart McFeeters.

Because of the continuous interaction between noncommunal and communal Hutterites during the first forty years in North America, it surprises observers that in the 2000s there is so little contact and that the groups have moved in radically different directions. An important reason for this is the movement of communal Hutterites to Canada during and after World War I. For a number of years into the 1920s and 1930s there were almost no communal friends and relatives with whom to converse. During this time Prairieleut second generation immigrants were heavily influenced by the forces of American assimilation.

Some Schmiedeleut Hutterites returned to South Dakota in the mid-1930s, but the other two Hutterite branches, the Lehrerleut and Dariusleut, never came back. This is significant because the Prairieleut had fewer relatives in the Schmiedeleut group than in the other two communal societies. With reduced informal contacts, marriages and conversions across the colony/prairie divide ended although as late as 1932 Prairieleut Samuel and Susanna Hofer joined the Rockport Colony.[36] One even later exception is Jacob Waldner, who left the Clark

---

36. A. Kleinsasser, ed., *Our Journey of Faith*, 6, 9.

Colony in 1955, joined a noncommunal Hutterite church and, five years later, married Prairieleut Macy Gross.[37] The map below shows the present location of 480 Hutterite colonies in the United States and Canada. Note that the Schmiedeleut Hutterites divided into two groups in 1992.

During World War I, many Hutterite ministers called on Tschetter to seek advice on how to respond to the military draft, the push to buy Liberty Bonds that supported the war effort and harassment from patriotic neighbors. Justina Guericke recalled that men "with long beards" called on her grandfather on a "daily" basis. "As a child I thought they were Pharisees or High Priests from the Bible."[38] These kinds of contacts had disappeared by the World War II era.

But during Paul Tschetter's lifetime ties between communal and noncommunal groups were strong. The groups agreed on most Hutterite beliefs and practices. The two groups spoke the same language, read the same sermons, ate the same foods and operated within similar cognitive and emotional frameworks.[39] Add to this the multitude of ways that people were related to each other. Paul Tschetter insisted that one could be a true Hutterite without living communally but he did not condemn his communal brothers and sisters for following a different pathway. Unlike increasing numbers of Prairieleut, Tschetter never questioned the integrity of the communal Hutterite way of life.

37. R. Janzen, *The Prairie People*, 173.
38. Guericke, *Precious Memories of a Historical House*, 3.
39. NHCRB, 825.

8

Leading the Neu Hutterthaler Church

> The Lord God be with you
> And strengthen you in everything.
> His spirit guide you forth
> On level path and thoroughfare[1]
>
> —Paul Tschetter, 1873

PAUL AND MARIA TSCHETTER HAD FIVE SONS AND FIVE DAUGHTERS who lived beyond infancy. Their first child, Susanna, was born in 1861 at the Hutterthal village. First-born son Jacob followed but he died in infancy. A second son, also named Jacob, died at age five while Paul was on his 1873 trip to North America. According to daughter-in-law Katherina Tschetter, Maria did not notify her husband of this death out of "fear" that "it might disturb father too much in his work."[2] This death was followed in 1877 by daughter six-year-old Barbara who got caught in a threshing machine in Dakota Territory. According to Katherina Tschetter,

> She stepped over the tumbling-rod that connected the horse-power with the threshing machine. Her dress was caught by the running rod and broke most of her bones... Her flesh was quivering till four o'clock in the morning. That was the only sign that there was still life in the body.[3]

Afterward Paul Tschetter is the one who carried his stricken daughter into their house.

---

1. Paul Tschetter, hymn #2, stanza one (1873). HHMA.
2. Mrs. Joseph W. Tschetter, *My Life Story*, 41.
3. Ibid.

Paul and Maria's third son, Paul W., was nicknamed "Big Paul" because of his large frame.[4] The lifelong bachelor was later described as intelligent, wealthy, honest and a benefactor to his brothers and sisters as well as the church. Paul Tschetter's other three sons were the following: a third Jacob (Jacob W.), Joseph W., later a minister and evangelist, and David W., also a pastor and evangelist.

In addition to Susanna and Barbara, Paul and Maria Tschetter's daughters included Maria, a second Barbara, and Justina. The second "Barbara" had an unnamed twin brother who died at birth. Thus Paul and Maria Tschetter had a total of twelve children. Now living in Dakota Territory, Paul and Maria Tschetter focused their attention on three major responsibilities; the raising of a large family, maintaining a successful farming operation and serving the Prairieleut church.

The Prairieleut Churches in Dakota Territory

One of Paul Tschetter's most important responsibilities was to establish a church for families who in Ukraine had lived in the Neu Hutterthal village. He also ministered to noncommunalists for other Ukrainian villages who homesteaded in the Wolf Creek area. With the arrival of the largest group of Neu Hutterthal residents on August 23, 1875, most of that village's inhabitants were now in the United States. As the church record book puts it, the church "was together again."[5]

From the outset the church that was established was called "Neu Hutterthaler," instead of "Neu Hutterthal," using a form of the Ukrainian village name that denoted its inhabitants. Having put down roots in a different part of the globe the Neu Hutterthalers wanted to differentiate, even if slightly, the name of their new congregation from the village of the same name in south Ukraine. In addition to establishing the Neu Hutterthaler Church, Paul Tschetter started two small house congregations for families that lived too far away to attend services at the church since travel by oxcart or horse-drawn wagon was slow. One house congregation was located near Olivet; the other northeast of the town of Bridgewater. Tschetter and other Neu Hutterthaler ministers took turns preaching at these congregations.

4. Much of the information concerning Paul Tschetter's children comes from D. J. Tschetter, "The Paul Tschetter family." David J. Tschetter is a son of Jacob W. Tschetter. WTC.

5. NHCRB, 18.

Paul Tschetter also served as the unofficial leader of the entire noncommunal Hutterite community. By the end of the 1870s, there were three established Prairieleut congregations: Neu Hutterthaler, Hutterdorf and Hutterthal, loosely corresponding to three Ukrainian village churches. Residents of a fourth Ukrainian village, Johannesruh, did not establish a separate church in North America. Instead members joined one of the other congregations or the Elmspring Colony. The fifth Russian village, Scheromet, was structured communally from the start. Its residents were part of the first Hutterite group to leave Russia and in Dakota Territory they established the Bon Homme Colony.

The new world provided many choices. Hutterites could live communally in one of the three colonies or they could settle on private farms and attend one of the noncommunal churches. As noted, this was a difficult decision and individuals, even within the same family, moved in different directions. By the 1880s, another choice had emerged; one that was especially attractive to noncommunal Hutterians. This third option was the Krimmer Mennonite Brethren (KMB) Church.

Krimmer Mennonite Brethren believed strongly that neither Hutterite group (communal or noncommunal) was preaching or living the true Christian faith. The evangelical KMB movement (discussed in the next chapter) presented a theological and ecclesial alternative for Hutterites who not only rejected communal life but questioned the value of other historic beliefs and practices as well. Paul Tschetter quickly found himself positioned in the middle, with the colony Hutterites on one side and the Krimmer Mennonite Brethren on the other.

Evangelically-minded Mennonites like the KMB group had a hard time understanding the Prairieleut. Most of them could not see the value of reading seventeenth-century sermons and they did not agree with the latter-day Hutterian disinterest in evangelism (at least outside of the ethno-religious community). Mennonites in general criticized Prairieleut Hutterites for poor church attendance and lack of Bible knowledge.

General Conference Mennonite evangelist Samuel Haury was particularly critical. Based on a mission trip to Dakota Territory in 1877, Haury described Dakota Anabaptists generally as "spiritually dead." He saw "spiritual deterioration" and materialism but he was particularly shocked by the lack of spirituality found among the people he called *Hutterische*, i.e., the Hutterites who did not live in colonies; the Prairieleut.[6] Haury called the Hutterite settlement "one big mission field."

During the early immigrant years there were indeed many distractions that might have caused Haury to question Prairieleut spiritual commitments. As in any religious group, some people in the Prairieleut community lived less than perfect lives and some did not attend church services regularly. Yet men and women like Paul and Maria Tschetter, and hundreds of others, do not fit Haury's characterization.

The reliability and accuracy of Haury's assessment invites critical review. According to John D. Unruh, Haury believed that God had given him the gift of "spiritual determination," and missionaries like Haury often find their audiences spiritually deficient.[7] We do not know whether Haury attended a single Prairieleut church service or met with any of the ministers. Traditional Hutterianism likely made little sense to him but this does not mean that the Prairieleut did not take their faith seriously or that it was not extremely meaningful to them.

Perhaps Haury had difficulty understanding the spiritual value of the Hutterian mixed cultural/religious heritage, where the secular and spiritual were closely intertwined, even though he was associated with an ethno-religious group himself. Representatives of one group are often blind to the significance of the folk traditions of another. From a Mennonite or evangelical Protestant perspective, then and now, traditional Hutterianism is difficult to comprehend, and for many, hard to appreciate. It was probably difficult for Haury to understand the contemporary value of reading seventeenth-century sermons; to believe that the Holy Spirit had given special insight to Hutterite ministers that could be relevant two hundred years later. On Sunday mornings Paul Tschetter read the sacred *Lehren* and nothing else. He did not see any reason to create an updated substitute. Haury likely viewed the sermon reading as dry and spiritually dead.

The *Lehren* are central, however, to the Hutterite understanding of the Christian faith. They typically begin with a section from the Bible adding contextual interpretations and contemporary (seventeenth century) applications. For Hutterites the sermons are almost as important as the Bible itself. The fact that communal Hutterites continue to read

---

6. Unruh, *A Century of Mennonites in Dakota*, 62. Smith, *The Story of the Mennonites*, 49.

7. Unruh, *A Century of Mennonites in Dakota*, 62.

them at every church service means that beliefs and practices are clear and do not change; traditions are maintained. Approaching the Word of God through the sermons ensures a stable interpretation and makes it easier to maintain a unified Christian community.

From the Hutterite perspective ministers and priests who write their own sermons expose themselves to multiple interpretations of the Bible and heretical side paths. When ministers compose sermons filled with personal examples and nuanced exegesis, there is a greater likelihood that theological chaos will ensue.

Samuel Haury was not impressed with the Hutterites. Born to a Mennonite family in Ingolstadt, Germany, he migrated to the United States at a young age and grew up in Sommerfield, Illinois. Powerfully influenced by Pietism he was a strong advocate of the "new birth" experience, which Hutterians would not have understood. In addition to receiving ordination as a minister and evangelist, Haury also held a medical degree, spent time working with the Arapaho Indians, and ultimately retired to an orange ranch in Upland, California.[8]

One of Haury's complaints was that Dakota ministers operated like "little popes in their congregations." According to Haury, "The whole congregation is supposed to bend the knee to his every notion, even though it is often contrary to scripture."[9] Which ministers was Haury targeting? Most likely it was men like Paul Tschetter, who did function with a sense of God-given authority.

Haury wrote that Prairieleut Hutterians were following nonbiblical teachings. But this was Haury's mantra wherever he went, not only in Dakota Territory. He was continually concerned about what he called the "Christian heathen around us" and "those who call themselves Mennonites but who with seeing eyes do not see."[10] Haury did not like church services where there were no personal testimonies (i.e. most Anabaptist congregations at the time). Haury was also a prohibitionist, something that would not have sat well in any 1870s-era Hutterite church in Dakota Territory.[11]

---

8. Shenk, ed., *Samuel S. Haury*.
9. Ibid., 7.
10. Ibid., 27, 39.
11. Kaufman, ed. *General Conference Mennonite Pioneers*, 322.

Leading the Neu Hutterthaler Church 147

Figure 8.1 Neu Hutterthaler Church, original building, circa 1890. Photograph courtesy of Neu Hutterthaler Mennonite Church Centennial Committee.

Organizing a Congregation

Before they left Russia, residents of Neu Hutterthal had agreed to re-establish their village church in North America.[12] From 1874–1880 they gathered in the homes of different members, often at Paul Tschetter's own house; on other occasions at the homes of Jacob Mendel, Joseph Hofer or Paul's father, Jacob J. Tschetter.[13] For the next eight years (from 1880–1888) the congregation met in the Riverside District #29 country schoolhouse and at another school near the Paul Tschetter homestead.[14]

Finally on November 11, 1888, the Neu Hutterthaler Church held its first "preaching service" in a newly-constructed building.[15] The church was built on Paul Tschetter's own land and served the congregation for the remainder of his life. It consisted of a simple thirty by forty-

---

12. J. E. Hofer, "A History of the Neu Hutterthaler Church, 11. HHMA.
13. Ibid., 12.
14. Glanzer, Wipf and Hofer, eds., *A Century of God's Blessing*, 10.
15. NHCRB, 25.

eight foot building, constructed of wood purchased from the Shanard Lumber Yard in Bridgewater.[16]

For unknown reasons, the congregation did not submit an official charter until 1902. It contains Paul Tschetter's signature as well as those of D. M. Hofer and Elias Wipf. We know that the Neu Hutterthaler church building cost $1,300.00 and that all of the funds were secured by free-will offerings. The sanctuary was constructed by volunteer labor, by members of the church.[17] Joseph W. Tschetter recalled that at age twelve he helped build the foundation and "hauled water" to make the mortar.[18]

Throughout Paul Tschetter's lifetime church services at Neu Hutterthaler were conducted in German, which became a problem for second generation children, not only because they attended public schools where instruction after the first few years was in English but because the Hutterite first language is the *Hutterisch* Tirolean/Carinthian dialect, which originated in southeastern Austria. Unlike at the colonies, where German School classes were established and met on a daily basis, Prairieleut young people rarely studied standard German. Instead they spent much time with their English-speaking neighbors or Hutterisch-speaking relatives and other church members. Neu Hutterthaler provided German classes only in special summer school programs and on Sunday mornings but these classes were discontinued in the early 1900s.

The Neu Hutterthaler church building was divided into men's and women's sections, with separate pews placed on either side of a main aisle. The congregation's children sat in the front rows as one finds in twenty-first-century Hutterite colonies. In front of the sanctuary there was an elevated platform with chairs for the ministers and an oak pulpit for the pastor who delivered the sermon. The church was heated by a stove placed near the center of the building. Light was provided by gasoline lamps suspended from the ceiling. The interior was adorned with simple wallpaper.

The Neu Hutterthaler Church also had a "ministers room" (*Prediger Stiebel*) to the right of the lobby near the front door but it was

---

16. J. E. Hofer, "A History of the Neu Hutterthaler Church," 13. Glanzer, Wipf, and Hofer, eds., *A Century of God's Blessing*, 10.

17. Hofer, "A History of the Neu Hutterthaler Church," 14.

18. Ibid.

used primarily for storage. Jacob E. Hofer also recalled the presence of a spittoon, which was used for the crude but then-accepted practice of "spitting" and was totally unrelated to the use of chewing tobacco.[19] Hutterite males commonly and publicly emptied their mouths (and throats) of excess saliva and dust. Neu Hutterthaler members also constructed five horse barns, a number of hitching posts and outhouses near the church building.

As in south Ukraine, the Neu Hutterthaler Church was originally served by two ministers: Paul Tschetter and Joseph Wipf.[20] Another pastor, Johann Hofer, was selected in 1884. As noted, during their sojourn in Russia Hutterians had not consistently selected ministers by casting lots. Paul Tschetter wrote positively about the practice in his 1873 diary but there is no record that the lot was ever used by noncommunal Hutterites in North America. In the new world environment, perhaps influenced by Mennonite practice, the Prairieleut selected ministers on the basis of democratically determined congregational discernment just as they had started to do in Ukraine. Following tradition ministers were always selected from within the congregation, under the assumption that God would provide someone with appropriate gifts. After a period of "probation" (one to five years) men chosen for leadership were formally ordained. They served for life unless there were serious moral infractions, which was a rare occurrence. An affiliated Neu Hutterthaler house fellowship, near Olivet, was led by the Rev. Martin Waldner.

Paul Tschetter was ordained as a minister in 1866. On January 28, 1883, he received further ordination as a church "elder." Historically Hutterites used the term "elder" to designate the person who served as the senior spiritual leader for the entire Hutterite community. In Ukraine Michael Stahl served in this position, although his leadership was not recognized by the emerging communal groups. But in Dakota Territory, Stahl joined the Wolf Creek Colony leaving the Prairieleut with no central leader.

The election of a single elder was one of Paul Tschetter's personal goals and he hoped to fill this position himself. But not enough Prairieleut agreed with him to make Tschetter's aim attainable. Instead, in North America the term "elder" began to take on a different meaning. From the 1880s into the first half of the twentieth century the term

19. Ibid.
20. NHCRB, 4.

designated the person who served as senior minister in a Prairieleut congregation. This was also the practice of Russian Mennonites.

Paul Tschetter was ordained to the position of elder by the Mennonite minister Friedrich Schartner at a service conducted at the Wolf Creek schoolhouse. This time the reason that Tschetter was ordained by a Mennonite, and not by a Hutterite, is clearer: There were no noncommunal Hutterite elders left (Michael Stahl had joined a colony), and Hutterite colony elders would not have agreed to do it.

We assume that Paul Tschetter's elder ordination was actively encouraged by members at Neu Hutterthaler, and that a process of congregational discernment preceded ordination but the records provide no details nor do any personal memoirs or oral histories. In his diary, "Yos" Hofer uses the word "elected" to describe Tschetter's selection as elder and says that the event took place on January 7, 1883.[21] Tschetter's formal ordination followed three weeks later (on January 28).

The man who performed the ordination, Friedrich Schartner, was born in Karlswalde, Poland, in 1842. He immigrated to Dakota Territory in 1875 with the Tobias Unruh group, which chose to settle in Dakota Territory due to the influence of Daniel Unruh and Andreas Schrag.[22] Schartner himself was a controversial figure, however, who was involved in many internecine church conflicts. Only ordained as an elder himself in 1880, Schartner eventually established a separate Mennonite congregation (in the Marion area), which brought together a few Low German Mennonites from the Russian Molotschna colonies, his own followers from Poland and a few adherents from the Crimea.

During his service as elder, Paul Tschetter participated in the ordination of eleven ministers in the Neu Hutterthaler congregation.[23] He also ordained two Mennonite pastors (Jacob Schartner and David Tiesen). But Tschetter ordained only one minister in the other two large Prairieleut congregations. He ordained no one at the Hutterthal Church and only one pastor (Peter Stahl) at the Hutterdorf Church. The leaders of the Hutterthal and Hutterdorf churches refused to recognize Tschetter's formal leadership as a senior elder with supervisory power.

The first minister ordained at Neu Hutterthaler was the aforementioned Johann Hofer, in 1884. Others are listed in Table 8.1. Tschetter's

---

21. A. M. Hofer, ed., *The Diary of Joseph "Yos" Hofer,* January 7, 1883 entry.
22. Centennial Book Committee, ed., *A Tale of Three Cities,* 112.
23. NHCRB, 4, 5.

last ordination (Jacob Walter) was performed on September 15, 1918, one year before his death.

Table 8.1 Ministers ordained by Paul Tschetter

1884–1918	
1884	Johann Hofer
1909	Joseph Hofer
1910	Jacob Schartner
1910	David Wipf
1910	Paul J. Tschetter
1912	Elias Wipf
1914	David Tiesen
1914	Paul Kleinsasser
1914	Paul John Hofer
1914	Paul Gross
1914	Johann Kleinsasser
1917	Peter Stahl
1918	Jacob I. Walter

Paul Tschetter had no formal authority over any congregation except Neu Hutterthaler, his primary spiritual charge. But in a broad sense, Tschetter considered all noncommunal Hutterites to be his "church," and many Prairieleut viewed him as the final authority on Hutterian cultural and religious traditions.[24] In his writings Tschetter often speaks to the larger noncommunal brother and sisterhood. He kept a record of ministers that includes names and years of service of all Prairieleut ministers as well as those communal Hutterite ministers that were selected in Russia.[25]

At Neu Hutterthaler Paul Tschetter was the senior administrator with assistant ministers providing support as needed. Tschetter started with a single assistant minister but by the time he died there were six ordained pastors in the congregation. With a multiple ministry model, pastors took turns reading the sermons and/or presiding at services.

24. J. E. Hofer, "A History of the Neu Hutterthaler Church, 60.
25. NHCRB, 3, 4.

Paul Tschetter's additional janitorial responsibilities were not typical for a Hutterite minister. He likely took this job because he lived nearby on the same homestead land. Tschetter kept the fires going in the church building, lit the lamps before services, and cleaned the sanctuary as needed.

Early on the Neu Huttherthaler Church was often called the "Wolf Creek *Gemeinde*" due to its location.[26] In 1888, members of what was also called "the congregation of Elder Paul Tschetter," established the office of *Waisenvorsteher* or orphan administrator.[27] This church official helped determine what happened to young children when their parents died. Tschetter himself administered divisions of property in cases where church members died without wills.

The Neu Hutterthaler Church made participation in the *Waisenordnung* optional so that members could follow United States civil law instead if they wanted to. Heads of Neu Hutterthaler families were given "ten days after the congregational decision" to decide whether or not to commit themselves.[28] In Paul Tschetter's view this decision had significant religious implications. Church records indicate that "If someone joins our Orphan Regulation and later wants to withdraw and join in the worldly regulation, he will be considered as disobedient and will no longer be recognized as a member in the church."[29] But even if a member opted not to participate at all, he/she would be choosing what was described as a "worldly" civic practice. Paul Tschetter instituted the regulation in order to promote community and accountability among the Neu Hutterthaler membership.

Organization

During Paul Tschetter's lifetime the responsibilities and duties of Neu Hutterthaler ministers were not written down or well-defined. There was no job description or formal evaluations. Based on interviews with older members in the late 1940s and early 1950s, Jacob E. Hofer found that during Paul Tschetter's time the minister had "great influence if not final authority" with regard to many matters, including church disci-

---

26. "Hutterthal Mennonite Church Family Records," 269. HHMA.
27. Paul E. Glanzer, et. al., *A Century of God's Blessing*, 4.
28. Jacob E. Hofer, "A History of the Neu Hutterthaler Church, 21.
29. NHCRB, 21.

pline.³⁰ Church governance was in some sense a mix of democracy and executive enforcement. But under Tschetter's leadership there was little formal consultation and debate.

During Tschetter's lifetime Neu Hutterthaler Church budgets were not formalized nor did the congregation hold regular business meetings. A spirit of voluntarism ensured that buildings and facilities were repaired as needed. In addition to serving as the unofficial church janitor, Paul Tschetter was also the congregation's treasurer and secretary.³¹ To ensure financial support Neu Hutterthaler instituted a "dues" system to support the basic upkeep of facilities. As late as 1914 these assessments were set at fifty cents per family with widows exempted.³²

It is impossible to secure reliable Neu Hutterthaler membership and attendance figures for the late nineteenth and early twentieth centuries because of the lack of detailed records. Jacob E. Hofer describes a "healthy growth and a substantial increase" by the year 1900 but he provides no statistics.³³ General estimates indicate a membership of about 250 by the turn of the century.

Problems at Neu Hutterthaler

The Neu Hutterthaler church record book delineates four problems that confronted the congregation in the late 1800s. The first was related to the historic Hutterite peace position but focused specifically on gun ownership.

One of the main reasons for leaving Russia was to keep Hutterite males out of the armed forces and most Neu Hutterhtler members were fervent pacifists. Paul Tschetter portrayed conscription requirements in Russia as divine chastisement meant to "awaken people from their sleep."³⁴ But Tschetter was just as upset by what he called the "spirit of gun ownership" that had crept into his congregation in Dakota Territory.³⁵

---

30. Jacob E. Hofer, "A History of the Neu Hutterthaler Church," 23, 24.
31. Ibid., 28.
32. Ibid., 58.
33. Ibid., 63.
34. NHCRB, 8; and Ibid., 39.
35. NHCRB, 19.

Tschetter believed that a position of nonresistance implied a proscription on owning and using guns for any reason, including hunting. Here he followed historic Hutterite belief and practice, as outlined in the Riedemann confession of faith and confirmed by the Chronicle. In 1633 Hutterite elder Andreas Ehrenpreis made the following statement: "There is also rumor that some brethren ... own and use guns. This should not be, for what profit is a gun to the brother? It has never been permitted in the *Gemein* in the past and shall also not be permitted in the future."[36]

But on the North American plains gun ownership was extremely popular. And in the 1880s, a *Flinten Geist* (spirit of gun ownership) swept through the Neu Hutterthaler Church. Tschetter had trouble containing it. Adding to Tschetter's discomfort was the fact that on Sunday, the day of rest, some members went hunting instead of attending church services. Some of those who hunted said they did so to provide "food" for their families.[37] Tschetter considered this a highly debatable justification; God would provide food in other ways.

According to the church record book, it was Tschetters' strong and unrelenting position on guns that was a primary reason that the three noncommunal Hutterite churches (Neu Hutterthaler, Hutterthal, and Hutterdorf) never selected a common elder. While this was not the only or even most important reason, the gun controversy was at least one factor that forestalled the creation of an official noncommunal church alliance. An important opponent of the single elder structure, for example, was the Rev. Johann Waldner, the senior pastor at the Hutterthal Church, who also supported some forms of hunting with guns. Ironically, Waldner later joined a Dariusleut colony and apparently changed his position on guns.[38] But while he was a Prairieleut minister, Waldner, exemplifying a power struggle that likely had many components, resisted Tschetter's general proscription on gun ownership. As Tschetter later wrote, Waldner "saw it unnecessary to put away all guns. So we couldn't become united and remained one congregation and put away weapons in our congregation."

---

36. Andreas Ehrenpreis, in Brock, *Pacifism in Europe to 1914*, 244.

37. J. E. Hofer, "A History of the Neu Hutterthaler Church," 39.

38. Mendel, *A History of the People of East Freeman Silver Lake and West Freeman*, 16.

On the gun issue, the Neu Hutterthaler Church acted on its own. One Sunday Tschetter announced, "Members shall not have weapons. If any continue to do so they shall have to forfeit their membership."[39] The congregation then passed a gun ordinance, which every member was required to sign. It reads in part:

> Because we claim to be a nonresistant people who carry no weapons according to our Confession of Faith, and since we left Russia for that very reason, it appears inappropriate for us to carry guns because it contradicts our Articles of Faith; also because our youth could easily be led astray if they become accustomed to carry a weapon, and it if would happen that they would be drafted into military duty, it would be easier for them to comply. For this reason we have come to see it a great mistake in the Church, and we Church leaders are responsible due to our solemn promise to order such evil to be abandoned in the Church. All who do not agree with us, but consider it a right and privilege to own a gun will be separated from the church until they admit that they were in error. The parents of such children who are not yet Church members but own or carry a gun will be held responsible because as Christian parents they have not kept their children in better order.

The ordinance ends with the following statement: "All those Church members who agree with us should sign the above Church Regulation in their own handwriting without being forced."[40] Signatures of seventy-five members follow in the church record book. Paul Tschetter reminded congregants that "no guns" had always been the Hutterite position in Europe. "As it was ordered" [in Russia] he noted, "so were the two guns that were found among us immediately destroyed."

A second controversial issue at Neu Hutterthaler was the sport of baseball. Some members at Neu Hutterthaler played the popular game recreationally and this upset Tschetter and others who believed that the activity was too frivolous for adults. Baseball was brought to the attention of the entire congregation where it was acknowledged as "an evil" that should be "discontinued."[41] Paul Tschetter was also opposed to bowling.

---

39. J. E. Hofer, "A History of the Neu Hutterthaler Church," 39.
40. NHCRB, 20.
41. J. E. Hofer, "A History of the Neu Hutterthaler Church," 23.

A third problem at Neu Hutterthaler surrounded the game of pool. In a section titled "Report of An Event in the Church" (in 1884), Tschetter describes pool as "a great evil and black spot."[42] The church took action deciding that anyone shooting pool had to apologize in front of the church for first and second offences. A third offense meant formal separation from the congregation.

A fourth problem was the purchase of musical instruments and bicycles, which some members owned. Tschetter's opposition to instruments followed traditional Hutterian practice, which emphasized a cappella singing and associated musical instruments with secularism. With regard to bicycles, conservative Hutterite colonies in the 2000s continue to oppose their use because it makes it more difficult to know exactly where children are spending their time. At Neu Hutterthaler it was decided that ownership of musical instruments or bicycles could lead to excommunication.[43]

In addition to the "problems" listed above, Tschetter also fought an ongoing battle against tobacco. He refused a donation from congregant John Hofer, for example, because Hofer grew tobacco in his garden.[44] Tschetter also spoke out against some business practices. On May 5, 1888, "Yos" Hofer wrote the following: "[Paul Tschetter] withdrew from preaching position. Promised to again preach if the church members would give up smoking tobacco and occupy no store [i.e. not go into business]."[45]

The latter part of the quote (to "occupy no store") displays a cautionary Hutterite position on business dealings. In the early 1900s many Prairieleut started small businesses and stores in local towns. The city of Freeman, for example, had a Prairieleut-owned butcher shop, harness shop, creamery, drugstore and livery barn. Hutterians also owned a grain elevator as well as implement and furniture stores, a nursery, a barbershop and even a tavern. Paul Tschetter's son, "Big Paul," co-owned grain elevators in the towns of Emery and Bridgewater. Prairieleut Jacob J. Mendel began publishing the Freeman *Courier* weekly in 1903.

---

42. NHCRB, 21.

43. J. E. Hofer, "A History of the Neu Hutterthaler Church.," 24.

44. A. M. Hofer and Pauline Becker, *The John Hofer and Anna Wurtz Family Record* (Freeman, SD: self-published, 1991), 8.

45. A. M. Hofer, ed., *The Diaries of Joseph "Yos" Hofer,* May 10, 1888 entry.

All of these business developments concerned Paul Tschetter. Tschetter was an agrarian, who understood that surplus farm products had to find markets in a capitalistic national and international economy. But he was skeptical of the profit margins taken by local Prairieleut businessmen and their regular interactions with non-Anabaptists. He likely recalled the negative impact of buying and selling on member of the Raditschewa community during the early 1800s.

A number of noncommunal Hutterites also got involved in politics, taking positions on city councils and school boards; some of the early Freeman city council minutes were written in German. Paul Tschetter was opposed to this involvement believing that political activity necessitated moral compromises, which he did not think Christians should make. Tschetter watched this development carefully and viewed it skeptically.

Paul Tschetter took hardline positions on many issues. In early 1899, for example, the Olivet house church decided to select a new minister. When he heard about this, Paul Tschetter's response was that the person should be chosen from within the Neu Hutterthaler Church membership, not from the small Olivet assembly. This led to conflict with members of the Olivet group, who did not favor this restriction. In March 1899, "Yos" Hofer, a member of the Olivet group, attacked Paul Tschetter's "reoccurring new narrowness," and says that he personally "got a bad reception," when he talked to Tschetter about the ministerial selection issue.[46] Soon thereafter, on Easter Sunday, April 2, 1899, there was "no preaching [at the Olivet house church] "due to dissension" and ten weeks later at Pentecost, there was "still no preaching."[47] Yos Hofer notes that Tschetter refused to meet with Olivet members to discuss the ministerial selection process further and he describes this action as "dishonorable."[48] Conflict between Olivet and Paul Tschetter emerged again during the 1899 Christmas season.

In April 6, 1900, the Olivet congregation took matters into its own hands overriding Tschetter's objections and electing a minister without his approval. They selected the aforementioned ex-communitarian, Joseph "Yos" Hofer. Perhaps this had been the underlying problem all along: Paul Tschetter's refusal to recognize the ministerial gifts of the

46. Ibid., March 22, 1899 entry.
47. Ibid., April 2, 1899 entry.
48. Ibid., April 23, 1899 entry.

man whom he knew would be selected by the Olivet house church if they were given the opportunity to do so. Tschetter likely questioned the ministerial suitability of someone who had changed church affiliations three times within a decade. The full story probably lies somewhere between Yos Hofer's subjective account and what actually happened. Paul Tschetter responded to the Olivet action by declaring "Yos" election "invalid."[49]

Paul Tschetter held a traditional Hutterite line on most matters as long as he was living. South Dakota historian John D. Unruh describes him as "not only very conservative but quite dogmatic."[50] Unruh wrote that Tschetter refused on one occasion to perform a wedding because the groom wore a mustache (Hutterites associated this with the military in Europe) and a "stiff collar and stiff cuffs on his shirt."[51] But Paul Tschetter was not totally intransigent. He was open to new practices if the ideological fit made sense to him and if the new direction was taken after a certain amount of deliberation. In 1908, for example, Neu Hutterthaler established a Sunday School program; an afternoon class for young people. Jacob E. Hofer notes, "It [the Sunday School] was heartily accepted by everyone, including the Pastor Tschetter."[52] In 1912, Sunday School was moved to the morning since, as Paul Tschetter himself put it, too many people spent Sunday afternoons fishing.[53] The Sunday School curriculum included Bible study and a review of church history.

With regard to evangelism, Paul Tschetter followed the isolationist post-seventeenth-century Hutterite position. This approach focused on faith modeling without active proselytizing. In his 1953 history of the Neu Hutterthaler congregation, Jacob E. Hofer excuses Tschetter and early congregants, noting the difficult economic times faced by the prairie pioneers. But the philosophy of separatism they exhibited was nothing new. It had typified Hutterite thinking and practice for two hundred years, since the Thirty Years War period (1618–1648).[54] Regardless of

---

49. Ibid., April 6, 1900 entry.
50. Unruh, *A Century of Mennonites in Dakota,* 101.
51. Ibid.
52. J. E. Hofer, "A History of the Neu Hutterthaler Church," 29.
53. NHCRB, 16.
54. J. E. Hofer, "A History of the Neu Hutterthaler Church," 59.

economic conditions, why should things have been any different in Dakota Territory?

Paul Tschetter's conservative approach to missions does not mean that the Christian faith was not important to him in terms of belief or practice. There was a strong effort to evangelize the community's own youth, for example, as well as those individuals who did not attend church regularly. One of Tschetter's primary responsibilities was to visit his parishioners on weekends. But Tschetter did not look beyond the boundaries of his own ethno-religious group.

At the Neu Hutterthaler Church an "awakening of the missionary spirit" had to wait until after Paul Tschetter's death and the first church missionary organization was not founded until 1926.[55] During his lifetime Tschetter was too occupied with the affairs of his flock even though most of his own children disagreed with him and joined the more evangelistic Krimmer Mennonite Brethren denomination. With the exception of the Sunday School, Neu Hutterthaler did not establish special youth programs until 1923.[56]

After Paul Tschetter's death in 1919, Neu Hutterthaler changed course in a number of areas. There was a greater sense of shared decision-making and a commensurate decrease in ministerial authority. Church discipline was not as rigidly enforced and Neu Hutterthaler operated more bureaucratically with written procedures covering all aspects of congregational life. In 1923, Neu Hutterthaler started paying salaries to its ministers.

The German language, however, was used in Neu Hutterthaler church services until 1940 just before the onset of World War II. Prairieleut Hutterians were simply not accustomed to addressing God, reading sermons or singing hymns in other languages. In everyday life they conversed in the Hutterisch dialect, the first language of all Hutterians. As young people learned English in school, however, there was a strong push for change, which eventually led to the demise of German (and Hutterisch). None of this happened during Paul Tschetter's lifetime.

Paul Tschetter's imprint remained even after his death. The Neu Hutterthaler Church was always known as the most conservative of the Prairieleut congregations and the Hutterite *Lehren* were read at most

---

55. Glanzer, Wipf, and Hofer, eds., *A Century of God's Blessing*, 25.
56. Ibid., 26.

worship services into the early 1940s. There were no musical instruments in the church until 1946. All of these manifestations show the continuing influence of Paul Tschetter.

Worshiping God in Dakota Territory

At the Neu Hutterthaler Church, worship services followed the traditional Hutterite pattern. The service began with a brief welcome and introduction (*Einleitung*) followed by prayer (*Gebet*), a hymn (*Lied*) from the Hutterite *Gesangbuch*, and the morning sermon (*Lehr*). The church serviced ended with a closing prayer, with congregants kneeling on the floor.

Church services were originally about two hours in length. While Bible reading and prayer were important components of worship the sermon was central. As noted, the traditional *Lehren* were likely the only sermons delivered by the Rev. Tschetter. With the exception of the aforementioned "extemporaneous" talk given in Elkhart in 1873, there is no hard evidence that Tschetter delivered any other sermon during his lifetime.[57] The Elkhart sermon too probably consisted of Tschetter's remembrance of parts of one of the *Lehren*. It was perhaps nuanced since Tschetter was not known to have memorized any of his sermons. Neu Hutterthaler minister Kenneth Ontjes, who has served the Neu Hutterthler congregation since 1979, confirms that Tschetter did not compose any of his own sermons.[58]

There are alternative opinions. Jacob E. Hofer said that older members told him Paul Tschetter did not "read" all of his sermons. "Nor was he confined to any book of sermons," writes Hofer.[59] In a 1989 presentation, Tschetter's grandson, Paul G. Tschetter also stated that the Rev. Tschetter wrote "some" of his own sermons.[60] Prairieleut folk tradition says that at times even colony members requested sermons composed by Tschetter. But there is no documentation or original source evidence supporting any of these suggestions. The Hutterite request was likely for Tschetter's handwritten copies of the *Lehren*. The special emphasis that Hutterians placed on the *Lehren* was powerful and we assume that Paul

---

57. J. E. Hofer, "A History of the Neu Hutterthaler Church," 65.
58. Kenneth Ontjes, interview, July 2005.
59. J. E. Hofer, "A History of the Neu Hutterthaler Church," 65.
60. Paul G. Tschetter, "Monologue," tape (June 1989), Mitchell, SD. HHMA.

Figure 8.2 Paul Tschetter's first sermon book.
Photograph courtesy of Gideon Bertsch and Wesley Tschetter.

Tschetter did not stray from this perspective. Like ministers in Hutterite colonies, he read from a sermon collection that had been composed substantially in the seventeenth century.

Colony Hutterites continue to believe that the *Lehren* represent a primary and sufficient way to find out what the Bible means. In the late nineteenth century most Hutterite ministers familiarized themselves with the sermon content by creating personal handwritten copies. As Clifford Walter put it, "Ministers spent many a long winter evening copying sermons into books in German script."[61] Paul Tschetter followed this practice.

Where Tschetter's many sermon collections ended up is another of the mysteries that surround his life. The only Paul Tschetter sermon book that has been found is his first sermon collection. It is in the possession of Gideon Bertsch (Menno, South Dakota) whose first wife, Mabel, was Paul Tschetter's youngest granddaughter. This collection was written while Tschetter was still living in south Ukraine. It is dated 1870, is well-used and shows clear and beautiful penmanship, using both black and red ink. Amazingly, Bertsch keeps the sermon book in a cardboard box on the shelf of a closet.

We know that Paul Tschetter used this 1870 sermon collection for the rest of his life because there are many handwritten notes in the mar-

---

61. Clifford Walter, correspondence, March 2003.

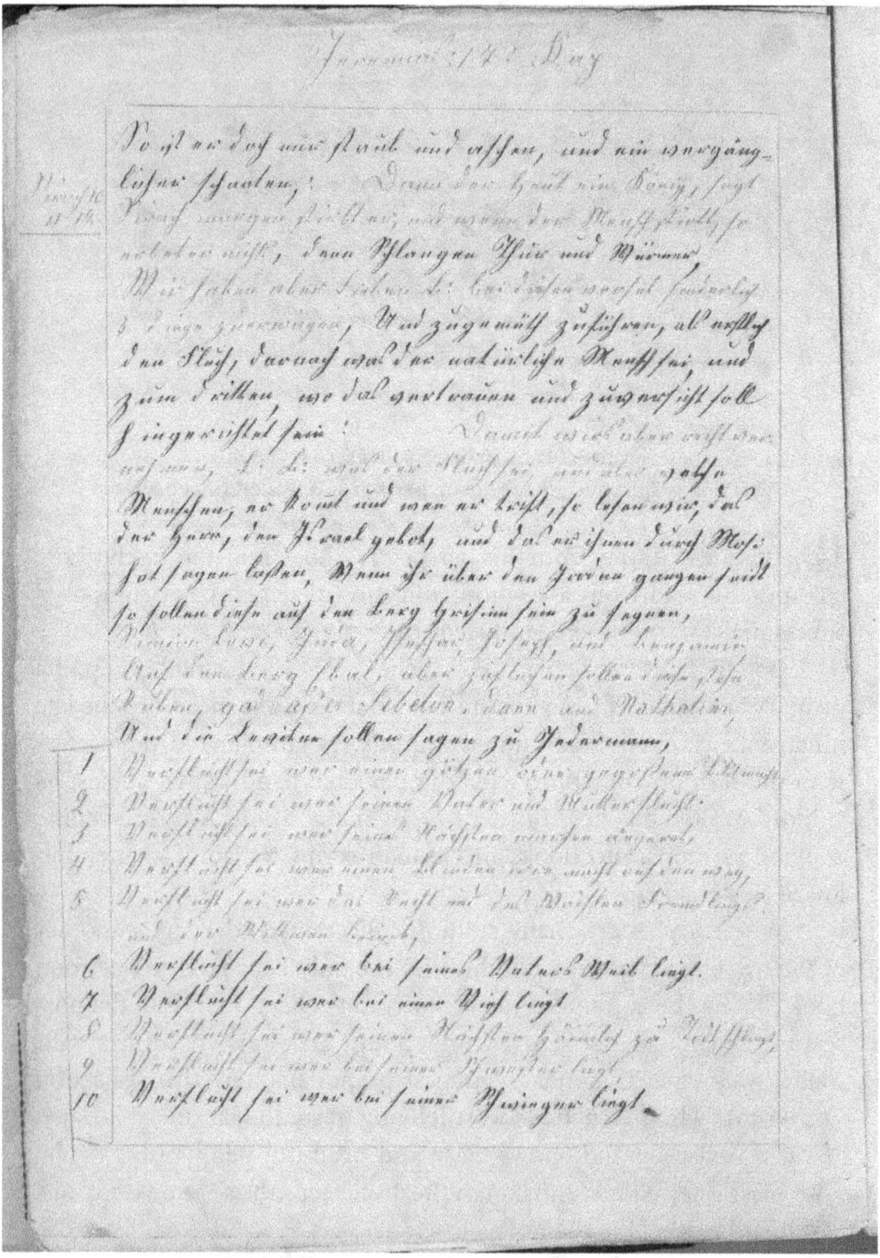

Figure 8.3 Paul Tschetter's first sermon book, title page.
Photograph courtesy of Gideon Bertsche and Wesley Tschetter.

gins, including Neu Hutterthaler Church membership lists as well as baptism, marriage, and death records. One entry describes the death of Tschetter's daughter, Barbara. A 1916 entry lists the dates that Tschetter delivered specific sermons. When one compares this handwriting to that found in his diary, one finds basic similarities in form. But the 1870 sermon book contains only nine sermons, far too few to last a lifetime of ministry, even when one considers that some sermons took more than one Sunday service to read.

Hutterite minister Mike Wipf suggests that Tschetter likely had at least one hundred sermons in his possession, which he would have used in a variety of rotations.[62] All of the sermons in the existent Tschetter collection are used by communal Hutterites in the 2000s. In addition to nine sermons, the 1870 book has many blank pages, which Mike Wipf says is unusual. "X"'s placed in columns emphasize sermon points that Tschetter considered important.

The Paul Tschetter sermon book is 145 pages in length and includes *Lehren* on Old and New Testament chapters, including Psalms 139, Isaiah, 58, Isaiah 60, Jeremiah 17, Sirach 3, Luke 8, Galatians 5, James 5, and 1 Corinthians.[63] Mike Wipf's analysis indicates that three of the nine sermons are somewhat shorter versions of those found in colony books.[64] Most of the others are word-for-word copies. According to Schmiedeleut Hutterite Patrick Murphy, prior to the modern era of published manuscripts, ministers sometimes broke the *Lehren* into smaller mini-sermons to accommodate church services that were much shorter than those held in the seventeenth century.[65] Tschetter likely did the same thing.

But these are not the only sermons that Tschetter delivered. In addition to the nine sermons in the 1870 Paul Tschetter compendium, "Yos" Hofer's diary includes specific reference to eleven additional sermons that he heard the Rev. Tschetter deliver. These sermons are all based on biblical references and include the following: Exodus 12, Psalm 75, Proverbs, Matthew 6, Matthew 7, Luke 2, John 3, Acts 2, Hebrews 12, 1 Thessalonians 5, and Titus 2.[66] Paul Tschetter's own 1873

---

62. Mike Wipf, interview, Oak Lane Colony, Alexandria, SD, July, 2006.
63. "Paul Tschetter Sermon Book" (1870).
64. Mike Wipf, interview, Oak Lane Colony, Alexandria, SD, July 2006.
65. Patrick Murphy, correspondence, April, 2007.
66. A. M. Hofer, ed., *The Diaries of Joseph "Yos" Hofer*.

diary indicates that Tschetter read (additionally) sermons on Acts 2, 1 John 5 and Colossians 2 while in the United States. This is the sum of documentation about Tschetter's sermon choices (twenty-three in all) but it confirms the existence of additional sermon collections, the whereabouts of which are unknown. Perhaps descendents or later ministers donated them to a Hutterite colony or sold them at an auction not realizing their historical importance. When Paul Tschetter's son, David W. died in 1955, for example, all of David's hand-written sermons and German books were donated to a nearby Hutterite colony.[67]

Music

Vocal music has always been an important part of Hutterite worship. The Neu Hutterthaler Church continued this tradition and did so without the use of musical instruments until long after Paul Tschetter's death. There were also no choirs or singing groups since Hutterites believed that public performances nurtured feelings of pride.

The Hutterite hymns were sung from memory since the *Gesangbuch* was not published until 1895. Until then only Neu Hutterthaler ministers had copies, again handwritten, of the hymnbook. The Neu Hutterthaler Church did not purchase the *Gesangbuch mit Noten* (a hymnal with musical notes) until 1912.[68] Prior to this the general practice was for one of the preachers to recite the words of a stanza, line by line ("lining it out") after which "someone with a strong voice and some musical ability would begin the singing and the rest of the congregation would join in.[69] Melodies were passed down from generation to generation.

The hymns themselves are filled with practical theological statements as well as stories of those willing to suffer martyrdom. One of the favorite Hutterite hymns is *Lobt Gott ihr Christen all zu Gleich*, which appears on page forty-four of the *Gesangbuch*. In 1912 Neu Hutterthaler also purchased the evangelical Protestant *Evangeliums Lieder* hymnal. Communal Hutterites in the 2000s continue to sing the traditional hymns and they do so a cappella, without reserve and with emotional

---

67. Norma Jean Tschetter Parlier, interview with Wesley Tschetter, December 2008.

68. *Gesangbuch: Eine Sammlung Geistlicher Lieder zur Allgemeinen Erbauung und zum Lobe Gottes*. Elkhart, IN: Mennonitischen Verlagshandlung (1895).

69. Historical Committee, eds., *History of the Neu Hutterthaler Church* (Freeman, SD: Pine Hill Press, 1968), 10.

fervor, just as the hymns would have been sung at Neu Hutterthaler during Paul Tschetter's lifetime.

Observing the Sacraments

At the Neu Hutterthaler Church, baptism was conducted by pouring water on a woman or man's head inside of a church building. Between 1871 and 1919, the year of his death, Paul Tschetter baptized 328 people. The last group of nineteen young men and women were baptized on June 16, 1918. During this time only one individual at Neu Hutterthaler was baptized by someone other than Paul Tschetter. Baptisms were performed once a year in early summer with preparatory catechism classes beginning on Easter Sunday.

The Lord's Supper was observed two times each year; on Good Friday and on Ascension Day.[70] About two weeks before communion Neu Hutterthaler's ministers emphasized the importance of individual spiritual preparation at the Sunday morning church service. Each member was asked to talk to anyone he or she had offended before participating in communion in order to be at peace with one another and with God.[71]

Other important ministerial responsibilities included the conducting of weddings and funerals. Justina Guericke attended a funeral as a child where the "ministers" (one of whom was probably Paul Tschetter) preached sermons that emphasized that a recently deceased infant was "now in heaven as an angel."[72]

With regard to marriage, Prairieleut parents continued to be actively involved in the selection of dates and potential mates, notwithstanding Johann Cornies' condemnation of the Hutterite arranged marriage structure sixty years earlier.[73] Practices did not change overnight. As Jacob E. Hofer notes, "At the beginning of this century the selection of a partner was largely but not entirely the responsibility of the parents."[74] Suitors were well-known to all parties although in a horse-and-buggy world, contacts between boys and girls were not always easy to arrange

---

70. J. E. Hofer, "A History of the Neu Hutterthaler Church," 51.
71. Ibid.
72. Guericke, *Precious Memories*, 11.
73. Jacob E. Hofer, "A History of the Neu Hutterthaler Church," 69.
74. Ibid.

or to maintain. Most conversations took place at church and other celebratory events and involved friends and relatives. Couples desiring marriage were expected to first join the church by studying the catechism and being baptized.

Paul Tschetter married eighty-nine couples during his ministry, including five at one time on January 16, 1909. Tschetter performed his last marriage in January 1916. To some extent wedding ceremonies were simple events with no bridal veils or expensive rings. Yet the weddings were also huge gatherings that were often held in tents that could accommodate as many as 500–600 guests. Meals that accompanied weddings were substantial and often included roast beef, sauerkraut, potatoes, coffee, and cake.[75] Alcoholic beverages flowed freely.

Holy Days

Holidays commemorated in the Hutterite community replicated those observed in their Eastern European villages. Easter was given special emphasis and observances began on the morning of Good Friday with the celebration of the Lord's Supper, and continued for the next three days through Monday. Forty days after Easter the Neu Hutterthaler Church celebrated Ascension Day.

Christmas was also a three-day celebration, from December 25–27. This continued to be the Neu Hutterthaler practice until 1924. The church also held a one-hour service on New Year's Day and a special meeting on January 6 (Epiphany) the traditional date designating the arrival of the Wise Men at Jesus' stable.[76] "Yos" Hofer refers to Epiphany as the "Holiday of the Three Kings."[77]

The Neu Hutterthaler Church also followed Hutterian tradition in emphasizing Pentecost and celebrating it for three full days; Sunday through Tuesday.[78] Noncommunal Hutterians did not emphasize the communal life aspect of Pentecost but they believed that the energizing power of the Holy Spirit's arrival was a seminal event in church history. Six separate *Lehren* were delivered at Pentecost, concluding with the Acts 2 sermon.

75. Ibid., 70.
76. Ibid., 51.
77. Arnold M. Hofer, ed., *The Diaries of Joseph "Yos" Hofer*, 83.
78. NHCRB, 664, 820.

Figure 8.4 Jacob W. and Susanna Decker Tschetter, wedding photograph, 1899. Photograph courtesy of Wesley Tschetter.

Dress

The Neu Hutterthaler Church expected members to exhibit plainness in dress and general lifestyle. In Paul Tschetter's view an individual's outward appearance should show humility and religious devotion and was not to be influenced by fashionable trends. The outward man or woman reflected an inward reality and dress did matter. It was a public reminder of identification with a particular religious group. It showed commitment and assisted the process of maintaining communal control over individual behavior.

In terms of general attire Prairieleut women at Neu Hutterthaler did not cut their hair. They wore it combed back or braided and covered with a veil or shawl. Women wore ankle-length gathered skirts, long aprons, a blouse, and a long-sleeved vest or jacket. Jacob E. Hofer said that a typical head-covering was made out of sheer black net material, a "kerchief" with fringes, and was adorned with beautiful flowers.[79] Paul Tschetter

---

79. Jacob E. Hofer, "A History of the Neu Hutterthaler Church," 68.

Figure 8.5 Traditional shawl worn by Katherina Wollman Decker. Photograph courtesy of Wesley Tschetter.

was initially adamant that women always cover their heads and wear long dresses. But in the United States he was fighting a losing battle.

Neu Hutterthaler men sported trimmed beards and simple dark clothing. They wore suspenders instead of belts and initially used hooks and eyes on their shirts and coats instead of buttons. One sees the hooks and eyes in the 1873 Paul Tschetter photograph. Hutterites did not traditionally wear ties but social customs changed rapidly in Dakota Territory. By the 1890s many women were not wearing a shawl outside of church services and some men wore ties when engaged in business activities. Buttons replaced hooks and eyes.

Photographs

Paul Tschetter was opposed to personal photographs, and, as noted, he allowed himself to be photographed only once or twice. Tschetter viewed photographs as idolatrous and against the Ten Commandment injunction forbidding graven images. Thus Tschetter became enraged one Sunday morning when he discovered that one of his parishioners had hung a wall-papered picture with a religious theme inside the Neu Hutterthaler Church. Tschetter immediately took a hammer and nailed small pieces of wood over the top of the picture. Son David W. noticed his father's handiwork before the church service and removed the wood to avoid conflict.[80] But although the Rev. Tschetter later admitted that he had exhibited "foolish behavior" in covering the picture, he never softened his stand against photographic images.[81]

In theory, the colony Hutterites continue to hold a no-photograph position although it is abrogated openly and regularly. In July 2005, a Dariusleut minister exclaimed surprise that the author did not own a digital camera and did not come prepared to take photographs while touring his colony. Hutterites usually limit photographs, however, to wedding albums and small journals. One does not see family photographs lining the hallways.

Some older Hutterites continue to frown on photographs. In 1982 an older Hutterite woman became so distraught when a distant Prairieleut relative took her picture that she prayed as hard as she could that God would intervene. Miraculously, the tripod holding the man's camera kept falling down during the photo-session and when the film came back from the developer it was blank.[82] Prairieleut individuals involved attribute the lack of a photograph to camera malfunction and/or film developer incompetence; the Hutterites suggest divine intervention.

Practicing Church Discipline

Paul Tschetter was a stickler on behavioral norms and he was committed to work toward the creation of a body of believers without spot or wrinkle. Thus when Tschetter discovered that parishioner Joe A. Hofer had purchased a piano he informed him that he was "out of the church."[83] Tschetter did the same, as noted, when a member was found

---

80. Paul G. Tschetter, "Monologue."
81. Paul G. Tschetter, interview, July 1998.
82. Phil Glanzer, interview, July, 1998. For a more detailed rendition of this story, see R. Janzen, *The Prairie People*, 98.
83. R. Janzen, *The Prairie People*, 24.

growing tobacco in his garden, even though benefactor Johann Cornies had encouraged Hutterites to cultivate this crop in Russia.

The Neu Hutterthaler Church never adopted an ordinance that penalize tobacco use, however, because so many members smoked or chewed. Tschetter lost this battle. Maria Tschetter's physically handicapped brother, Henry Walter, was known not only to walk with a crutch but to smoke tobacco "western style, roll your own."[84] But this does not mean that Paul Tschetter liked what he saw and he worked hard to eradicate the practice. In his diary, as noted, "Yos" Hofer writes that in November, 1891, Paul Tschetter threatened that he would not preach until members of his congregation quit smoking.[85]

With regard to other church discipline issues, granddaughter Justina Guericke recalled, "Several church members were dismissed from church membership because they shaved their beard off and got a haircut by the barber."[86] In one case the man excommunicated never returned, nor did he join another church. Tschetter preferred that men have beards and wear their hair moderately long. He once refused to marry a couple because the groom wore a starched collar, which to Tschetter showed a lack of humility. Tschetter was also opposed to members frequenting bars although he was not a teetotaler, and he greatly disliked dancing.

The picture of a hardened traditionalist is softened by memories of granddaughter, Anna Fisher who reminded the author that when her mother Justina fell in love with the non-Hutterite farm laborer, Christ Hofman, many at Neu Hutterthaler were opposed to this relationship. But the Rev. Tschetter announced that he would approve it "as long as," he told his daughter, "you get along and you love him."[87] Paul Tschetter was unable to stop the forces of change. In 1916, son Jacob W. purchased a piano for Paul Tschetter's granddaughter, Maria. In 1917 Jacob W.'s sons, David and Emil purchased a camera without their parents' permission and for a time were able to take photographs secretly by intercepting developed images from the postman before he arrived at their

---

84. Paul G. Tschetter, "The Life Story of David W. Tschetter," no date, unpublished manuscript in the possession of Gideon Bertsche, Menno, South Dakota.

85. A. M. Hofer, ed., *The Diary of Joseph "Yos" Hofer*, November, 1891 entry.

86. Justina Guericke, "History of the Rev. Paul P. Tschetter," presentation, Paul Tschetter Descendents Reunion (Freeman, SD: 1960). WTC.

87. Anna Hofman Fisher, interview, May 2004.

home.[88] Ten years earlier (in 1907) a photograph of Neu Hutterthaler member John Deckers' home shows that Decker too owned a piano.[89]

Spirituality in Different Forms

Notwithstanding the fervor with which Paul Tschetter and his congregants practiced their faith, evangelical Protestants and Mennonites complained about a state of spiritual decline in his congregation. Some of the criticism was an attack on Hutterite cultural practices; the dialect, the dress. Tschetter was criticized frequently for his rigid enforcement of church rules and regulations. Critics pointed to poor church attendance, over-consumption of alcohol, and the lack of emphasis on a personal relationship with Jesus. Tschetter, like all traditional Hutterites, viewed the Christian's relationship with God more communally. Also criticized was the absence of sermons that included examples from contemporary life.

The story of Prairieleut spirituality or lack thereof, is complicated. The Neu Hutterthaler Church did have problems with congregants who were not fully committed to the church. But this was also the case in the Krimmer Mennonite Brethren and evangelical Protestant denominations which many ex-Hutterians joined, especially after the excitement of the conversion experience diminished. These were the people that were most critical of Paul Tschetter.

There is no question about Paul Tschetter's own spiritual commitment. Tschetter focused most of his attention on the supernatural realm of existence and the relationship between human behavior and biblical standards. He was greatly concerned with the religious vitality of his community in Russia as well as in the United States. Tschetter was also conservative and inflexible on lifestyle and many cultural issues, which he believed had religious implications. Members interviewed by Jacob E. Hofer in the late 1940s said that Neu Hutterthaler functioned as a "monarchy" during Paul Tschetter's tenure as elder. "The preacher was almost the controlling force and his authority was practically final," notes Hofer.[90] But this does not mean that Tschetter was not seriously committed to the life and teachings of Jesus.

---

88. Wesley Tschetter, correspondence, October, 2008.
89. Historical Committee, eds., *Menno*, 254.
90. J. E. Hofer, "A History of the Neu Hutterthaler Church," 24.

9

The Evangelical Alternative

> John Tschetter was said to be the first one among the Hutterite people to have a personal conversion experience with the Lord and to openly confess Christ as his personal Savior.[1]
>
> —Mrs. Paul S. Gross, 1986

BEGINNING IN THE 1880S, PAUL TSCHETTER HAD TO CONFRONT THE fact that many of his congregants were defecting to the Krimmer Mennonite Brethren (KMB) denomination. This included many members of his immediate family. In addition to dealing with the communal/noncommunal divide that had also existed in Ukraine, Tschetter now found himself doing battle with evangelical Mennonites. He found himself positioned between the colony Hutterites on one side and the KMBs on the other.

Unlike communal and noncommunal Hutterites, the KMB had minimal interest in preserving uniquely Hutterite teachings or practices. Because so many Prairieleut joined KMB congregations, they often maintained Hutterite cultural traditions, including the Hutterisch dialect, foods and some modes of dress. Some historic beliefs were also retained within the KMB context, for example, an emphasis on church discipline. But much of the communal theology and ecclesiology was given up.

People in both the communal Hutterite and KMB ranks recognized Paul Tschetter's spiritual stature and they tried to convince him to come over to their side. But Tschetter held his ground, justifying the noncommunal Hutterite position while trying not to come down too harshly on either of the other groups. As noted, in the early settlement

---

1. Mrs. Paul S. Gross, *A History of the Salem MB Church, 1886–1986*, 4.

years, many Prairieleut were attracted to communalism and the security that accompanied a life lived as one large extended family. Many people left the Prairieleut churches and moved into the colonies. By the mid-1880s there was a second option.

The KMB sect was founded by Jacob A. Wiebe in the Russian Crimea in 1869, just a few years before the mass emigration from Russia. Wiebe's group promoted a more evangelical type of Christianity than was found in either the colonies or in the independent Prairieleut congregations. Since KMBs practiced immersion baptism, Hutterites often called them "Baptists."

Krimmer Mennonite Brethren evangelists brought their message to the Dakotas via revival services beginning in 1881. They found a receptive audience among some Low German Mennonites but "especially among the Hutterites" [the noncommunal Prairieleut].[2] Evangelists visited Prairieleut families in their homes bringing Bibles and songbooks. They emphasized a personal relationship with Jesus as well as strict holy living and adherence to church rules and regulations. More than other Russian Mennonite groups the KMBs practiced, as C. J. Dyck puts it, "rigorous austerity in dress and life" as well as church discipline.[3] These positions were comforting to many Prairieleut. The KMBs also emphasized evangelism, which was not stressed by Hutterites.

The personal salvation emphasis was especially attractive. KMBs talked about being "saved," asking Jesus to "come into their hearts" and of a warm, emotional connection to God. At the Neu Hutterthaler Church Paul Tschetter too taught "spiritual regeneration" but he did so within the context of Hutterian traditions. The latter were deemed unimportant or even a spiritual hindrance to KMB converts, who viewed Hutterite traditions as cold and legalistic and ultimately embarrassing in the New World context. They referred to Neu Hutterthaler as "the old church."

Paul Tschetter's brother, John, was the first "Tschetter" and the first Hutterian to join the KMB Church. After being converted, in late November, 1886, he was re-baptized in the Wolf Creek after the ice was cut.[4] The Neu Hutterthaler Church had not met John Tschetter's spiritual needs. As his spouse, Susanna Mendel put it in a personal memoir,

---

2. Plett, *The Story of the Krimmer Mennonite Brethren Church*, 151.
3. Dyck, *An Introduction to Mennonite History*, 284.
4. Plett, *The Story of the Krimmer Mennonite Brethren Church*, 154.

> The new birth was not preached in our Church where my brother-in-law, Paul Tschetter was the preacher. Our Huterish (sic) people thought that all that was necessary to please God was to live a good clean life. To become a new creature in Christ Jesus; to be born into God's family; to have peace with God; and to have sins forgiven was something altogether unknown."[5]

For John Tschetter this was the critical difference: a direct and emotional personal relationship with God. In her memoir, spouse Susanna describes her non-KMB parents as "God-fearing people" who "lived a devotional life."[6] But they were not "saved" or "born-again," i.e. they had not experienced a complete, emotion-laden and deeply spiritual internal regeneration according to KMB understandings. In that same year (1886), Paul Tschetter's brothers, Jacob and David, also joined the KMBs and other Prairieleut followed. They liked the greater emphasis on grace, as opposed to legalistic forms. They liked the faster, catchier tunes of the KMB gospel songs and viewed worship there as more vibrant and meaningful. There were tearful personal "testimonies" and encouraging slaps on the back.

Susanna Tschetter wrote that she was at first opposed to the "new" teaching as was Paul Tschetter's mother, Barbara (with whom they lived). "At first I did not understand my husband" [John Tschetter] "because he started to pray and read the Bible."[7] But Susanna changed her mind as did Barbara Kleinsasser Tschetter.

John Tschetter found what Susanna described as the "blessed assurance" of salvation, after which his happiness "was so great that he could hardly sleep for joy. The Lord was so near to him because he was the first one of our people who had the assurance of salvation." Susanna continues, "Often the Lord appeared unto him, as it seemed, in a vision of brightness of an angel, as he was meditating in prayer before the Lord." Soon Susanna followed, undergoing a conversion experience of her own. In his autobiography John Tschetter described his pilgrimage as follows:

> tried hard to be good but it didn't work . . . I also tried to quit bad habits like smoking, and so forth—then via prayer and

---

5. Susanna Tschetter, "Mother's Manuscript," in Jacob A. Tschetter, ed., "Family History," unpublished manuscript, 1952. WTC.

6. Susanna Tschetter, "Mother's Manuscript."

7. Ibid.

Bible reading . . . I started to constrain myself to live simple; I quit smoking, yet this habit caused me such trouble. When I was in company, I smoked again; especially on weddings and such occasions.[8]

Tschetter goes on to describe what he calls "darkness" among the Prairieleut and says that he was searching for something more spiritual. Then one day,

In our cellar under our house I found a quiet place to pray. It was dark there because to keep the frost out we closed the windows . . . Once when I prayed, a light as bright as the sun brightened the cellar. It seemed as if an angel stood at my side. A wonderful joy came over me. It filled my entire being, yet I told no one about it.[9]

After this occurrence Tschetter talked with local "Baptists" (i.e. KMB) about what had happened. He wrote that "the new birth was not preached in our church," implying that his brother's sermons (the seventeenth-century *Lehren*) did not call for a personal salvation experience.[10] He also noted, "We had no Sunday School [true before 1908] and so we drifted along."

Paul Tschetter's mother, Barbara, was also "saved"—at seventy years of age, though she never withdrew her membership from the Neu Hutterthaler Church. After his father, Jacob, died in 1882, Barbara remained with son John and his wife Susanna on the family farm. Hutterite tradition gave the parents' land to the youngest son but also expected him to take care of them during their waning years. Living with her KMB son and daughter-in-law, Barbara was exposed to different religious interpretations and expressions. According to John Tschetter, after being converted, his mother exclaimed: "I always wanted to be good, but anything like this I have never experienced." Barbara had at first feared that her youngest son was "going too deep."[11] Now she too experienced the grace of God in an entirely new way. It is hard to underestimate the depth of the soul-wrenching experience that caused so many of

---

8. J. A. Tschetter, ed., "Rev. John Tschetter's Autobiography," n.d. WTC.
9. Ibid.
10. Ibid.
11. Ibid.

Neu Hutterthaler's members, and eventually so many members of Paul Tschetter's own family, to leave Hutterite traditions behind.

The KMB were dynamic and they eventually attracted all but one of Paul and Maria Tschetter's children. Sons David W., Jacob W. and daughter, Justina left Neu Hutterthaler in 1904; Joseph W. followed in 1906. All four of them had initially joined the Neu Hutterthaler Church and this congregation had been an integral part of their lives since birth.[12] Joseph W. had helped to construct the Neu Hutterthaler Church building, "haul[ing] water to make the mortar."[13] But now they felt truly "saved" and believed that God was calling them to join a different religious body.

Joining the KMB meant that Paul Tschetter's children had to be re-baptized because their first adult baptism, by their own father, was not recognized by the new religious group. This is perhaps one reason why the Rev. Tschetter once referred to the KMBs as "a wild religious movement."[14] Tschetter's sons were re-baptized on their knees by immersion, in a river. They were dunked forward three times, in the name of Father, the Son, and the Holy Spirit.

The only child who did not join the KMB was daughter, Maria. She married Joshua Hofer and later moved to Beadle County, where she and her husband joined the Hutterthal Church, near Carpenter. Out of respect, oldest son "Big Paul" also did not leave Neu Hutterthaler until after his father's death. But six years later, on August 25, 1925, he too took the plunge (at age fifty-nine) and was re-baptized by his first cousin, Jacob M. Tschetter.[15]

So many Tschetters joined the KMB in the Bridgewater area that one of the early meeting places was referred to in Jacob J. Hofer's diary, as "the congregation by the Tschetter Brethren" although officially the congregation was known as the "Salem Krimmer Mennonite Brethren Church."[16] Present Neu Hutterthaler pastor Kenneth Ontjes calls the Salem Church a Neu Hutterthaler "split-off."[17] Amazingly, the

12. Mrs. Paul S. Gross, *A History of the Salem MB Church*, 99.
13. Mrs. Joseph W. Tschetter, *My Life's Story*, 5.
14. Paul G. Tschetter, "A Legacy," 2.
15. Mrs. Joseph W. Tschetter, *My Life's Story*, 12.
16. A. M. Hofer, ed., "Diary of Rev. Jacob J. Hofer, 1900–1920." Unpublished document. HHMA.
17. Kenneth Ontjes, interview, October 2005.

The Evangelical Alternative 177

Figure 9.1 The Salem Krimmer Mennonite Brethren Church, 1917. Photograph courtesy of Salem Mennonite Brethren Church Centennial Committee.

Salem KMB Church building itself was constructed on the homestead property of Paul Tschetter's father Jacob and within sight of the Neu Hutterthaler Church.

On December 20, 1900, John Tschetter preached a sermon at the Salem Church based on the Old Testament Book of Lamentations, chapter 3.[18] Other early pastors at the KMB congregation were Low German Mennonites Henry Goossen (who served from 1885–1899) and Dietrich Goossen (from 1895–1907). Dietrich Goossen's son, Jacob, married Paul Tschetter's niece, Anna, in 1902.

The KMB movement presented a dilemma for Paul Tschetter, who tried to maintain good relations with converts even as they turned their backs on his ministry and many Hutterite theological traditions. Some ex-Neu Hutterthaler members were very close friends of Paul and Maria. When immediate family members left the impact was even more dramatic.

There were many surprises in store for Paul and Maria Tschetter. In 1901 for example, the Rev. Johann Hofer performed the wedding ceremony of Tschetter's son, Joseph W., to Katherina Hofer at the Neu

---

18. A. M. Hofer, ed., "Diary of Rev. Jacob J. Hofer, 1900–1920," 3.

Hutterthaler Church.[19] Afterward the couple lived with Paul and Maria during their first year of marriage while Joseph W. was employed as a schoolteacher. Joseph W. and Katherina worked "their own land" but resided in the same house as their parents.[20]

In 1903, however, the newlyweds moved onto their own property two miles east, constructed a house and farm buildings and began attending meetings at the KMB Church. One evening after attending a revival service, Joseph told Katherina that "he wanted to take a firm stand of the Lord, get assurance of his soul's salvation."[21] The couple prayed about it and in the quiet of their home they "found salvation."[22] In spring 1904 they left the Neu Hutterthaler Church. In his diary "Yos" Hofer says that he attended a service at Neu Hutterthaler on June 12, 1904 where Joseph W. Tschetter "explained himself" in front of the congregation. Hofer describes "great resistance" to Joseph W.'s testimony.[23] Four years later, Joseph W. was elected minister at the Salem KMB Church.[24]

Justina S. W. Glanzer wrote that Samuel Glanzer (her father-in-law), a Neu Hutterthaler member, was converted after conversations with KMB friends as well as much prayer and Bible reading. When Glanzer (like Joseph W. Tschetter earlier) attempted to give his personal testimony during a Neu Hutterthaler service, the Rev. Paul J. Tschetter yelled out, "Samuel, be seated, your place is there by the Baptists."[25] According to Justina, this led to an "uproar" in the audience and led to many bad feelings between acquaintances and even members of her own family.

Justina said that her father, Joseph Hofer, once asked three "colony brethren" (ministers) from Bon Homme and Rockport colonies to come to their house to help him point out errors in Samuel Glanzer's newfound KMB faith. When they arrived Glanzer's exasperated cry was as follows: "They are colony people—What should I, poor child, just converted do? Lord!"[26] One of the ministers told Glanzer that he had

19. NHCRB, 781.
20. Mrs. Joseph W. Tschetter, *My Life's Story*, 8, 39.
21. Ibid., 8.
22. Ibid.
23. A. M. Hofer, ed., *The Diary of Joseph "Yos" Hofer*, June 12, 1904 entry.
24. A. M. Hofer, ed., "Diary of Rev. Jacob J. Hofer, 1900–1920," 23.
25. Guericke, *Precious Memories of a Historical House*, 3.
26. Glanzer, *Life's Story of Samuel W. Glanzer and Justina S. W. Glanzer*, 3.

been invited by Joseph Hofer to "correct your ways." Glanzer could not understand why the Hutterites did not keep to themselves. As he put it, "If you believe in communal living as the correct way to heaven, why do you work for other congregations' [i.e. Neu Hutterthaler's] foundation? You don't let minister Paul Tschetter step upon your platform, you don't pray with him."[27] One colony minister said that talking to Glanzer was not accomplishing anything. It was like "throwing peas against a wall—[they] all come back."[28]

This amazing interchange shows that at least one Neu Hutterthaler member (Joseph Hofer) enlisted the support of colony Hutterites to combat the evangelical challenge that was taking away so many members from his and other Prairieleut congregations. Joseph Hofer himself was married to Susanna, a sister of Paul Tschetter. In later years Joseph and Susanna too left the Neu Hutterthaler Church but they did not join the KMBs. Instead they moved into a colony. (But they did not stay there long. After a few years they returned to Neu Hutterthaler.[29])

With regard to the "born-again" experience, Paul Tschetter's view was that for some people it was difficult to remember a particular point in time when they were "saved." To Tschetter the Christian faith was transformative yet complicated and involved an intricate set of ethical commitments and cultural forms. It was unnecessary to throw out the *Lehren* as the KMBs wanted to do. The sermons too stipulated that individuals make personal commitments to Christ. Tschetter did not use "born again" language in daily conversation but one of his hymns indicates belief in the importance of a strong inner faith. Tschetter writes,

> But also give us more
> That the sun would shine,
> Deep inside my heart
> That is the Lord, Jesus Christ,
> He is the true flame
> The eternal light.[30]

We can imagine how hurt Paul Tschetter must have been when his younger brother John, as well as John's fiancé, Susanna left Neu Hutterthaler for a denomination they insisted was closer to the truth.

27. Ibid.
28. Ibid., 4
29. Ibid.
30. Paul Tschetter, hymn #4, stanza five (1873). HMA.

John and Susanna had studied the catechism with the Rev. Tschetter. He had baptized and married them. This pattern was repeated by Paul Tschetters' son, David W., who was re-baptized in the Wolf Creek by the Rev. Heinrich Wiebe on May 22, 1904.[31] David started attending the Salem Church while he was still living in his father's house.[32] On the same date in May (1904), Paul and Maria Tschetter's daughter, Justina, was also baptized by immersion, as was the man she was dating and would soon marry (Christ Hofman) as well as Jacob W. and Susanna Tschetter. Son Joseph W. and his wife Katherina followed as noted two years later.

Paul Tschetter was also aware that even Neu Hutterthaler members who remained sometimes attended Salem KMB church meetings. Many older KMB Prairieleut say that Tschetter admitted that this had an energizing effect on church life at Neu Hutterthaler and that he did not oppose it. Relationships between members of the two groups were in any case impossible to avoid. The Salem Church building was situated right next door. On Sunday mornings, members of the two congregations could see each other outside their respective sanctuaries that were built on the adjoining homesteaded properties of the Rev. Paul Tschetter and his parents!

One woman said that as a girl she attended Sunday morning services at Neu Hutterthaler, then (in the afternoon) walked over to the Salem Church for Sunday School classes. In 1886, Neu Hutterthaler's sister congregation, Hutterthal, decided that if members attended KMB services and "neglected" their own church, they would be excommunicated.[33] Neu Hutterthaler never went this far but there was always tension in the air.

The KMB church periodical, *Wahrheitsfreund* is filled with the names of Prairieleut individuals who left the independent Hutterite churches to join the KMBs. Similar notations are found in almost every Prairieleut family history as well as in obituaries published in local newspapers. D. M. Hofer, for example, one of those who signed the 1902 Neu Hutterthaler Church incorporation documents, later joined the

---

31. Paul G. Tschetter, "The Life Story of David W. Tschetter." Unpublished document. HHMA.

32. A. M. Hofer, ed., "Diary of Jacob J. Hofer, 1900–1920," March 1902 entury.

33. Kleinsasser, ed., *Our Journey of Faith*, 91.

Salem KMB Church.³⁴ Hofer's wife, Barbara, was Paul Tschetter's niece. Jacob I. Walter, one of the last ministers ordained by Paul Tschetter, left Neu Hutterthaler in the same year that he was ordained (1918) and spent the next thirty-three years serving as a KMB minister. Some colony Hutterites also joined the evangelical group. Paul G. Tschetter said that his grandfather was "deeply hurt" by all that was going on but that he decided to "leave it to God."³⁵

Assurance of Salvation

An important KMB position was the doctrine of the assurance of salvation. This stance suggested that once you "accepted Jesus into your life" God would give you "complete assurance" that you would go to heaven after you died.

In this regard if you were a colony Hutterite, the community itself provided a foundational kind of security, sometimes compared to Noah's Ark in the Old Testament. The ark metaphor was first used by Hutterite leader Peter Walpot in the sixteenth century and reiterated by Michael Waldner in the 1850s. In the colonies spiritual status is exemplified by willingness to share material belongings and live in an extended ethno-religious family. God makes the final determination about whether an individual is accepted into heaven (Hutterites do not believe they speak for God) but members feel secure in their faith nonetheless.

Noncommunal Hutterites had more difficulty believing that their congregations could guarantee eternal status. As in the colonies Christian salvation was defined collectively. It was based not only on a personal relationship with God but mediated by church members as representatives of Jesus on earth. Still this faith was not institutionalized in a communal way of life. There was a lot more room for personal angst.

External indicators confirming Christian faith were more discernible in the colonies (institutionally) and in the KMB congregations (emotionally) than in the noncommunal Hutterite churches. In the colonies Hutterites made a public commitment to live communally in separation from the rest of the world; in the KMB congregations spiritual security came as a result of an emotional encounter with God. There was nothing like this in noncommunal Hutterianism, the third or

---

34. Glanzer, et. al., *A Century of God's Blessing.*
35. Paul G. Tschetter, "Monologue."

middle path, even though the sermons encouraged members to worship God and follow the teachings of Jesus.

The search for spiritual security had already presented a dilemma for members while they were living in Eastern Europe. In Dakota Territory, social and economic uncertainties during the settlement years exacerbated this ideological/religious quandary. And in North America the Prairieleut did not have an integrated village support system. The basic dilemma was how to live a Christian life with a strong sense that one's worship practices and general lifestyle were adequate to take one to heaven after death. Many Prairieleut wanted a greater sense of security than was found in the independent churches. Those who left the Neu Hutterthaler Church saw hypocrisy, shallow faith and cultural rigidity there.

Many KMB accepted the popular late nineteenth-century teaching of "assurance of salvation," which guaranteed that, as a result of a personal relationship with God, one could "claim" eternal security in heaven. This position is sometimes described as "once saved, always saved," although the KMB Conference did not go this far. Still assurance of salvation was confirmed by an emotional experience in which Jesus "came into one's heart." For many this teaching provided spiritual comfort and a new sense of purpose. It often led to moral improvement as well.

The assurance of salvation teaching was also found to cure the condition of spiritual malaise that Hutterites refer to as *Anfechtung*. This emotionally destabilizing form of depression literally means "temptation" and is believed to be the result of an individual's deep struggle with sin, sometimes with Satan himself. According to the Neu Hutterthaler Church Record Book, one Susanna Gross Hofer "went to sleep in the Lord" in 1892, after first experiencing "many temptations (*Anfechtungen*) to suffer in this life" and having "wished very much to be released from this world."[36] In 1902, sixty-one-year-old Michael Hofer (father of Katherina Tschetter) too "endured a serious spiritual struggle."[37]

In the 1950s researchers Bert Kaplan and Thomas Plaut described Hutterite *Anfechtung* as a psychosis resulting from a heavy sense of guilt leading to "a weakening of the ego's ability to deal with the moral struggle

36. NHCRB, 825
37. Ibid., 664.

between ideology and impulse."³⁸ Hutterites consider *Anfechtung* to be part of the life struggle that some people have to endure; mental illness is viewed as only a temporary spiritual defeat. One of the Hutterite sermons puts it this way: "The great art is to obey the Lord Jesus Christ and to never oppose him, so long as one lives, and to endure everything in patience, whatever *Anfechtung* or suffering may come."³⁹ But the KMB suggested that what the Hutterites called *Anfechtung* was the result of an overly negative or pessimistic attitude toward life, resulting from a lack of assurance that one was a true Christian. KMB founder Jacob A. Wiebe believed that "deep experiences," that is, *Anfechtungen*, could be avoided if one experienced "joy in Christ" and accepted the certainty of one's faith.⁴⁰

To become a member of a KMB congregation thus involved careful discernment about one's relationship with God and whether or not one was "saved." In his diary Jacob J. Hofer describes the case of "four persons" who were "examined" in order to determine whether they were ready for baptism.⁴¹ As Hofer put it, "They [the baptismal candidates] gave testimony of their conversion and asked to be baptized."⁴²

Personal relations between Hutterite traditionalists and Hutterite KMB did continue in different forms. In 1902, KMB pastor, Jacob J. Hofer attended a service at Neu Hutterthaler where Paul Tschetter distributed the communion elements.⁴³ Tschetter in turn joined his uncle, John, in preaching sermons at the funeral of Hofer's father three years later, on August 29, 1905.⁴⁴ But since KMBs practiced "closed communion," no member at Neu Hutterthaler, Hutterthal or Hutterdorf could participate in the Lord's Supper at a KMB church. With regard to the 1905 funeral service Jacob J. Hofer referred to the KMB ministers involved as "Brother" John Tschetter and "Brother" John Wipf but he does not use the "brother" appellation when referring to Paul Tschetter since the latter was not "in fellowship."

38. Kaplan and Plaut, *Personality and Communal Society*.
39. Hans Friedrich Kuentsche, in Anderson, "The Pentecost Preaching of Acts 2," 261.
40. Plett, *Story of the Krimmer Mennonite Brethren*, 25–27.
41. A. M. Hofer, ed., "The Diary of Rev. Jacob J. Hofer," 21.
42. Ibid., 19.
43. Ibid., 18.
44. Ibid., 32

Hutterite theological emphases were not entirely disregarded by the KMB. In her autobiography, Paul Tschetter's daughter-in-law, Katharina Tschetter, continues to use the language of Hutterian *Gelassenheit*. When describing a "call" to full-time evangelism, for example, she describes "a dying to self."[45] From 1911 to 1915, Katharina and Joseph W. served as missionaries to the African-American community in North Carolina.[46] The KMBs also retained German as the language of the church.

But there was more to the Christian faith than this. During Paul Tschetter's lifetime he was continually bombarded with stories of people going forward at revival services, getting "saved," then designating as unnecessary, if not unholy, a wide variety of Hutterite ecclesiastical traditions that he himself thought valuable. Throughout the 1880s, 1890s and early 1900s Paul and Maria watched as hundreds of people left the noncommunal Hutterite churches for the KMB. One wonders how they felt about all of this.

The relationship between the two groups was further complicated when marriages crossed the denominational divide. In mixed marriages the KMB member was always immediately accepted into the independent Hutterite church as a full participant. KMB-administered baptisms were recognized as valid. But the reverse was not the case. If a Neu Hutterthaler member married a KMB woman, he was not immediately admitted to membership in a KMB church. Not even the acknowledgment of a personal relationship with God and a belief in the assurance of salvation would bring him into the fold; not even an adult baptism. First he had to be re-baptized by the proper mode (immersion).

To independent Hutterites all of this indicated a position of Krimmer spiritual superiority. The KMB position, alternatively, was that they were simply making sure that the church was comprised of true believers and that since Jesus was baptized by immersion in the Jordan River, his followers should be baptized in the same manner. Traditional Hutterians were viewed with suspicion; as people who were unduly wedded to the past, like Judaizers in the Early Church, like the people the Apostle Paul battled against in the Book of Galatians and elsewhere. Hutterites needed a religious reawakening; a new start

---

45. Mrs. Joseph W. Tschetter, *My Life Story*, 9. In the book the words, "a dying to self" are published in bold print.

46. Ibid., 1.

spiritually. Requesting a new baptism confirmed an individual's spiritual commitment. This was not asking too much of a new member.

Alcohol and the Christian Faith

The KMB also took a strong stand against the use of alcohol. This contrasted with the Hutterite position that allowed alcohol consumption in moderation. Anyone who visits Hutterite colonies is aware of this. A glass of homemade fruit wine is often offered before the guest indicates whether or not he imbibes. The Hutterite Chronice notes that since Jesus commanded his disciples to drink wine in the New Testament that he will expect his followers to do likewise when they meet him in heaven. The biblical reference supporting this position is Matthew 26-29 (RSV): "And I tell you I shall not drink again of this fruit of the vine until that day when I drink it new with you in my Father's kingdom." "Now Rod, a Hutterite minister once told me with a glimmer in his eye, 'how can we question what Jesus has told us?'"[47]

The Rev. Paul Tschetter was no teetotaler. He drank a jigger of schnapps every day before lunch. Granddaughter Anna Fisher said that each evening before retiring he asked for a glass of wine.[48] Anna felt honored that she was allowed to take the glass to him. (Anna told the author that her KMB father "snuck" drinks inside the barn.) Another granddaughter, Justina Guericke, recalled that when Hutterite colony ministers visited Tschetter during World War I, that he "served each a glass of wine or even a stronger drink—whiskey." She continued, "How those elders hung around that room until the bottle of liquor was gone. Then they departed without making any decisions. Were they interested in the War situation or in the drinks is a question that remains unanswered."[49]

Arnold M. Hofer, who grew up at the Neu Hutterthaler Church, and who later joined the KMB, said that when he was young it was his job to take the wine grapes off the back of a truck and to "stomp them" with his bare feet.[50] The wine was then aged in a large barrel in the basement. On one occasion the wine barrel developed a leak, causing wine to run

---

47. Hans Decker, interview, July, 1988.
48. Paul G. Tschetter, "Die Auswanderer."
49. Guericke, *Precious Memories of a Historical House*, 3.
50. Arnold M. Hofer, interview, May 2004.

out onto the floor and down under the foundation to a small enclosure where his father deposited important documents. These papers were kept in a metal box and included the deed to his land. Bridgewater farmer Tim Glanzer, who eventually purchased this land from Hofer, holds the original deed, which is permanently stained with the color purple.

In reality persons who joined the KMB Church were most concerned about the free-flowing consumption of liquor that was found at some Hutterite events, for example, weddings, where, as one older Prairieleut man told the author, "they served beer from five or ten gallon kegs."[51] But to quit using alcohol entirely seemed unnecessary to Paul Tschetter. And some KMBs continued to make wine for medicinal purposes. California KMB Egon Hofer recalls helping his grandmother make wine from Muscat grapes.[52]

Other Krimmer Mennonite Brethren Distinctives

The way that KMB selected ministers also reflected a more individualistic spiritual ethic. Members believed that God called individuals both directly and through the affirmation of the body of believers. Individual and communal angles intertwined, whereas in traditional Hutterite practice, the communal structure dominated. In the Hutterite context no one talked about a personal call from God. This was looked on as an indication of pride and took away the authenticating power of the church as the body of Christ. If someone ever said he "wanted" to become a minister he would likely never be nominated for the position. This continues to be the case in Hutterite colonies in the twenty-first century.

KMB sermons were also different; they were written by the ministers themselves, assumably under the direction of God's Spirit. They were generally delivered without notes, some extemporaneously, although ministers usually created a rough outline during the week. KMB believed that Paul Tschetter and the Neu Hutterthaler congregation was limiting the power of God's Spirit by reading sermons written by ministers in past centuries and with outdated references. Paul Tschetter was being idolatrous when he viewed the *Lehren* as holy writ.

---

51. Andrew Hofer, interview, November 1985.
52. Egon Hofer, interview, July 1997.

The Hutterian response was to ask KMBs why they believed that the Bible itself, written hundreds of years earlier with its own singular examples, could speak to Christians in the late 1800s. In the Hutterian view the *Lehren* did not replace the Bible, but like the Bible, the sermons were inspired by the Holy Spirit. This attempt reminded KMBs of the Roman Catholic justification for what they considered to be extra-biblical teachings. The debate continued.

At worship services, the KMB sang bouncy gospel hymns with positive messages, as compared to the slow, though emotion-laden and loud, drone and heavy lyrics that characterized Hutterite hymns. The latter often emphasized the heroic experiences of suffering for the faith of the ancient martyrs. The new hymns praised God joyfully and spoke about personal transformation.

KMB spirituality placed significant emphasis on the "heart" and this bothered Paul Tschetter. His own stance on emotionalism in the Christian faith is shown in negative comments that are included in his 1873 diary. Tschetter was more concerned about the tangible practice of the faith, the works that should accompany religious commitment. He did not give much credence to individual feelings or verbal expressions. This does not indicate a lack of deep spirituality; he just expressed his faith in a different way. Tschetter was more interested in the fact that many KMBs showed moral improvement in the lives after being "saved." This he could admire.

A similarly critical opinion on the place of emotions in worship was expressed by Mennonite Peter Jansen in his reflections on a summer 1873 visit to North America. With reference to an experience in Ontario he notes:

> Something entirely new to us were the "revivals" which were being held during the long winter evenings at the various churches. We were not accustomed to the emotional and sensational religion which was being expounded here, and it seemed ridiculous to see the antics some of the newly "converted" cut up. Father, although a devout Christian, did not believe in this kind of religion, but we children had lots of fun.[53]

Emotional revival services were central to KMB evangelism and this was upsetting to Paul Tschetter. Still he never cut off relationships with his KMB children. "He was never hostile," as Paul G. Tschetter puts

---

53. Jansen, *Memoirs of Peter Jansen*, 40.

it.[54] In fact Tschetter was attracted to many KMB emphases, especially, as noted, a strong focus on morality and individual ethics. He liked the KMB emphasis on a personal relationship with Christ even though he thought this could be developed within the context of Hutterian church traditions. Tschetter admired the pastoral and evangelistic work undertaken by two of his sons, although he did not feel called to do the same. According to older KMB Prairieleut, Tschetter often expressed that he was impressed by the spirituality exhibited in the daily lives of many KMB members.

Many descendents contend that Paul Tschetter told family members that he would have left the Neu Hutterthaler Church and joined the KMB if his own "flock" had not needed him so much. Dozens of people have told me this story and, whether true or not, it is now part of Prairieleut KMB folklore. It is true that Tschetter engaged in little public criticism of the KMB. But the story of a desired denominational transfer has not been authenticated. No one has located any first person accounts. Grandson Paul G. Tschetter (a KMB) insisted that Paul Tschetter never discussed this with him and that it may reflect wishful thinking. Instead, according to this KMB grandson, the Rev. Tschetter expressed distress that his family did not stay at Neu Hutterthaler to "help me out."[55] It is hard to imagine Paul Tschetter being rebaptized in the Wolf Creek. In the fourth volume of the *Mennonite Encyclopedia,* published in 1959, Melvin Gingerich inaccurately refers to Paul Tschetter as "a leader in the group which joined the Krimmer Mennonite Brethren."[56] As Paul G. Tschetter put it, "If he [the Rev. Tschetter] thought this were said of him he would turn over in his grave."[57]

---

54. Paul G. Tschetter, "The Legacy of Paul Tschetter," 6.

55. Paul G. Tschetter, interview, July 1998.

56. *MennEncy,* 4:753. The entry on Paul Tschetter was written by Melvin Gingerich.

57. Paul G. Tschetter, "The Legacy of Paul Tschetter," 3.

10

The Final Years

> It is clear ... that a Christian may neither go to war nor seek revenge. Anyone who does has abandoned Christ and His way ... The sword of this world removes the person from earthly life, depriving him for evermore of the chance to repent.
>
> —Peter Walpot, 1547

The World War I Years

DURING HIS FINAL TWO YEARS OF LIFE PAUL TSCHETTER WAS CONFRONTed with military service demands related to the United States involvement in World War I. This meant confrontations with government officials at national, state and local levels. It also meant many conversations with church members, especially young men. Colony ministers as well sought Paul Tschetter's counsel.

On April 6, 1917, the United States declared war on Germany and beginning in June 1917, the United States Government required that all males between the ages of twenty-one and thirty-one register for the draft as the country prepared to enter the world conflict. The wartime milieu and required military service led to a series of "earnest prayer meetings" at the Neu Hutterthaler Church and what Jacob E. Hofer describes as an "awakening among the Mennonites."[1] For the first time since arriving in North America the historic Anabaptist commitment to pacifism was put to the test.[2] It was a difficult struggle for many Prairieleut, who enjoyed life in the United States and considered themselves model citizens, yet had been taught never to take up arms,

---

1. NHCRB, 29.
2. J. E. Hofer, "A History of the Neu Hutterthaler Church," 41.

not even in self-defense. Equally problematic was the Hutterian identification with the German language and German culture in general.

Soon after declaring war, the state of South Dakota prohibited the use of the German language in church services, schools, and even telephone conversations, showing what Paul Tschetter described as "hatred toward the German people."[3] George Rath notes a wave of hysteria in the state that led to a general hatred of all things German.[4] South Dakota historian Herbert Schell describes a "spirit of intolerance" that led patriotic citizens to "dump German textbooks into the Missouri River," rename frankfurters "hot dogs," and express concern about the loyalty of all German-speaking people.[5] Especially disconcerting were German-speaking pacifists (i.e. Hutterites and Mennonites), who refused to support the war effort with their lives.

Paul Tschetter described the conflict in general as "the so-called World War."[6] His two-page discussion of the war period is found in Appendix B. According to Tschetter,

> After our Church had practiced its faith in peace and quiet for 40 years, the so called World War broke out in Europe on August 4, 1914, which here and there caused much anxiety among the brethren because the older brethren knew from experience that God would punish his people.[7]

Tshetter hated war and he wrote against what he now described as "the murder and slaughter of people." The Neu Hutterthaler Church, furthermore, never obeyed the law against the use of German in services.[8] As the Rev. Tschetter put it, "In spite of the fact that this ordinance gave us much grief, we never abided by it in our Church, even though the minister of this particular day approached the pulpit with a heavy heart. The spirit of the Lord reminded us that we must obey God more than man."[9] Neu Hutterthaler members were cautioned, however, not to speak German or Hutterisch when people who were not well-known were listening. Paul's

---

3. NHCRB, 29.
4. Rath, *The Black Sea Germans in Dakota*.
5. Schell, *A History of South Dakota*, 273.
6. NHCRB, 25.
7. Ibid.
8. Ibid.
9. Ibid., 30.

youngest brother, Bethel KMB Church (Huron, South Dakota) pastor John Tschetter, took a stronger stand saying the authorities were welcome "to arrest him" but he too would not quit speaking German.[10] It is also true that some Prairieleut had divided loyalties, not recognizing significant differences between the Central Powers (Germany and Austria-Hungary) and the United Kingdom and France. From 1914 to 1917, Jacob J. Mendel's Freeman *Courier* advocated neutrality in the war effort, and before the war began one national Mennonite periodical placed Germany's Kaiser Wilhelm on the front cover.[11]

Ironically, at the same time, distant Hutterian relatives in Habaner communities in Slovakia faced similar legislation against the use of German as a result of popular and ethnocentric sentiments in those regions.[12] The state of South Dakota did eventually authorize German-speaking ministers to give a fifteen minute review of their sermons in German at the end of each Sunday morning service.[13]

According to Paul Tschetter the Bible passage that reads "Rachel weeping for her children refused to be comforted" was never truer than at this difficult time.[14] As Jacob E. Hofer writes, "Sons were torn from the arms of their mothers. Fathers had to carry their sons from the house because they did not want go and give military service."[15] Paul Tschetter wrote that the "grief brought both young and old upon their knees and many tears were shed."[16] The biggest problem was the absence of alternative service options for conscientious objectors, which in later years provided a way for patriotic Hutterians to show their love of country in other ways. But in 1917 and 1918 the South Dakota Council of Defense and local defense councils were diligent in making sure that all qualified men reported for duty and the United States Government did not provide exceptions for pacifists. There were no forms of alternative national service for conscientious objectors.

According to the Neu Hutterthaler church record book, the war "caused much anxiety." Justina Glanzer describes "fear and trembling" as

10. Kleinsasser, *A History of the Bethel Mennonite Church, 1919-1979*, 22.
11. M. J. F. Funk, "Divided Loyalites," 28.
12. Waltner, "Among the Habaner of Czechoslovakia," 89.
13. Schell, *A History of South Dakota*, 273.
14. NHCRB, 29.
15. J. E. Hofer, "History of the Neu Hutterthaler Church," 42.
16. NHCRB, 28.

young men were drafted."[17] There were many meetings, much counseling, and written petitions were sent to President Woodrow Wilson, one as early as June 5, 1917. Unlike forty-four years earlier, Tschetter did not seek a personal meeting with a United States President. But the issues were the same; U.S. Grant's "no war for fifty years" prediction did not hold. It had already been abrogated in 1898, with the Spanish-American War and the Philippines civil war that followed. Prairieleut Alex Wipf enlisted and served in the Philippine conflict.[18]

Paul Tschetter did his part for the pacifist cause by helping young males complete registration forms, locate baptism dates, and seek conscientious objector status. Tschetter also held many special prayer meetings at the Neu Hutterthaler Church. As a result very few non-KMB Prairieleut enlisted in the armed forces during World War I.[19] But they were drafted nonetheless. Two men from Neu Hutterthaler, Joseph Gross and Jacob Hofer, were the first called to duty (on September 22, 1917). Many others followed.[20] To escape the draft at least thirty Prairieleut males fled to Canada, some of the accompanied by their families.[21] One of Paul Tschetter's cousins, Daniel Wurz, was one of these men. Paul Tschetter's assistant minister, Johann Hofer, accompanied another young man, Peter J. S. Hofer, on his journey across the northern border.[22] Other Prairieleut were more fortunate securing family, medical, and farm deferments.

Colony, KMB, and independent church Hutterians were ordered to report to the railroad station at Parkston, South Dakota, where they boarded trains that took them to the military training camps. The men were then often transferred from one place to another.[23] In the military camps there were many temptations and unrelenting discrimination. Young Hutterians were constantly asked to display their patriotism and

---

17. Guericke, *Precious Memories*, 5.

18. Mendel, *A History of the People of East Freeman, Silver Lake and West Freeman*, 117.

19. Guericke, *Precious Memories*, 3.

20. NHCRB, 28.

21. A. M. Hofer, ed., "The Diary of Rev. Jacob J. Hofer Diary, 1900–1920," August 1918 entry.

22. R. Janzen, *The Prairie People*, 146.

23. NHCRB, 30.

they were called "yellow" or "slackers" for their nonresistant beliefs.[24] Most draftees suffered personal insults and taunts and many endured physical attacks. Because Prairieleut and communal Hutterite young men often refused to carry guns and perform requested drills a number of them were court-martialed.[25] Others were placed in solitary confinement and some served time in federal prison.

One young man, Jacob Hofer, joined the military as a combatant and was killed and buried at the Battle of Verdun.[26] A few others served in noncombatant positions, wearing uniforms in medical, forestry, and engineering units. In contrast, among the Prairieleut KMB congregations, forty-eight percent of the draftees performed 1-A military service, a striking phenomenon that went against the conference's own pacifist position, although it is important to note that when one adds young men who secured legal deferments, the total percentage of KMB young men who performed military service is reduced fifteen to twenty percent. Comparative statistics for men in the independent Hutterite churches are not available, but church records and memoirs indicate a much stronger commitment to the peace position. Much of this is likely due to the influence of Paul Tschetter (and others) who took a strong pacifist stand. This was not easy to do.

During World War I, many prominent Prairieleut exhibited superpatriotic attitudes and actions that were highly supportive of the war. For example, Jacob J. Mendel, editor of the Freeman *Courier*, served on the Hutchinson County Council of Defense, an organization that did not allow family deferments for colony Hutterites.[27] Mendel did not support the pacifist position that his parents fled Russia to preserve. This shows the powerful impact of American democracy and the American way of life.

The response to World War I illuminated profound differences within the Prairieleut community and even to some extent at the Neu Hutterthaler Church, although this was not the case in Paul Tschetter's own family. In 1918, son, Joseph W., by then a KMB minister, vis-

24. Ibid.

25. Homan, "Mennonites and Military Justice in World War I," 368. Peter M. Waldner court papers. HHMA.

26. NHCRB, 30. Arnold M. Hofer and Norman Hofer, taped interview with Paul L. Hofer, 1991. HMCC.

27. M. J. F. Funk, "Divided Loyalties," 30.

ited imprisoned communal Hutterite conscientious objectors at Fort Leavenworth, Kansas.

The communal Hutterites suffered the most in the military camps because they refused to wear uniforms and were thus accused of insubordination. Colony Hutterite men also wore beards for religious reasons and refused to shave them off. They were forcibly removed nonetheless after recruits first had fun pulling on them and cutting them into ridiculous shapes. The distinctive style of dress and strong dialects of the often naïve colony members made them perfect targets for verbal and physical abuse. Two young men from Rockport Colony were treated so badly that they died at Fort Leavenworth after being forced to stand outside for hours during a cold Kansas winter. The two men, Joseph and Michael Hofer, had been transferred to Leavenworth as criminals after previously being locked up in the high-security prison on Alcatraz Island in San Francisco Bay because they refused to drill and wear the uniform.[28]

Many colony Hutterites and some Prairieleut also refused to purchase Liberty Bonds, which helped support the war effort. We do not know Paul Tschetter's position on this issue, but other Prairieleut ministers instructed their congregants to purchase bonds as an example of good citizenship. We know that Neu Hutterthaler member Samuel S. W. Glanzer and his brother, Jacob, refused to do this and as a result they were temporarily thrown in a jail cell, where they sang hymns like their imprisoned ancestors in Europe. According to Glanzer's daughter, "There (in jail) he sat and cried and prayed. Then they wanted to lock the door but couldn't. The key wouldn't work. Then they said that he was no bad man, he won't run away. They swore. A woman said that we ought to cut out the tongue of the man."[29]

The Glanzers were released from jail after paying a $1000 fine. Jacob Glanzer went home and told his family that they were moving to Saskatchewan, which they did immediately, not even bothering to remove food from their dining room table. A number of Prairieleut families moved to Canada so that their sons would not be conscripted. These included the William J. Walter, Henry C. Gross, Joseph E. Wipf, and Andrew Gross families.[30] Neu Hutterthaler Church records indi-

---

28. American Industrial Company, eds., *Crucifixions in the 20th Century*.
29. Glanzer, *Life's Story of Samuel W. Glanzer and Justina S. W. Glanzer*, 5–6.
30. R. Janzen, *The Prairie People*, 137.

cate that many young men from the congregation fled to Saskatchewan. These included Paul L. and Jacob Hofer. In a 1991 taped interview, Paul L. noted that in early August 1918, his father "with no warning" announced one evening that he and his two sons would be taking a train to Canada the next morning. "Fill up your trunks with clothes you think you might need," he instructed.[31] There were also local investigations by the FBI, which sent agents to the Freeman community to assess subversive activities.[32]

Due to constant harassment most of the Hutterite colonies relocated to Canada during or following the World War I period. In 1918, for example, members of the aforementioned Kutter Colony moved to Redlands, Alberta, where they established the Rosebud Colony. This was the colony constructed on Peter Tschetter's original homestead.

After the armistice on November 11, 1918, Paul Tschetter wrote that "the joy of the parents was indescribable as their sons returned."[33] On October 19, 1919, the Neu Hutterthaler congregation met for a special evening of Thanksgiving (*Dankfest*), exactly one year after the last young man from the congregation returned from the military camps. Unfortunately the Neu Hutterthaler Church was hit simultaneously by the "Spanish influenza" or swine flu epidemic that spread across the United States after the war ended. Paul Tschetter described the epidemic as "a pestilence that covered the wide earth."[34] It led to the death of his niece, Anna Tschetter Hofer, as well as Neu Hutterthaler member Andreas Walter.[35]

The Final Years

Arnold M. Hofer recalled that as a boy of three, his parents took him to the funeral of "a very important person."[36] Looking back he believed this person was probably the Rev. Paul Tschetter.

For many years Paul Tschetter's youngest son, David W., his spouse Anna Tschetter, and their family lived with Paul and Maria at the home

---

31. Arnold M. Hofer and Norman Hofer, taped interview with Paul L. Hofer, 1991). HHMA.

32. Ibid.

33. J. E. Hofer, "A History of the Neu Hutterthaler Church," 48.

34. NHCRB, 30.

35. J. A. Tschetter, "Family History," 2.

36. Arnold M. Hofer, interview, May 2004.

place. They assisted with the farming operation and cared for their parents even while they attended a different church (the Salem KMB Church). Paul G. Tschetter, a son of David W., had fond memories of these years when he was living in the same house as his grandfather. "During long and often cold winter evenings," Paul G. said, he and his brother gathered around the stove, while the Rev. Tschetter entertained them with stories. Paul G. recalled the "coal embers glaring bright red, visible through the mica doors" and apples baking on the ledge "where the chimney left the stove."[37] The two boys listened while their grandfather told Bible stories as well as many tales about life in Russia.[38] Paul G. said that the Bible stories "came to life" and that they included "Daniel in the Lion's Den" and "Joseph sold by his brothers."[39]

In 1914, however, David W. felt called to the ministry. So he left the home place and enrolled at the Mennonite Tabor College (in Hillsboro, Kansas) for formal Bible instruction. Paul and Maria were now in their early seventies and unable to take care of the farm by themselves. They needed assistance with other personal needs as well. So they moved in with their daughter, Justina, and her husband Christian (Christ) Hofman and hired a local laborer, Gustav Schulz, to farm their land.[40] Ironically, Gustav was a heavy smoker and drinker and Christ Hofman often brought cans of tobacco for him when he was in town. Granddaughter, Justina, often wondered, "What if grandfather was in the dining room and he would see all that tobacco?"[41]

This decision of David W. to move to Kansas was heavily criticized by Paul and Maria's son, "Big Paul," who felt that his brother was deserting his parents and turning his back on a sacred obligation. "Big Paul" was incensed that David W., as the youngest son in the family, was reneging on the responsibility to take care of his parents until their respective deaths. In "Big Paul's" view, the family farm was theirs to inherit, but only if they kept their part of this important charge.[42]

Paul G. Tschetter recalled that his grandfather was devastated by son David W.'s decision to leave South Dakota. As Paul G. noted,

37. Paul G. Tschetter, "Anecdotes."
38. Ibid., 1.
39. Ibid., 2.
40. Guericke, *Precious Memories*, 48.
41. Ibid., 49.
42. Paul G. Tschetter, interview, July 1998.

"I will always remember that cold night in fall with all boxes packed when grandpa [Paul Tschetter] came to the barn, looked it over and shook his head."[43] Still relationships were not cut off. Paul G. said that on one occasion the Rev. Tschetter visited them at their new home in central Kansas.

A bigger blow for the Rev. Tschetter was the loss of his wife, Maria. She died at 4:40 A.M., on December 21, 1915, from the aftereffects of a stroke that included cardiac failure and pneumonia.[44] At the time of her death Maria was seventy-two years of age. The Neu Hutterthaler record book notes "[Maria] suffered much for nine days. She had to sit day and night. Because of her breath[ing] she could not lay down."[45] During the previous summer son, David W. and family returned to the home place from Kansas to help take care of her.

Paul and Maria were married for over fifty-five years. In her autobiography, Katharina Tschetter said that she and her husband, Joseph W., traveled from Chicago to visit Maria as late as in mid-December 1915. They found Maria "sitting in a chair with heart trouble."[46] Yet she greeted them "heartily" saying, "I thought after I will see you both and hear your voices I will die; now I live on just the same."[47] But Maria died a few days later "while sitting in a chair and talking." Her body was kept in a cemetery building until all of her children could attend the funeral. This was possible due to the extremely cold winter climate. Susanna Decker (who resided in Langham, Saskatchewan) was the only child of Paul and Maria Tschetter who was unable to attend the funeral.

After Maria's death Paul Tschetter remained with the Hofman family. All the rest of Paul and Maria's children, with the exception of the single "Big Paul" and the Jacob W. Tschetter family, had left the Freeman area and were now living in various parts of the United States and Canada.

Granddaughter Anna Hofman Fisher recalled a number of incidents from these final four "lonely" years of Paul Tschetter's life. Interviewed in a nursing home in Ashley, North Dakota a few weeks before her death in June 2004, Anna said she was between the ages of

43. Paul G. Tschetter, "The Legacy of Paul Tschetter," 2.
44. Ibid.
45. NHCRB, 831
46. Mrs. Joseph W. Tschetter, *My Life Story*, 28.
47. Ibid.

three and seven when her grandfather lived with them. The Hofman's owned a large six-bedroom house so there was plenty of room and it was situated only a couple of hundred yards from Paul Tschetter's original residence. Anna said that her parents gave Tschetter a private room (the "grandpa room") on the first floor, where he spent most of his time, even eating meals separately, just like a Hutterite colony minister. Anna talked to her grandfather often, however, and he continued to do "some physical work" on the farm.

Anna's older sister, Justina, recalled how overjoyed her grandfather was when, in the fall of 1917 her mother gave birth to a daughter she named "Maria." Paul Tschetter was "so proud" of his wife's namesake, she wrote that "he purchased a fancy baby buggy with a top."[48] Justina also recalled, "Since he was a minister and was still preaching at that time, we children enjoyed him. Daily we sat in his room and devoured with the greatest interest the bible stories he told us. These precious memories stayed with us throughout our entire lives."[49]

On October 25, 1918, Paul Tschetter suffered an incapacitating stroke in the midst of the influenza epidemic. Soon thereafter Joseph W. and Katharina received a telegram in Chicago requesting that they return immediately to South Dakota. On arrival they found the seventy-seven year-old Tschetter lying "helpless in bed" and unable to speak.[50] As granddaughter Justina put it, "He needed much attention from this time on."[51] Daughter Barbara and husband A. A. Stahl came from Saskatchewan to assist during this time when a number of family members were suffering from influenza.

After the stroke, Paul Tschetter spoke very little though he could still walk slowly around the property. According to the Neu Hutterthaler record book, the stroke not only caused Tschetter to lose his voice; it also "lamed his right hand."[52] Later, at least periodically, his speech returned in the form of a loud whisper. He continued to attend church whenever he was able to do so.

Anna Fisher said that her grandfather's inability to speak made it difficult for her mother to tell what he wanted to eat. On one occasion

48. Guericke, *Precious Memories*, 15.
49. Ibid., 49.
50. Mrs. Joseph W. Tschetter, *My Life Story*, 29.
51. Guericke, *Precious Memories*, 22.
52. NHCRB, 32.

the Rev. Tschetter kept pointing toward the barn, as Anna's exasperated mother, Justina, tried to guess what he was asking them to cook. She tried the words "beef," "chicken" and various garden vegetables but the Rev. Tschetter continued to shake his head. Finally, Justina said the word "milk" and she received an affirmative nod. Further nonverbal communication indicated that Tschetter wanted her to pour the milk into a bowl of rice.

On another occasion, the family found Paul Tschetter climbing precariously up the side of a windmill for no discernible reason. Fortunately, when family members "yelled for him to get down," he did so.[53] Anna also remembered her grandfather driving around in a buggy with a top carried by "a little brownish horse" named "Buller" (named after the man who sold them the horse). Before his stroke, Tschetter hitched "Buller" up regularly to visit members of his congregation. When he conducted church services in the Olivet area he typically stayed overnight, returning on Monday morning.

Anna said that on one occasion her grandfather took a ride in an automobile. This was unexpected since family members say that Paul Tschetter commonly referred to automated vehicles as "devil's fire wagons" and said that he would never step foot in one. After his stroke, however, he insisted on attending a funeral in the Olivet area and Christ Hofman said that he would only take him if he agreed to ride in Christ's Ford automobile, which had been purchased for 400 dollars in September, 1917.[54] Paul Tschetter reluctantly agreed but church members later criticized Christ heavily for making this demand on his father-in-law.[55]

Anna said that her grandfather was a kind old man who expressed deep concern for her personal welfare after she contracted polio at age five. The disease affected Anna's ability to walk but she often crawled into her grandfather's room even though she was instructed not to bother him. Anna remembered that the Rev. Tschetter responded to her presence with comforting glances even though he was unable to communicate verbally. Anna also recalled her grandfathers' specific admonition (later) that as a woman she should always wear a scarf tied in front and fastened with a pin.

53. Anna Hofman Fisher, interview, May 2004.
54. Ibid.
55. Guericke, *Precious Memories*, 21.

In contrast to the image of a rigid unforgiving traditionalist, granddaughter Anna Fisher described a man who on occasion exhibited a spirit of toleration. She reminded that her mother Justina's marriage to a non-Hutterian, Christ Hofman, was not well-accepted at the Neu Hutterthaler Church or in the Prairieleut community at-large. Justina was told by many people not to marry "that Russian" (Hofman came from Germans-from-Russia Lutheran background).[56] As noted Tschetter's response was that "as long as you love him" he would support the marriage. Tschetter also instructed Justina to "treat him (Christ) well."

Anna said that her father, Christ, once accompanied the now-silent Rev. Tschetter to a service at the Neu Hutterthaler Church. That same afternoon, at his home, the KMB, Christ expressed great frustration with the very traditional Neu Hutterthaler service. He told his daughter, Justina, that the preacher had even misspoken at one point stating that Jesus died at "California." This had led someone in the congregation to yell out "No, it was at Golgotha." In later years this story provoked much laughter (at least for Christ).[57]

During his last years of life, at least before the stroke, Anna said that many people visited her grandfather in his bedroom seeking advice and counsel. On one occasion she recalled a number of people lined up waiting to see him. In 1916, Paul Tschetter presided over his last marriage ceremony, the nuptials of Jacob J. S. Hofer and Sarah Pollman.[58] Two years later, in 1918, he baptized a final group of twenty young people.[59] Grandson, Paul G. Tschetter stated that his grandfather prepared for Neu Hutterthaler's future by "naming" David J. Wipf as his successor as senior minister.[60] Paul G. likely meant that the Rev. Tschetter "recommended" Wipf. In any case Tschetter's health was never the same after October 1918, and a little over one year later, on the morning of November 17, 1919, he was found "dead in bed" at the Hofman house after suffering a second, this time fatal, stroke.[61]

Paul G. Tschetter, who was twelve at the time, said that right before experiencing this terminal stroke his grandfather felt "light-headed and

56. Anna Hofman Fisher, interview, May 2004.
57. Mrs. Joseph W. Tschetter, *My Life Story*, 30.
58. NHCRB, 789.
59. Ibid., 672.
60. Paul G. Tschetter, "Monologue."
61. NHCRB, 833.

heard voices." Later Paul G. created an imaginative metaphorical account of this "vision" based on what Paul G. called a "personal incident," i.e. "suggestive" comments from his grandfather. The story has the soul of Paul Tschetter standing by a river with Maria motioning to him to cross over to the other side (to heaven). Jesus then appears, takes Paul's hand, and leads him across the water to Maria and his final place of rest.[62]

When Paul Tschetter died, Joseph W. and Katherina Tschetter received a telegram requesting that they be present at his funeral. According to spouse Katherina, Joseph W.'s initial response was that he was "too busy doing the Lord's work" to attend. Instead Joseph wired a personal statement to be read at the service. The extended family was not happy with this response, however, and would not take "no" for an answer. A second telegram to Joseph W. stated firmly, "The grave is not covered yet, please come." Joseph relented and was present at the "closing the grave" ceremony. Following Hutterite custom, Paul Tschetter was not buried until two days after the funeral when he was laid to rest at the Neu Hutterthaler Church cemetery. In 1974 a special historical marker was placed near his grave. The complete "Hutterite Memorial" text is found in Appendix D. Some of the words on the marker read as follows:

> After centuries of religious persecution in various parts of Europe, God's providence through the leadership of Rev. Paul Tschetter 1842–1919 and Lorenz Tschetter 1819–1878, brought them to America between 1874–1879. Rev. Paul Tschetter settled near this site and his grave is near by. Lorenz Tschetter settled near Olivet, So. Dak., where a simple slab marks his grave on a lonely hill one mile Southeast of Olivet.

At Paul Tschetter's gravesite Anna Fisher broke down in tears. She said that she cried so much and made so much noise that her mother told her if she did not stop they would have to place Anna in the grave alongside her grandfather.[63]

Afterward

After Paul Tschetter's death, the Neu Hutterthaler Church went through a slow process of assimilation moving slowly in evangelical Protestant

---

62. Paul G. Tschetter, "Monologue." Paul G. Tschetter, interview, June 1998.
63. Anna Hofman Fisher, interview, May 2004.

directions. Neu Hutterthaler members continued to speak Hutterisch at home and with friends, and to worship God in German, but they increasingly accepted most American social norms. Developing personal and business relationships with non-Hutterites led to corresponding changes in belief and practice.

These developments led to internal conflict between evangelicals and traditionalists. Jacob E. Hofer (writing in 1953) noted: "Whether we like it or not the fact remains that for some time there [has been] lack of harmony, discord and disagreement among the members."[64] For many years after Paul Tschetter's death Neu Hutterthaler ministers held the line with regard to Hutterian traditions. They read the *Lehren* until 1947 (though an increasing number of comments "off the sermon" were added). Members followed Hutterian social and ecclesiastical customs until mid-century as the congregation continued to be known as the most traditional of the Prairieleut churches.

The first movement toward significant change occurred in 1941, with the onset of World War II. At this time Neu Hutterthaler joined the General Conference Mennonite denomination due to the benefit of collective peace church negotiation in support of alternative nonmilitary service. Although the church conducted services in German throughout the war, the installation of the congregation's first non-Hutterian minister (Albert Ewert, in 1947) meant not only the beginning of English services but the end of seventeenth-century Huterites sermons.

Albert Ewert's pastorate was a significant juncture; when the congregation moved from specifically Hutterian theological interpretations in the traditional sermons to the exegetical and oratorical skills of individual preachers. The church moved away from institutionalized, and relatively unquestioned, communal historical traditions as it adopted a more democratic approach to decision-making and allowed greater input from members. These changes caused some attenders much turmoil as they saw innovations they did not like or understand. In the process many harsh words were said; many tears shed.

With reference to social issues the Neu Hutterthaler Church took a stand against bowling, gun ownership and musical instruments into the 1920s but without Paul Tschetter's presence these prohibitions were soon rescinded. Beginning in the 1920s Neu Hutterthaler also made small payments to supplant the income of its ministers. The first English

---

64. J. E. Hofer, "A History of the Neu Hutterthaler Church," 64.

language hymnal, *The Tabernacle Hymnal* was introduced in 1945 and the church purchased its first piano in 1946.

Theologically, the Neu Hutterthaler Church moved in evangelical directions. In 1951, Jacob E. Hofer wrote (apologetically), "Some persons familiar with the history of the church may be tempted to say that this congregation has not always believed in regeneration. I would admit that it has not received due emphasis. However to say that the church did not believe in it seems to be an untruth." Hofer wanted people to know that, at least in principle, Neu Hutterthaler had always been an "evangelical" congregation. Hofer continues, "Granting that there were members who did not approve of revival meetings there have also always been others to let their light shine."[65] Paul Tschetter was one of those who did not let his light shine, at least not in this way. Traditional ways of thinking were hard to give up.

From the 1920s to the 1960s the Neu Hutterthaler Church functioned as a vibrant body of believers with attendance figures hovering at the 150 mark. During the last thirty years of the twentieth century, however, Neu Hutterthaler saw its membership dwindle to a few stalwart families. In the 2000s Neu Hutterthaler continues to hold church services but with an average attendance of thirty or forty people and only a few young members. Ironically Neu Hutterthaler adolescents today attend youth group activities at the Salem Church and participate in regional and national Mennonite Brethren youth conventions.[66] The once-opposing churches hold joint pre-Easter services and Vacation Bible School programs.

Neu Hutterthaler's pastor, Kenneth Ontjes, previously pastored the Emery (South Dakota) Baptist Church and he is married to Alice Wipf, a great-granddaughter of early Neu Hutterthaler minister Johann Hofer.[67] Ontjes refers to Neu Hutterthaler as a "Sunday morning congregation" but notes there is still a core of committed members. Still Ontjes predicts that the church will cease to function when he retires.

The last Neu Hutterthaler Church constitution was published in 1974 and is basically a reprint of the congregation's 1948 *Constitution*.[68]

---

65. Ibid., 37.
66. The KMB merged with the Mennonite Brethren conference in 1960.
67. Glanzer, Wipf, and Hofer, eds., *A Century of God's Blessing*, 31.
68. *Constitution for the Neu Hutterthaler Mennonite Church* (March 1948). HHMA.

The document shows congregational adherence to evangelical and even fundamentalist theological positions including belief in the verbal inspiration and infallibility of the Bible. The church continues to adhere to Anabaptist "non-resistance."[69] In comparison to the lot-casting pastoral selection process that was never used by the Prairieleut in North America, Neu Hutterthaler selects its pastors by a two-thirds vote of the membership. The term of office is no longer for life; each assignment is three years in length with a vote of confidence held near the end of each term.[70]

In the end, whether noncommunal Hutterites stayed at Neu Hutterthaler, joined another independent Hutterite church or associated with the Krimmer Mennonite Brethren, the merger of all of these churches and conferences with much larger Mennonite groups led to the demise of distinctively Hutterian beliefs and practices. This happened in the independent Hutterite churches after they joined the General Conference Mennonites in the 1920s, 1930s and 1940s. It happened for KMB Hutterians when that denomination merged with the Mennonite Brethren in 1960.

Marriage outside of the ethnic group sealed the transformation to a multi-cultural identity that was no longer purely Hutterian. As noted in the book *The Prairie People: Forgotten Anabaptists*, a study of the Hutterite population in the Zion KMB Church (Dinuba, California) showed that in this mixed Hutterian/Low German Mennonite congregation, there was no marriage between someone of Hutterite and Mennonite background before the year 1940. After this date Hutterite/Mennonite marriages were the norm with Hutterite/Hutterite marriages almost non-existent by the late 1950s.[71] The Mennonitization that Paul Tschetter feared and actively fought against much of his life, in Ukraine and in South Dakota, proceeded forward in the end, although Hutterians gave many Mennonite congregations a special cultural and theological flavor for a long period of time.

---

69. Ibid., Article IV (April, 1974). HHMA.
70. Ibid., Article X.
71. R. Janzen, *The Prairie People*, 238.

The Descendents of Paul Tschetter

Descendents of Paul Tschetter and Maria Walter held regularly-scheduled extended family reunions between 1960 and 1995. These events included many stories from older descendents, some of which were preserved in handwritten statements. At the 1993 reunion a group of girls from the Oak Lane Colony (Alexandria, South Dakota) sang a number of hymns, reminding the Tschetter descendents of their communitarian past. A primary focus of the reunions is to ensure that younger family members do not forget their heritage. After one gathering, farmer and active Mennonite Brethren church leader, Ben Hofer, pulled out a dusty, framed portrait of the Rev. Tschetter, his great-grandfather and hung it up in his living room. After a ten-year lapse, another Paul Tschetter reunion was held in late April, 2005. About seventy-five people attended this event, which included a tour of the elder's original homestead and the nearby properties of his siblings and parents. Participants also visited the Neu Hutterthaler and Salem KMB church sites and cemeteries.

What follows is a brief review of the life and activities of Paul and Maria Tschetter's twelve children, according to their order of birth. Paul and Maria's first child was daughter, Susanna, born in 1861 at the

Figure 10.1 Paul and Susanna Tschetter Decker and Family.
Photograph courtesy of Wesley Tschetter.

Figure 10.2 "Big Paul" Tschetter. Photograph courtesy of Wesley Tschetter.

Hutterthal village in south Ukraine. In May, 1880, Susanna married Paul Decker at the Neu Hutterthaler Church. They moved to Langham, Saskatchewan in 1901.[72] Before relocating, Paul Decker, a school teacher, taught many of Maria Tschetter's younger brothers and sisters. Susanna Decker died in 1943 at age eighty-two.

A second child, named Jacob, was born in 1863 but he did not survive infancy.[73] Paul and Maria's third child was Paul W., nicknamed "Big Paul" because of his large frame. "Big Paul" was born in 1865 and lived until 1943. He never married and was known throughout his life as an important counsel to members of his family, including many of his nieces and nephews.[74] Often noted is Big Paul's refusal to leave the Neu Hutterthaler Church until six years after the death of his father.

---

72. Wurtz and Masuk, *Rooted and Grounded in Love*, 80.
73. D. J. Tschetter, "The Rev. Paul Tschetter Family," 57. WTC.
74. Ibid.

The Final Years 207

Figure 10.3 Joshua M. and Marie Tschetter Hofer.
Photograph courtesy of Goldie Wedel.

The terms of "Big Paul's" will provided significant financial assistance to most of his immediate family members.

Paul and Maria Tschetter's fourth child, a second "Jacob," followed in 1867. Jacob died at age five, in the summer of 1873, while the Rev. Tschetter was investigating settlement possibilities in North America. The fifth child, Maria, was born in 1870. She married Joshua M. Hofer in November, 1889 and they farmed in the Bridgewater area for many years before moving to Beadle County (South Dakota) along with many other Prairieleut. Maria died in 1949 at age seventy-nine. She is the only child of Paul and Maria Tschetter who did not join the Krimmer Mennonite Brethren. Her membership was at the Hutterthal Prairieleut Church near Carpenter.

Next, and sixth in order of birth, was a daughter, Barbara, born in 1871. Barbara was killed in 1877, at age six, in the threshing ma-

Figure 10.4 Jacob W. and Susanna Decker Tschetter family.
Photograph courtesy of Wesley Tschetter.

chine accident described in chapter eight. A seventh child, Jacob W. (the third child that Paul and Maria named "Jacob") followed in 1874. Jacob married Susanna Decker in February, 1899 and farmed land south of the town of Emery. Jacob W. was the longest-lived of Paul and Maria Tschetter's immediate family. He died in 1960 at the age of eighty-five.

Paul and Maria Tschetter's eighth child, son Joseph W., was born in 1876. He was married to Katherina Hofer in December, 1901. Joseph W. and Katherina joined the KMB denomination in 1906 and committed themselves to life-long missionary work, first in North Carolina and later in the city of Chicago, where Joseph died in 1955. The church that Joseph W. Tschetter established in North Carolina continues to thrive in the 2000s.

Much information about Joseph W.'s life is included in spouse, Katherina's autobiography, *My Life Story*.[75] Joseph W. Tschetter's no holds barred approach to matters of faith is shown in his preaching and it shows clearly that he was the son of his father. In the middle of a sermon Joseph W. once told members of the Salem KMB Church that

---

75. Mrs. Joseph W. Tschetter, *My Life's Story*.

Figure 10.5 Joseph W. Tschetter
Photograph courtesy of Wesley Tschetter.

they were spending too much time watching the clock. He pointed to it and yelled out, "Now throw that thing out and let the Spirit work."[76]

Particularly noteworthy is Joseph W. and Katherina Tschetter's work supporting progressive race relations and peace as they ministered to African-Americans in North Carolina. The Tschetters adhered to segregationist principles by establishing a Black-only congregation. But the very fact that they were working with African-Americans was upsetting to local citizens, a few of whom threatened to hang Tschetter if he continued to evangelize in the Black community. On one occasion a white man offered to provide armed protection.[77] Joseph's response: "Bring your son along, but leave your guns at home. They will make

---

76. Wesley Tschetter, interview, May 2004.

77. Mrs. Joseph W. Tschetter, *My Life Story*, 12–14. A detailed account of Joseph W. Tschetter's life is Wesley Tschetter, "Biography of Rev. Joseph W. Tschetter (1876–1955). WTC.

Figure 10.6 North Carolina KMB Mission Church, 1919
Photograph courtesy of Wesley Tschetter

more trouble. Jesus nowhere teaches that we should force our way through with guns." On another occasion the mission church received a visit from members of the Ku Klux Klan. Joseph invited them into the church defusing any potential conflict. On a third occasion Joseph was knocked to the ground by someone who "pounded with his fist on my head." As he later put it, "Jesus teaches that we should not resist evil. I took the beating."

Joseph W. was followed by a sister Barbara (a second "Barbara"), Paul and Maria Tschetter's ninth child. Barbara was born in 1878 and in 1903 she married the Rev. Andrew A. Stahl who later pastored the Emmanuel KMB Church near Langham, Saskatchewan. Barbara returned to South Dakota only twice during her lifetime and died in 1954 at seventy-six years of age. One of her sons, Albert, the last living grandchild of Paul Tschetter, died in October, 2008. Barbara also had an unnamed twin brother who died at birth.

Paul and Maria Tschetter's eleventh child was Justina, born in 1880. Justina married the non-Hutterite, Christian (Christ) Hofman in 1905. Amazingly, the bride and groom walked from their respective homes to the Neu Hutterthaler Church for the wedding service. Before marrying Justina, Christ Hofman worked in the community as a farm laborer. He was raised as a Lutheran but later joined the Salem KMB Church, as did Justina. It was the Hofmans who took Paul and Maria Tschetter into

Figure 10.7 Andrew A. and Barbara Tschetter Stahl.
Photograph courtesy of Harold Stahl.

their home in 1914, and with whom Paul Tschetter lived for the rest of his life. Justina died in 1952 at age seventy-one.

Paul and Maria Tschetter's last child, their twelfth, was the aforementioned David W. Tschetter, born in 1882, when Maria was thirty-nine years of age. David W. married Anna Glanzer on the same date (December 7, 1905) that his sister Justina married Christ Hofman, in a joint ceremony conducted by the KMB Elder Dietrich Goossen. David died in August, 1955, at age seventy-two.

The Tschetter Persona

By the time of the mass immigration to North America the Hutterian ethno-religious group included nineteen family surnames. These included the following: Decker, Entz, Fast, Glanzer, Gross, Hofer, Janzen,

Figure 10.8 Christian and Justina Tschetter Hofman family. Photograph courtesy of Edith Hofer Tschetter.

Kleinsasser, Knels, Mendel, Miller, Pollman, Stahl, Tschetter, Waldner, Walter, Wipf, Wollman, and Wurz.

Like in many small communities throughout the world, certain Hutterite clans came to be associated with particular intellectual and emotional traits. Paul Tschetter's granddaughter, Justina Guericke suggested that the "Tschetter" surname was associated with loquaciousness. "When you hear a lot of noise—talking all at once, there is a group of Tschetters," she said, indicating a talkative, if not always courteous, method of social intercourse. Guericke also noted that "when you see doors not closed, that's Tschetters," showing a spirit of openness and hospitality.

Guericke also described her family as a "stormy" people who had difficulty focusing on a single issue. "Tschetters" were people who liked to travel and they were, unlike Paul Tschetter, very "mission-minded." Colony Hutterites interviewed suggest that "Tschetters" are known for

Figure 10.9 David W. and Anna Glanzer Tschetter family
Photograph courtesy of Wesley Tschetter

their natural intelligence and an ability to learn new things quickly. Peter Gordon Clark's study of Schmiedeleut Hutterite patronymic groups found that the surname "Tschetter" was found infrequently among those holding the highest level jobs in the colonies but this is not the case among the Dariusleut Hutterites, with whom most colony Tschetters are associated. Dariusleut Tschetters are as well-represented in leadership positions as any other clan.[78]

The Tschetter extended family is especially well-represented in eastern South Dakota. A review of the Sioux Falls, South Dakota phone book, for example, shows thirty-six separate entries for the surname

---

78. Clark, "Leadership Succession among the Hutterites," 298. An analysis of Dariusleut Tschetter family members and positions of leadership was done by anthropologist Max Stanton in July 2007.

"Tschetter" and this does not include the many unlisted Tschetters who rely on cell phones.[79] This information is provided in Table 10.1. The table includes a mix of people from noncommunal and colony Hutterite backgrounds. Other Hutterite surnames appear as well, indicating a large ex-Hutterian population in the area. With the exception of the surname "Hofer," however, "Tschetter" is the Hutterite surname listed most, if one assumes that the last name "Walter," a common German name, includes more non-Hutterians than Hutterians.

Decker	21
Glanzer	4
Gross	43
Hofer	55
Kleinsasser	9
Maendel	10
Stahl	12
Tschetter	36
Waldner	17
Walter	31
Wipf	23
Wollman	20
Wurz	8
Total	289

Table 10.1 Hutterian Surnames: Sioux Falls (South Dakota) Telephone Directory, 2007

Paul and Maria Tschetter's Descendents

Paul Tschetter's descendents include people in many walks of life, from medical doctors, ministers and professors to athletes and construction workers. There are many important accomplishments. Great-grandson Dr. Loren Tschetter, and spouse Jean, for example, are leaders in cancer

---

79. *DEX Official Directory: Sioux Falls and Surrounding Area* (Sioux Falls, SD, 2005).

research and treatment in Sioux Falls, South Dakota.[80] Great-grandson, Wesley Tschetter serves as Vice-President for Finance at South Dakota State University, in Brookings. Other examples include David J. Tschetter (a grandson of Paul Tschetter) who was a well-known Chicago-based radiologist. Professional golfer Kris Tschetter is a great-great niece of the Rev. Tschetter. And two grandsons of Paul Tschetter's brother Jacob are prominent political figures. Menno Tschetter served for over a decade as a South Dakota state legislator in the 1960s and 1970s. Ronald A. Tschetter presently serves as director of the Peace Corps.

On a sadder note, one of Paul Tschetter's grandsons, Alfred, joined Jim Jones' People's Temple religious organization. Alfred was the son of David W. Tschetter and a distinguished x-ray specialist at Baylor University. But Alfred ultimately followed Jim Jones to Guyana, where People's Temple member Catherine Thrash wrote that Tschetter continued to operate an "x-ray machine" and to practice medicine.[81] Tschetter participated in the mass suicide that took place in fall 1978.

A skeleton in Paul Tschetter's immediate family involves son-in-law Paul Decker, a teacher who was married to his daughter, Susanna. Decker had many financial and legal problems and one time when the police were looking for him he hid underneath the Neu Hutterthaler Church.[82] Decker and his family fled to Canada in 1901 to evade criminal prosecution.

Connections with the Eastern European Homeland

In the fall of 1922, Prairieleut KMB minister David M. Hofer visited Ukraine on behalf of the American Mennonite Relief Administration, a forerunner of the Mennonite Central Committee.[83] Hofer, who was married to one of Paul Tschetter's nieces, visited all five Hutterite village sites in south Ukraine, including Johannesruh, his place of birth, where he spent the first ten years of his life.[84]

But when Hofer arrived at the Neu Hutterthal village site where Paul Tschetter had served as senior minister he found almost complete

80. Sioux Valley Foundation Newsletter, eds., "Setting New Standards," Fall 2003.
81. Catherine Thrash, as told to Towne, *The Onliest One Alive*, 90.
82. David P. Gross, correspondence, September, 1987.
83. HMCC, eds., *A History of the Hutterite Mennonites*, 97–100.
84. D. M. Hofer, *Die Hungersnot in Russland und Unsere Reise um Die Welt*. (Chicago: K. M. B. Publishing House, 1924).

Figure 10.10 Raditschewa village, 2005.
Photograph courtesy of Wesley Tschetter.

destruction. Hofer located two dwellings that were in somewhat reasonable condition; everything else was in ruins. Amazingly Hofer found seven Ukrainian families (a total of forty people) living in these two Hutterite-built houses. While visiting the Mennonite Neuendorf village (in the former Chortitza Colony) Hofer also met a destitute man named "Tschetter" who, he said, was related to Paul Tschetter.[85]

Over fifty years later, in 1976, a large group of South Dakota Prairieleut visited the same south Ukraine Hutterite village sites. Arnold M. Hofer's notes from that trip are published in the book *Hutterite Roots*.[86] Hofer wrote that that there was nothing left at the Neu Hutterthal site. Other Prairieleut, many of them Paul and Maria Tschetter's descendents, have visited not only the five Ukrainian village sites north of the Black Sea, but the remains of earlier Hutterite settlements in Transylvania, Slovakia, and Moravia. On one of these trips, in 1991, Arnold M. Hofer found people with the surname "Tschetter" living in Sabatisch (now Sobotiste), Slovakia.

In 2003, Paul Tschetter descendent Wesley Tschetter and historian Arnold M. Hofer were some of the first Hutterians to re-visit the

---

85. Towne, *Jacob's Friends*, 236.
86. HMCC, eds., *Hutterite Roots*, 105–17.

Raditschewa and Wishenka sites, northeast of Kiev.[87] Tschetter returned to these villages in 2005 and he also visited Johannesruh and Hutterthal, where he found Hutterite-built houses and cellars still standing.

Figure 10.11 Hutterite-constructed residence, Johannesruh village site, 2005. Photograph courtesy of Wesley Tschetter.

11

The Legacy of Paul Tschetter

> What will you do with the world? World is world and will remain world until the Lord will come and end it all.
>
> —Paul Tschetter, 1873[1]

PAUL TSCHETTER WAS BORN AND RAISED IN A SMALL HUTTERITE FARMing village in Ukraine. He had only five or six years of formal schooling yet he became an important intellectual, administrative and spiritual force for the entire non-communal Hutterite community in North America. From the time of his arrival in Dakota Territory in 1875, until his death in the home of Christ and Justina Hofman in 1919, Paul Tschetter provided leadership for that initially larger group of Hutterites who decided not to live in colonies.

Paul Tschetter was married to Maria Walter in 1860, saw the birth of a daughter Susanna in 1861, and five years later, at age twenty-four he was ordained to the ministry. In 1868, after only two years of service as an assistant minister at the Hutterthal village he helped establish the village of Neu Hutterthal one hundred miles away. But major political changes initiated by the Russian Tsar in the 1870s caused Tschetter to fear for the integrity of the Hutterite way of life socially and theologically. This led Tschetter to visit St. Petersburg in 1872 and to join the Mennonite/Hutterite delegation to the United States and Canada in the summer of 1873.

During his trip to North America the thirty-one year-old Tschetter kept a diary that gives significant insight into the late 19th century Hutterite mind. He traveled from New York City to Dakota Territory in search of good land and favorable settlement opportuni-

1. JMH, 110.

Figure 11.1 Christian and Justina Hofman House where Paul Tschetter was living at the time of his death. Photograph courtesy of Justina Guericke.

ties and along the way he railed against urban immorality, Mennonite liberality, smoking, musical instruments and photography. He also met influential Americans like Jay Cooke and the President of the United States, Ulysses S. Grant. Since Tschetter was impressed with the quality of land and political prospects on the American Great Plains he proposed that the Hutterites emigrate when he returned to south Ukraine. Members of the Hutterite community-at-large agreed with him with near unanimity.

In the United States Paul Tschetter provided formal leadership for members of the Neu Hutterthaler Church. Informally, he served as an influential spiritual figure in the Prairieleut community-at-large. The Neu Hutterthaler Church and the other two non-communal Hutterite congregations in Hutchinson County later spawned daughter congregations in Beadle and Spink counties (in South Dakota) as well as in different parts of North Dakota and the province of Saskatchewan. The non-communal Hutterite churches are listed in Table 11.1. Most of these congregations later joined Mennonite conferences and members gave up most distinctively Hutterite beliefs and practices.

Table 11.1 Prairieleut Hutterite Congregations in North America

Congregation	Location	Date Established
Neu Hutterthaler	Bridgewater, SD	1875
Hutterdorf	Freeman, SD	1875
Hutterthal	Freeman, SD	1879
Hope	Chaseley, ND	1900
Bethany	Freeman, SD	1905
Hutterthal	Carpenter, SD	1906
Zion	Bridgewater, SD	1920
Emmanuel	Doland, SD	1922
Fairfield-Bethel	Hitchcock, SD	1927
Mt. Olivet	Huron, SD	1945

During his lifetime Paul Tschetter held fast to traditional Hutterite understandings of the faith and pushed the Prairieleut congregations to follow suit. He was a traditionalist devoted to the Hutterite sermons, epistles and Hutterite ecclesiastical traditions. The *Lehren*, as noted, are interpretive expansions of Biblical texts and are often filled with polemical, graphic and earthy agricultural and other references. Note the following passage from a sermon on Matthew 6, which includes a strong indictment of those who fantasize about inappropriate things during church services: "In the same way (the sermon puts it) that a woman who besides her husband, looks at young boys, hangs her mind on them…and wants to love them, is not true, honest and right…."[2]

Tschetter read sermons like these and he was not afraid to confront sin wherever he found it. The *Lehren* were at the center of Tschetter's understanding of the Christian faith and the sermon writers do not mince words. Communal Hutterites continue to read them as they also make sure that they are kept out of the public domain. The big issue for Hutterites who left the traditional church, however, was whether pre-written, centuries-old sermons could speak adequately to contemporary issues. Did they allow God to creatively break into history at any point? Paul Tschetter was convinced that they did and he refused to entertain other possibilities at the Neu Hutterthaler Church.

For Tschetter the Hutterite hymns were also important. They included stories of the ancestral martyrs and he hoped that they would

---

2. Peter Tschetter, ed., "Hutterite Sermon Collection," unpublished.

keep contemporary Hutterites from becoming complacent in their faith. Tschetter viewed them as motivational. The Hutterites had been pushed from place to place in Eastern Europe, and eventually to North America for the sake of a particular understanding of the Christian faith. The stories told in the hymns reminded that this faith bore a physical cost and that Hutterite Christians should be prepared to suffer for their faith again in the future.

But now that the Hutterites were living in a country that embraced the concept of religious freedom and the separation of church and state, many turned their backs on the theological and ecclesial traditions that had sustained them when they lived under the jurisdiction of dictatorial regimes. Given free religious choice, the Hutterite traditions made no sense to increasing numbers of Tschetter's congregants who spoke English, liked American democracy and were doing well economically.

Communal Hutterites who saw the impact of the assimilation process used the Prairieleut as cautionary tale of what happens to Hutterian Anabaptism when community of goods is given up. They continue to do this in the 2000s. Along with communalism, most Prairieleut gave up conservative dress, strict pacifism and a life in social and ideological isolation from "worldly" (i.e. non-Hutterite) people; from their ideas and ways of life.

Paul Tschetter's Impact: Holding the Center

Throughout his life Paul Tschetter watched members of the Prairieleut community look longingly in other directions. Some people joined the colonies; others the Krimmer Mennonite Brethren. Tschetter was left holding an increasingly small center.

From the Hutterite side Tschetter heard stories about the communal practices of the forefathers; from the Krimmer Mennonite Brethren, stories of people finding true salvation. He was introduced to the same "born again" evangelical emphases that in the 2000s have gained widespread support and are causing serious conflict in the Hutterite colonies. A list of Krimmer Mennonite Brethren churches with majority Hutterian ethnic compositions is shown in Table 11.2. In 1960 the KMBs merged with the Mennonite Brethren Conference.

Table 11.2 Prairieleut Congregations of the Krimmer Mennonite Brethren Conference

Congregation	Location	Date Established
Salem	Bridgewater, SD	1886
Bethel	Yale, SD	1902
Zion	Dinuba, CA	1922 (disbanded, 1990)
Emmanuel	Langham, SK	1917 (does not hold regular services)
Emmanuel	Onida, SD	1919
Immanuel	Chaseley, ND	1920 (disbanded, 1932)
Ebenezer	Doland, SD	1920 (disbanded, 1995)
Bethesda	Huron, SD	1943

Paul Tschetter did not join the Krimmer Mennonite Brethren nor did he join a Hutterite colony. But through social turmoil and human movement, Tschetter continued to believe in the concept of a separated, non-worldly life in a spiritual "ark" he sought to preserve in the non-communal Hutterite churches. He and Maria never wavered in this belief. But in the end all but one of their children left the Neu Hutterthaler Church.

Paul Tschetter's legacy is contained in a commitment to a particular understanding of the Christian faith, within the context of a unique ethno-religious group. It is important for a number of reasons.

First, Paul Tschetter was a pioneer. He was a risk-taker, a modern-day Joshua, who was willing to lead his people to a new place of residence thousands of miles from where they lived in their south Ukraine village. Never in their entire history had Hutterites journeyed this far from a previous place of residence. The fact that Tschetter was able to convince almost the entire Hutterite population to leave Ukraine shows an amazing self-confidence as well as charismatic authority based on recognized personal integrity.

Prior to making emigration decisions, Tschetter left his young family and embarked on a four month investigative exploration of North America. He did not shy away from walking through the streets of major urban centers, as much as he detested them; from interacting with heretical Christians and a variety of ethnic groups, even though he believed they exhibited sinful and/or misguided behavior. Tschetter was a man who operated with a strong sense of purpose and self-confidence, certain that God was directing whatever path he took.

Second, Paul Tschetter was a reflective writer. In his important 1873 diary he includes many comments (in the narrative and in the hymns) that analyze humanity's place in the world from a traditional, old order Anabaptist perspective. Tschetter gives very blunt appraisals of the human condition, the Christian faith and environmental issues.

As he crossed the North American continent Tschetter was constantly reminded of relevant Old and New Testament personalities, situations and aphorisms. He evaluated everything on spiritual grounds and from a biblical perspective. There is no light-heartedness, no jokes or funny stories in Tschetter's writing. There is no holding back when Tschetter assesses human hypocrisy and weakness.

Third, Paul Tschetter was a strong and forceful leader. He was an effective communicator and organizer during a time of great psychological stress and social disruption in the Hutterian community. Non-communal Hutterites were putting down roots on foreign soil in the midst of intemperate weather conditions, a national economic panic, competing religious organizations and the constant attraction of the communally organized colonies.

People looked to the Rev. Tschetter for advice and counsel during those difficult times. This was also the case during World War I when congregants (as well as colony Hutterites) sought Tschetter's counsel as they decided how to respond to the military draft and persistent requests to buy Liberty Bonds. How much should the pacifist Christians bend? Should they move to Canada or stay in the Dakotas and hope for the best?

Fourth, Paul Tschetter was deeply committed to the church. He took his role as minister very seriously and was extremely rigid in enforcing church discipline. He believed that the church held the keys to the kingdom of God and that everything that one said, did or wore was a witness to whether or not one was fully committed to God and the body of believers. Tschetter did not recognize boundaries between the natural and supernatural worlds. Everything done on earth impacted one's eternal state and was therefore of interest to him.

Tschetter demanded that members of his congregation see the world the way that he saw it. But this did not mean that he was uncaring or completely intolerant. When others questioned the marriage of his daughter Justina to a non-Hutterian, Tschetter was primarily concerned about whether or not Justina and Christian loved God and each other. Granddaughter Anna Fisher recalled the kindness displayed toward her when she had polio. But in general Tschetter was intransigent when it came to changing traditional Hutterian ways of viewing and practicing the Christian faith.

Fifth, Paul Tschetter was committed to Hutterian beliefs and practices, which he unfailingly supported even when others were moving in different directions. Tschetter believed in the viability of non-communal Hutterianism during a time when he was being attacked on the left (from communalists in the Hutterite colonies) and from the right (from evangelical Prairieleut in the Krimmer Mennonite Brethren denomination). Tschetter provided leadership for those who stayed in the center; for those who believed in moderation and the beauty of the status quo.

Paul Tschetter did not provide new theological perspectives or Biblical interpretations. Instead he was committed to the scriptural instruction provided in the *Lehren*. Tschetter read his Bible faithfully but believed, with humility, that it was not the role of ministers to write their own sermons. In humility, he did not consider himself inspired in this way.

Paul Tschetter was a traditionalist who did not budge on theology or ecclesiastical practice unless there had been considerable debate and conversation. By the early 1900s, however, especially after his own children began to leave the Neu Hutterthaler Church, Tschetter developed at least a guarded openness to innovations, for example, Sunday School programs and Gospel hymn books.

Paul Tschetter was the most influential non-communal Hutterian of his generation. In 1974, at the dedication of the 100-year Hutterian memorial at the Neu Hutterthaler Church, Wesley Tschetter summed it up in the following way: "The impact that Paul Tschetter had on our lives can't be measured in rods. I venture to say that no other Hutter in any generation since Paul Tschetter will have as significant an impact on all the Hutter people as did Paul Tschetter."[3]

This important pioneer demonstrated in his own life, in the life of his immediate family, and in the life of the entire non-communal Hutterite community, how difficult it is for any ethnic or religious group to establish the same kind of society, with the same belief patterns, in

---

3. W. Tschetter, "Reflections on the Life of Paul Tschetter."

the United States as in the community it left behind. But Paul Tschetter gave it his best shot.

Appendix A

Paul Tschetter's Summer 1873 Diary

Translated and Edited by Jacob M. Hofer and Rod Janzen[1]

Description of a Journey to America, April 14, 1873, with Lohrentz Tschetter, Accurately Recorded from Day to Day

Saturday, April 14. I began my momentous journey to America taking leave of my wife and dear children with a heavy heart and also took leave of all my brothers and sisters. Due to circumstances my brother Joseph Tschetter and my sister-in-law could not he present although they had planned to accompany me as far as Nikopol. Their son had taken sick at Hutterdorf and they wished to visit him there. There were two brethren visiting at our home at the time, George Hofer and Joseph Hofer and of these I also took leave. Love obliged my dear mother and father to accompany me as far as Nikopol and so we left with a sad and troubled heart only God knowing if I should ever see my loved ones

---

1. As noted in the text, J. M. (Jacob Mendel) Hofer's wife, Maria, was a granddaughter of Paul Tschetter. Hofer translated the 1873 diary into English while working on his doctorate at the University of Chicago, where he studied from 1927–1930. The Hofer translation was originally published in the *Mennonite Quarterly Review* in the July, 1931 (pages 112–27) and October, 1931 (pages 198–219) issues. Permission to reprint the diary was granted by John Roth, editor of the *Mennonite Quarterly Review*. Because much of the information is dated, this printing of the translation does not include Joseph W. Tschetter's short biography of the Rev. Tschetter nor J. M. Hofer's introductory or concluding comments. I have also omitted J. M. Hofer's footnotes and parenthetical explanations as well as "corrections" made by *Mennonite Quarterly Review* editors. The diary appears as it was written.

again. I put all my trust in the Lord that He might send His angels to guide and protect me.

There were also three brethren from Hutterthal at our home, Peter Tschetter, Peter Mendel and Christian Hofer, who accompanied us as far as Nikopol for it seemed the will of the Lord to have a number of our brethren present when we departed. At 5 P.M. we arrived at Nikopol. We immediately went to see the steamship and purchased our tickets to Cherson, second class, costing three rubles, sixty kopecks.

Sunday, April 15. Early Sunday morning we all boarded the steamship which was named *Listalscha*. At six o'clock I took leave of my dear father and mother who embraced me and wept bitterly. So also Lohrentz's daughter wept loudly and embraced her father. After this, we departed in God's name arriving safely at Cherson before evening. We remained for the night at a European hotel. Cherson is a large city, well-built and has paved streets.

Monday, April 16. After awaking all well, praise the Lord we went to our steamship at eight o'clock and purchased tickets to Odessa, second class and paid two rubles, forty kopecks. The name of the ship was *Gibson*. There was quite a wind, but the ship did not rock much until we came upon the Black Sea. Here the wind became stronger, the waves rolled furiously, and the ship swayed violently to and fro. Lohrentz went to the upper deck, but soon returned and said that the ship was very unsteady and the waves high. I also went on deck but soon began to feel bad since I was not accustomed to traveling on the sea. After a short while I returned to our cabin below. Then I again went to the upper deck for better air, as I had a severe headache. I remained there until we arrived at Odessa at five o'clock in the afternoon. Odessa is a large city, and we made our headquarters at the Maiback Nerro Lazar Hotel.

Klassen and myself, called upon Toews to get information in regard to our journey. He greeted us very cordially. Since it was late in the evening, he asked us to come again and see him early the next morning for further information.

Tuesday, April 17. In the morning after giving thanks to the Lord for His protection we called on Toews at nine o'clock and he went with us to the Exchange Bank in Odessa. He assisted us as much as possible. We exchanged only fifty-two rubles and fifty kopecks, one part into Austrian florins and the other part into francs. A florin is worth seventy kopecks silver and a franc five rubles and ninety-three kopecks. He gave us letters of introduction to Trütschler in Berlin, and Maier in Hamburg. We asked him whether it would be necessary to secure a different pass and he informed us that we might possibly have to exchange it for another in Hamburg and, if not, the pass we possessed was good clear to America, for the Russian authorities do not favor exchanging their passes in Germany. We thanked him for his assistance and left. That same evening at eight o'clock we arrived at Wolotschisk on the Austrian boundary line. We traveled throughout the night, third class with a mixed crowd of Jews, women and children. The train was so crowded that we were obliged to sit up all night and were unable to sleep much.

Wednesday, April 18. After traveling across long stretches of plains, hills, and valleys at a tremendous speed, we arrived at Wolotschisk at six o'clock in the evening. This city is on the boundary line between Austria and Russia. Our passes were examined here and our baggage inspected. We purchased a ticket to Podwotoczyska, costing ten kopecks and from there another ticket to Oswiecim on the Prussian boundary line, for which we paid nineteen gulden and eleven kreutzer. The Russian language became useless because no one understood it or could speak it. Most of the people spoke the Austrian language and some the German. This country is known as Galicia or Austrian Poland and is mostly wood land.

Thursday, April 19. At nine o'clock in the morning we arrived at Lemberg, the chief city of Galicia, where we changed cars and at seven in the evening came to Oswiecim. Here we purchased a ticket for Myslowitz, a short distance from Oswiecim, and remained for the night. We were tired from the journey for one cannot very well sleep on the train. We had a quiet room.

Friday, April 20. In the morning after we had praised and thanked the Lord for His protection, we departed for the station to proceed on our journey. We purchased tickets as far as Kassel and left at five o'clock in the morning from Myslowitz and came to Breslau, the chief city of Silesia. At Breslau we purchased tickets for Berlin, the chief city and capital of Prussia. We arrived in Berlin at eight o'clock in the evening in a large railroad station such as I had never seen in my life. This railroad station was even larger and more magnificent than the one at St. Petersburg. The railroad was crowded with thousands of people and there was great noise and bustle in and about the same. It was night and we were strangers in a city where, no doubt, plenty of wicked people can be found. Soon a man approached us, saying that he had quarters for us for the night nearby, and we entrusted ourselves to this stranger although with certain fear and distrust. We followed him rather reluctantly into the basement of a large five story structure, where we found great crowds of people and here he showed us a dingy, little room with four bedsteads and one window, where we were to spend the night.

The room did not particularly appeal to any of us, but being unable to find a better one, we decided to remain there for the night. The manager and his wife seemed to be respectable and honest people. We locked the doors and prayed to God that He might protect us during the night. We retired and slept well.

Saturday, April 21. After morning prayer, we called at the Hamburg railroad station about two versts distant, for Trütschler was to assist us in the matter of exchanging our money. We did not find him at the office and waited for him two hours. When he arrived he greeted us cordially and exchanged for each of us seven hundred rubles into American money. For the seven hundred rubles we received six hundred twenty American silver dollars. He advised us to again change these American silver dollars to American paper money and gain a further premium which we did. We purchased third class tickets from Berlin to Hamburg, but secured them at the fourth-class rate.

The distance from Berlin to Hamburg is one hundred thirty-seven miles. We left Berlin at 10 A.M. by train and arrived at Hamburg at seven in the evening. The country between Berlin and Hamburg is very low and woody, so low in fact that drainage canals around the fields are necessary and by means of windmills the water is drained from the fields. When we arrived at the Hamburg railway station, we again found the same noise and bustle that we had already experienced in Berlin. One cried, "Come to my quarters," another, "I have a room for you," etc. All of a sudden we heard someone's voice above all the rest, "Klassen, Toews, Tschetter, come to me." We were surprised to hear our names in a strange place like Hamburg but were informed that he represented the

German Company and had orders to accommodate us. We entered a spacious hall in a five story building, where boys and girls were dancing. I was almost terrified and shrank back. The man said, "Follow me, I will give you a room where you shall be undisturbed." This was true. I inquired of him as to who these people were who found so much pleasure in dancing, upon which he answered that they also expect to sail for America on April 24. I said, "They should rather pray than dance." "Yes," he said, "but we cannot always pray; we must enjoy ourselves." That is the way of the wicked world. We then went to our room and retired for the night.

Sunday, April 22. I remained in my room until noon, read the Word of God and meditated. In the afternoon we called upon the agent August Bolten and presented to him our letter of introduction from Toews of Odessa. After he had read the letter, he said that he would do everything possible to accommodate us. We purchased second-class return tickets from him, two hundred dollars each and he promised to ask the captain on the ship to give us a good cabin. We thanked him for his kind assistance and returned to our lodging place. The immigration building on one side faces the water front and rests upon strong piers.

Monday, April 23. During the night shortly before daybreak, many more emigrants arrived, mostly Germans, Mecklenburgers from Prussia, with women and children, numbering more than five hundred souls. They were emigrating for various reasons. Here at the immigration building all ate at one table and at a regular hour. Breakfast was served at seven in the morning and consisted of a large cup of coffee and white bread. At noon: soup, meat, and potatoes and in the evening a cup of coffee. The board was good.

In the afternoon I went out sight-seeing in the city and among other places I drifted into a bookstore, where I purchased a little book on Menno Simons. I walked through the city and observed the hustle and bustle of the city, for Hamburg is a great business and commercial center with many canals and bridges, large warehouses and an excellent harbor in which many ships were anchored. The people of Hamburg are mostly Lutherans. The city has large buildings, five, six, and seven stories in height. Most of the buildings face a waterfront and rest on piers. In the evening I again returned to my room and retired for the night.

Tuesday, April 24. I remained in my room practically the entire day, writing letters, and spent some time buying the necessities for the ocean voyage. I was also invited to visit Rev. Roosen but feared that I might get into an argument with him, for I knew that he was an unsound Mennonite. The Apostle warns us to "avoid those who may harm our souls."

Wednesday, April 25. In the morning we left our lodging place and drove to the ship which was harbored in the Elbe about two versts away. Here our passes were examined and we entered the ship with sighs and prayers to God, trusting our all in Him that He might guide and protect us on the wide and angry ocean. We departed at eight o'clock in the morning in a small ship and after sailing for two hours we came to a very large ship which we entered and were assigned to our cabins. There were six beds in the cabin and, since there were only four of us, two friends joined our company and shared the sleeping room with us. For a dining room and a sitting room there was a large hall. There was always plenty to eat, such as soup, meat, fish, cheese, butter, plums, cherries, nuts, apples, and many other things, the names of which I did not know. Meals were served four times daily, one hundred eating at each board. Words fail me to express the table manners and courtesy of both waiters and patrons. From the Elbe we sailed the first day into the North Sea. The sea was calm all day and we slept soundly that night.

Thursday, April 26. The sea was calm until ten o'clock in the morning, then the wind increased and the ship commenced to sway back and forth. I began to have a severe headache, but was able to partake of a good dinner. Some people had to leave the dinner table, and still others did not even leave their cabins. Of our companions, Toews did not eat a morsel all day. I was also able to eat lunch and supper. As our ship sailed into the English Channel, shortly before evening, the wind increased so that we were unable to sleep very much. I began to feel so bad that I had to go on deck to get better air. As I watched the rolling waves and the ship plowing through huge mountains of water, my spirit went up to God to whose care we had entrusted ourselves. The godless were little disturbed by the great storm. They continued dancing and were merry. After a while I returned to our cabin and retired for the night.

Friday, April 27. When I awoke Friday morning it was day and the ship stood still. I thanked my heavenly Father for His protection for another day and night. I went on deck and in the distance could see Havre, France, a beautiful city with a fine harbor in which many ships were anchored. At Havre we were detained for twenty-four hours and spent the time sight-seeing in the city. During this time our ship was loaded with a supply of coal and water. Around the city of Havre several fortresses are located.

Saturday, April 28. At eight o'clock in the morning we steamed out of the harbor of Havre. Our hearts went up to God, that He might protect us on our voyage and send His angels to guide us on the wide ocean. After a lapse of two hours we lost sight of all land and now only the blue heavens and the deep ocean could be seen. The ship moved along smoothly that day. The frivolous and gay crowd was happy and paraded up and down the deck, a thing I abhorred. I thought it would have been more appropriate to pray to God for His protection, but they had not the slightest thought of this. I went to bed and slept well that night.

Sunday, April 29. Awoke all well and thanked my Lord for His Fatherly protection. The ship sailed on smooth seas until ten o'clock in the morning when a storm arose which rocked the ship to and fro so that many of the passengers began to feel sick. Only those who were used to traveling on the sea and those who possessed a strong constitution were not affected. I, being frequently bothered with headaches, was also forced to retire to my room, although I was able to partake of a light dinner, lunch and also supper. Many left the table while others did not even appear at meal-time. I thought and remarked to some of the people, "Yesterday you were so jolly and gay and today you look so sad."

Monday, April 30. I did not feel well all day; remained in bed most of the day without eating much.

Tuesday, May 1. It rained in the morning. Felt good so that I could eat well. Had rain and storm in the evening so that the ship rocked considerably, but I was already getting accustomed to this.

Wednesday, May 2. The ocean was more calm than any day since our departure. The people recovered their former health, but at the same time became more godless. In the evening the wind became stronger.

Thursday, May 3. The sea was quiet. One of our brethren, Toews, had been in bed for eight days and during that time had hardly eaten anything. The other brother, Klassen, was not seasick at all.

Friday, May 4. Rain and storm today; the waves were so high that they seemed as mountains and the ship at times seemed to be moving between two walls. It was nearly impossible to eat for the tables were very unsteady. Many again became seasick, but I was not materially affected for I was already used to sea travel. The storm raged far into the night.

Saturday, May 5. Rain in the morning and the ocean was more calm. The wind blew from the east. The sails were put up and this greatly increased the speed of the ship so that we sailed three hundred forty miles in twenty-four hours, as formerly we made only two hundred ninety-eight to three hundred fifteen miles per day. The weather became colder for we began to approach the icebergs near Iceland.

Sunday, May 6. This was a beautiful Sunday morning. The sea was quiet. In the morning the pastor delivered a sermon on Psalm 50:14. The prayer which he offered was reverent and effective, but the sermon seemed much too mild for such godless rabble as that on the ship. His object in the sermon seemed merely to entertain the audience. At dinner an offering was taken for a family, whose father and husband had died on the voyage and who were in meager circumstances. I also gave a small donation. The orphans were four children, most of them already grown, the youngest being nine years old. At eleven o'clock in the night the corpse was lowered into the depths of the sea and buried beneath the waves. The burial was not public so as not to frighten the people on board the ship.

Monday, May 7. In the morning at ten o'clock the flag was raised and we met a small ship from New York which escorted our ship back to the city. Oh how the people all rejoiced that land was finally to be in sight soon. The pastor sang a song of thanksgiving with a group of men and women in which I heartily joined. It gave me great joy to know that there were at least some on board the ship, who thought of praising God for His guidance and protection during our long voyage.

Tuesday, May 8. Early in the morning, we sighted land toward the north after wandering on the large and stormy ocean for thirteen days. We all rejoiced at the sight of land. It was not until eleven o'clock that the magnificent *Silesia* stopped and we were all transferred to a smaller steamship and after steaming past more than one hundred ships in one hour we landed at Hoboken. At noon we left the ship, went to the city and found a lodging place in the Karles Unrein Hotel where we had dinner. During the afternoon and evening until twelve o'clock I wrote letters and then retired for the night in God's name.

Wednesday, May 9. After breakfast, at ten o'clock we called on Pastor Neumondt, crossing a small body of water in a steamboat in order to get to his house to get some information and advice. He greeted us cordially but his advice according to my opinion was too excessive. He spoke too much and acted too wise. He asked us to call again in the afternoon, when he would give us references and advise us as to exchanging our money. Klassen and Toews went but Lohrentz and I did not and exchanged our money without his assistance. For three hundred dollars in gold we received three hundred fifty dollars in paper money. New York is a magnificent and beautiful city with many large ships in the harbor and is very populous. The railroads run double-deck, supported by steel pillars. In the evening at eight o'clock we departed from Hoboken by train for Elkhart, Indiana. We passed through a tunnel two versts in length. Throughout the entire night we traveled through a mountainous region.

Thursday, May 10. At eight o'clock in the morning the locomotive suddenly lost the rest of the train but returned to pick us up. Throughout the day we again traversed a country with lofty mountains, some as high as six hundred feet. The mountains are rocky and are covered with trees. People are found living at the foot of the mountains, plowing such small patches as they have cleared. On the mountainsides there seem to be springs that develop into small rivulets flowing down the steep grades. The soil is chiefly of a yellowish color. The country with its many green trees seems not a bad region, very beautiful but probably not so suitable for agricultural purposes. That same midnight we arrived at Dunkirk where we remained for the night. We had a good night's rest. The lady at the hotel could speak German but in general the people were English speaking.

Friday, May 11. At nine o'clock in the morning we departed from Dunkirk. Dunkirk is near a large lake and the country is quite level with many orchards. The trees were in full bloom. At three o'clock we came near the lake and passed through the city of Ziehago in which there were many steel factories and foundries. At three in the morning we arrived at Elkhart and remained in the station until morning. We could sleep little for there was much noise caused by steam engines. From New York we traveled to Elkhart in forty-six hours.

Saturday, May 12. In the morning we called at the home of John Funk, a minister of the Old Mennonite Church. He was not at home, but we were cordially greeted by members of his family and given breakfast. The Old Mennonites have beards and shave around the mouth. They rather speak English than German. After breakfast we called at the Funk publishing house. I was given a little book and also purchased a song book. In the afternoon there was a street parade in Elkhart. Thirty-four wagons in which were all kinds of animals passed through the streets. Seven teams of horses were hitched to the first wagon. All the men and horses were decorated with plumes of red, white, and green colors. The wagon was as if made of gold and seated upon it were musicians and comedians who played tunes. The other wagons were all drawn by two and three teams. I have never seen such things in all my life. In the afternoon there was a circus. I did not attend for I considered it a sin to witness such devilish things.

I was glad that I had been relieved of the godless rabble with whom I was obliged to spend such a long time on the ocean. In the afternoon many Mennonites came to Elkhart and a man named Isaac became acquainted with us, and took us to his home. We wished to attend church services the next day and the church was not far away from Isaac's home. They do not live in villages like we do. Every one has his own piece of land which is fenced. Isaac's land is seven miles from the church. We arrived at his home just at sunset and were warmly welcomed. Isaac has a farm of two hundred acres of which one hundred acres is woodland. He also has a fine orchard.

Sunday, May 13. Awoke all well and gave praise to God for it. At nine o'clock we drove to church with Isaac where many people had already assembled. They gave me a seat among the ministers. It happened incidentally that an infant had recently died and so the funeral services commenced. Songs were sung for the opening, the first one in German and then another one in English. The first sermon was in German on the text, 1 Corinthians 15. Then followed an English sermon of which I understood nothing. Prayers were said aloud and the people knelt, although some remained seated. After this another song was sung and then the child was carried out and buried. While the child was being buried, the congregation sang another song.

The style of dress among the men is conservative. Their coats are somewhat short with buttons on the trousers and vests. The young men are well dressed, wearing breast shirts with green or blue neckties. They part their hair in the middle like we do and some part their hair on the side. Most of the men have beards. The women are dressed in a variety of styles and colors. Some wear white knitted caps with lace in front. Others wear hats of various colors. Girls wear straw hats with long ribbons. Some are dressed in white, others in blue, black, red, etc. The small children are also taken to church services, some sitting on their mother's lap while others walk around. After the services were over, one of the women repented for her sins. The minister then made a few remarks. The Old Mennonites address each other as "brethren" and "sisters." The ministers are elected, just as we do, and are finally chosen by lot. The Lord's Supper is taken twice a year, not at a specific time and not for the forgiveness of sin but in memory of the suffering and death of Christ. They baptize when an applicant calls for baptism. The ministers do not marry couples in cases where one is a member of the church and the other is not. Some marry couples if both are non-members and when they are later baptized they are accepted into the membership of the church and become brethren and sisters of the same. The ban is enforced as in our church. If the accused repents and confesses, he is again taken into the church.

There was one thing which I did not approve and that was the fact that some of the women smoked and chewed tobacco. They spoke mostly English for that is the language they study in school. They can speak only a broken German, even one of the ministers was unable to speak in German. We again went to the home of Isaac and a certain deacon went with us. I inquired of him why it was that they preach in the English language; whether it was against the law to preach in German. He said, "No, the government does not object, neither does the government care what one preaches. The chief reason is that so few of the people understand the German language." I asked him why. He told me, "Most of the people come from Holland and England and therefore know no German." I wondered whether these people realize how much they have lost by giving up their mother tongue. For dinner we were at Isaac's, fifteen in number.

At three o'clock we again assembled at the church, where I preached a Sermon on the text, 1 John 5:14: "For whosoever is born of God overcometh the world." I preached according to our custom because the ministers wished it that way. According to our custom I dictated the songs. After the services, one of the ministers, Daniel Brennemann invited me to his home. All the meals, breakfast, dinner and supper were the same: coffee, ham, butter, white bread, syrup, apple sauce, cherry cakes and blackberries. Prayer is said before mealtime but not after. After supper we sang a song, had a brief prayer service and then retired for the night.

Monday, May 14. In the morning after we had risen, Daniel led in prayer and then we had breakfast. After supper he took us to Isaac, who lived four miles away. The people in the community have good horses and strong harnesses, but the wagons are not so very good and convenient. The wagon boxes are long and look like a trough. The wheels have wooden axles and are very high, with only a little iron used as rims. The people have good cows which cost about forty dollars per head, also fine hogs, which as a rule are fat. They feed them corn. Only a few sheep can be seen and these are not very good. Most of the money is made on cattle and wheat. I also inquired about the matter of military service. The ministers said that their young men were now exempt but during the last war they had to pay three hundred dollars for every young man who was drafted. I asked about those who were unable to pay, and they said that the churches assisted those who were unable to pay that amount. During times of peace these three hundred dollars need not be paid. In America the soldiers are hired and paid a salary. In my travels in America so far, I have seen very few soldiers. They are stationed only near the boundary lines to protect the country against the Indians. A murderer in America is punished by hanging, if found guilty. A thief is imprisoned in a penitentiary for a time. I inquired if Mennonites bring suits into the courts and if they are required to vote. I was told that the Mennonites do not go to court, and the matter of voting is voluntary. In regard to taxes I was informed that a person's property is first assessed and then he pays according to the amount of property possessed, so much per one hundred dollars.

Isaac said that he owns one hundred forty-five acres of land and paid forty last year, payable to the county or district wherein one resides. I also asked in regard to insects that may prove injurious to the crops. He said that there were potato bugs, which he also showed to us. They were black and had white stripes with yellow heads and were about the size of a bean. They were first seen years ago and unless they are picked off, there is no potato crop. These bugs are very poisonous, but they are not injurious to wheat. In the afternoon Isaac took us to Elkhart, but Funk was not at home. As a matter of pastime I went to see his press. The machinery and the speed with which it works is a marvel. I have never seen anything like it. At ten o'clock the same evening, Funk came home.

Tuesday, May 15. In the morning Funk told us that Suderman of Berdjansk and Buller of Alexanderwohl had telegraphed that their ship would arrive in New York Wednesday and he advised us to wait until they had arrived and thus work with them together in our appeals to the government. Funk said that he would accompany us since we were unacquainted with the English language. In the evening two ministers and two other brethren from Pennsylvania came to Funk's house for the purpose of uniting the different churches in the community. In the morning these brethren led in the morning worship and prayer and after breakfast at eight we left, ten of us on two wagons to go out into the country a distance of ten miles to attend church services. One of the ministers of Pennsylvania preached a sermon. Then I followed with an extemporaneous sermon, as much as the Lord gave me grace, for it is customary here in America to preach from memory. After the sermons Funk gave the following report of what had been decided at the Conference:

1. That they should not chew tobacco during church services because spitting is obnoxious. 2. Not to run back and forth so much during the services and keep from vain talk. 3. Everyone should act as is fitting for a Christian. 4. Parents should raise their children in the fear of the Lord. 5. A minister should be elected and the brethren should pray so that the Lord may show whom to choose.

Brother Funk, four people from Pennsylvania and four of us were invited to dinner by one of the brethren. At three o'clock we again went to a church six miles away, where services were conducted and in the evening we had supper at the home of a man named Holdemann. There were nine of us at the table. In the evening we again went to church where I preached the first sermon, followed by the two Pennsylvania ministers. One of these ministers did not appeal to me because he smoked and as a whole seemed a rather cold Christian. We spent the night at Joseph Holdemann's.

Wednesday, May 16. In the morning after breakfast, David, one of the Old Mennonites, took us to the Amish Mennonites who live six miles away, and left us at the home of a minister named Mosi, where we had dinner and supper. After supper Mosi took us to another minister where we remained for the night. The Amish Mennonites are more plain in their style of dress as well as in their homes in comparison with the Old Mennonites. They are not permitted to wear loud-colored clothes or to dye anything in a gay color. Their clothes must be of one color. They use hooks and eyes instead of buttons except on trousers. The men must wear hats instead of caps. Their trousers are of a blue color and have a tight fit. The slit in the trousers is on the side instead of in front. They are not permitted to cut their beards around the mouth. The hair is worn long. Girls and women must cover their heads with a white hood. In their style of clothes the Amish Mennonites agree with our Hutterites. They have no church buildings but have their church services in the different homes. The man in whose house the services are held must then furnish dinner for the entire group. Visiting ministers may not preach in their services. The Old Mennonites are more hospitable to visitors than the Amish Mennonites but they also have their dark sides. The minister at whose home I stayed had three guns in his house and everyone in the house smoked, even the women. What is worst among the Old Mennonites is that even the ministers smoke.

The country in this community is very prosperous with fine orchards and pastures and beautiful fields of grain. The people seem pale and not very healthy. They have plenty to eat and in my opinion they eat too much, especially of sweets and fruits. If they would eat more sour foods, they would look healthier. They do most of the work themselves for I did not see many hired men and maids.

Thursday, May 17. In the morning after I had arisen from my bed and as I walked out into the yard I heard someone shooting. Who would be shooting so early in the morning I thought, and just then a gray-haired old minister emerged from the woods, gun in hand. I did not know what to think and much less what to say. What a fine example of a non-resistant Mennonite. We had breakfast at his house and I purchased from him a Martyr's Songbook for one dollar. After that he accompanied us to Elder David. Both David and his wife smoked. Here we had dinner and in the afternoon David took us to one of the Old Mennonites, a certain John Kreider, who was a very friendly man and he and his wife showed us great hospitality. Here we had supper and after that attended evening services in the church, where I preached the sermon. No other minister was present. After the services we again returned to the home of Kreider where we remained for the night. They had a large house. Most of the houses in the community are wooden, two-story structures. The upper story is used for bedrooms for visitors and the floors are covered with red and checked rugs. Many of the rooms have mirrors and the walls are papered.

Friday, May 18. In the morning we arose, all well, praise God for it. After breakfast John Kreider took us to Joseph Holdemann, six miles away where we had dinner and after that Kreider took us to Elkhart to Funk, where we remained for the night.

Saturday, May 19. Today I remained in my room the entire day and wrote a letter home.

Sunday, May 20. Today I felt somewhat ill. Immediately after breakfast I called on a certain Brennemann and went to church with him for this was Pentecost Sunday. I preached on Acts 2. After the sermon there was a short business meeting which dealt with two brethren, who had trouble amongst themselves. They said, however, that they had no differences and were ready to partake of the Lord's Supper. With this the meeting was dismissed, and we went home with Rev. Daniel Brennemann together with a large number of other guests. After returning to my room at Funk's house in the city, I attended evening services at the Evangelical Church which was located next to Funk's house. The Evangelicals differ from the Lutherans somewhat in their form of baptism. They do not emphasize infant baptism so much.

The pastor spoke on "Cast thy burden on the Lord, and he shall sustain thee: he shall never suffer the righteous to be moved. But thou, O God, shalt bring them down into the pit of destruction." The minister began to speak louder and louder and as I sat near the pulpit I was greatly bewildered; in fact I felt like running from the church. He marched back and forth behind the pulpit, once to this side and then to the other as if he was insane. He hammered on the pulpit with his fist, and pointing to his heart he cried: "Herein must the Lord live." At times he pointed toward heaven and then again down to hell, shouting like a mad man, for only a mad man could act like he did. His actions were not those of a minister of the Gospel but those of a general. Sometimes he praised everyone into heaven and then again he damned us all into hell. It is not in my power to describe this and my readers will doubt my statements, but it remains true nevertheless. I have been in many churches but have never witnessed the like. A comedy could hardly offer more entertainment. He preached the truth but with great indiscretion and lack of judgment.

Monday, July 21. As I awoke to-day I felt a headache and stomach pains. I praised the Lord for His protection and guidance. I feared a fever, because of the many places where one eats in traveling. After breakfast I went to a druggist for some medicine. The doctor said that I had quite a high fever but after taking the medicine I felt much better. In the afternoon I visited a paper mill. The paper is made of all sorts of old rags. At first the rags are moistened and then stuffed into a large container where they must remain for a time. It is then cut fine, run through rollers, and finally becomes paper. The Old Mennonites permit their people to have instrumental music. Last Sunday, when we visited at Brennemann's, the overseer of the poor, he asked us if we enjoyed music. We said, "No." He had a music box in his house and he began to play the instrument. After he had played several pieces, I remarked to him that the Apostle said, "Speak to yourselves in Psalms and hymns and spiritual songs, singing and making melody in your heart to the Lord" (Ephesians 5:19). He said that the Psalmist David also played on his harp and I replied that David was also a warrior and had shed much blood. Thereupon he became silent and did not say another word.

Tuesday, May 22. As we did not know the brethren, who had shortly arrived from Russia, we proceeded on our journey alone with John

Funk. We boarded the train at Elkhart at four-thirty in the morning and at eight we arrived in Chicago which is one hundred two miles from Elkhart. The city is located on Lake Michigan, and has a large navigable canal. This city was nearly all burned to the ground one and one-half years ago. The people say that since the creation of the world there never has been a fire like that. The loss of the fire was estimated at $200,000,000. Many people lost their lives. By this time large portions of the city have already been rebuilt. There are buildings from seven to eight stories in height. We went through many long and crowded streets and came into Chicago by a subway such as they have in Berlin. This passes under the Chicago River. It was a fathom high and one and one-half fathoms wide with an arched ceiling laid out with brick, like a cellar. The inside was cool. The street cars passed through the tunnel while over it passed boats and steamships. It took us fifteen minutes to walk through it. One's mind can hardly comprehend what man is able to construct.

According to all these things the end of the world must be nigh. Since I was very tired and did not feel well we went to a hotel to rest. Later in the day we went to the city to; look for the brethren but could not find them. We then looked up the railroad station agent and inquired about the land and then returned to our room. On our return from the station we saw in a tent on the street two wild and uncivilized men from a distant island, caged up. They were over 50 years old, very small, with long hair and short beards. The structure of their frames was as slight as that of a child of five years. I was much astonished when I saw one of these men raise tip another man of at least thirty puds weight. The thought came to me, as I looked upon these poor creatures, whether God would also demand an account of them on the Judgment Day. We remained that day and the following one in our rooms surrounded by so much noise and tumult that my head ached. How much relieved I would be if I were once again in my home, where everything is quiet and peaceful.

Wednesday, May 23. Since there was no hope of meeting the brethren in the city, we boarded the train at ten in the morning for St. Paul. This city lies in the state of Minnesota, four hundred eight miles from Chicago. We traveled through all kinds of territory. At first the land was beautiful and level with plenty of water and good thick woods. Then we came to a hilly region with many bridges over streams and then more level country. After twenty-one hours we arrived at St. Paul.

Thursday, May 24. At seven o'clock this morning we arrived at St. Paul and went to the business section of the city. We made our headquarters at a hotel. The hotel keeper's name was Wildenjager. In the forenoon we went to the courthouse to inquire for information. They treated us courteously, asked for our names and said that in the afternoon we could meet a man who had also lived in Russia. He would explain to us in regard to the different lands, here in America, for there are railroad lands, government lands, and school lands. He said that he would see us in our rooms at two o'clock in the afternoon. At that time the man came to our room and gave us much information in regard to the land. He took us to the railroad agent who also has millions of acres to sell at reasonable prices. We received telegraphic information that Suderman and Buller were also on their way to St. Paul.

This city was founded sixteen years ago. It is not a very large city, but has fine buildings and quite an important trade and commerce. One can buy everything that is needed. In the evening the Bergthaler deputies, Jacob Peters, the village mayor, Henry Wiebe, a minister, and Cornelius Boer came to our room. Oh how glad we were to see them. It seemed to me that they were of my own. They had already visited many parts of the country but as yet had not found homes. They had been in the south in the state of Texas and informed us that people in that state were already harvesting wheat, but they did not like that country. After talking over many matters, we retired to our rooms for the night.

Friday, May 25. Arose well, thanks only to God, the Almighty for His Fatherly protection and guidance. The Bergthaler brethren came to our room. We asked them to travel with us, but they said that they had already promised to join the Molotschna brethren who were to meet them in the city. In the morning we proceeded to the station, Wiebe helping me to carry my baggage. On the way we talked about non-resistance and how he liked the country here. He said the country did not appeal much to him and that after all the question of military service is the most important. We thought that it would not be possible to secure total exemption from military service in the United States but that the English government would be more liberal and grant a Charter guaranteeing exemption from military service which was better than what this country could offer. He spoke very sensibly, so that I immediately learned to love him. He said that one should not only consider the land question but also not forget the matter of freedom, for that is the reason why we came to this country and are making this long journey. Then we took leave, boarded the train and left St. Paul. The city lies on the Mississippi River and a long bridge several fathoms high spans the river at this point. Our destination was Duluth. At first the country was quite level but somewhat woody and then came many rocky cliffs. We crossed five different bridges, so high that one became dizzy when looking into the deep below. I estimated .the height over one hundred feet and the stream was so swift that it had the force of fifteen thousand horsepower. The name of the river was St. Louis. At four-thirty we arrived at Duluth. The city is located on a lake, which was full of floating ice. The city is only small, having been founded only four years ago. On one side the city lies on a high hill with many trees. The city is one hundred fifty-six miles north of St. Paul. Due to the ice, it was quite cold. We remained in the city for the night. There is also a large immigration house here, built by the railroad company for the welfare and comfort of the immigrants as well as for their own interest and profit.

Saturday, May 26. At seven in the morning we again took the train, traveling toward the southwest, because the country here seemed too cold to us and grain was planted too late in the season. We journeyed through level plains of woodland with many lakes. Here and there one could see a miserable hut inhabited by Indians. These Indians are quite civilized and would not hurt anyone. At two o'clock in the afternoon we arrived at the city of Bremont which was founded only two years ago. The town is only small and we had dinner. The woodland became thinner here and finally the land seemed clear altogether. The land at times was level and then again slightly hilly. The hilly land seemed to me the more fertile of the two. Here and there one could see a settlement of white people and small fields of grain. The wheat was yet very small. At eight o'clock in the evening we arrived at Glyndon, where a large immigration hail is located, built by the railroad company. We decided to remain here over Sunday because lodging is free and meals could be secured at very reasonable rates. The land around Glyndon is very level. It is probably too wet most of the year and that is a great drawback in spring plowing. Several people have already settled here. The distance from Duluth to Glyndon is two hundred fifty-eight miles and it took us thirteen hours to travel the distance by train. In the evening there was a great thunderstorm accompanied by rain and wind.

Sunday, May 27. In the morning when I awoke all well, thanks to God, the spirit told me that this was Pentecost. A longing immediately overtook me to be with my wife and children and celebrate Pentecost with them. I became very sad and began to think how I could possibly comfort myself in this wilderness. I took out my Martyr's Song Book and read a few songs. I then saw what people had been willing to suffer for the name of Christ. I took new courage and felt better. I re-consecrated myself wholly to God and to His Fatherly care. In the evening we attended a Lutheran church which was located in the neighborhood. Brother Funk preached a sermon in the English language of which we understood nothing. It was only a small congregation.

Monday, May 28. Awoke rested and much refreshed; praise to God. After breakfast we rode out for a distance of a few miles into the country on a wagon to see how the farmers were getting along in their work. There were as yet only a few pioneers settled in this region. Much of the land that had been plowed was yet under water. The wheat' had only a poor stand and was very weedy due to late seeding. The grass was only thin and small. The land was very level and the soil was black, hut somewhat sandy. It seemed to me that were we to settle here we should never be threatened with famine, and, provided we were industrious and God-fearing, the Lord would not withhold His rich blessings. Since the region seemed somewhat cold and spring came rather late, we decided to go further south to investigate conditions there. All Monday we had our lodging place at the immigration house. In the afternoon we again journeyed out into the country in another direction. The land here seemed better than that which we had seen in the morning because it was richer in grass. We drove around the fields the entire afternoon and in the evening we met our brethren Jacob Buller, Bernhardt Suderman, Wilhelm Ewert of Prussia; Tobias Unruh of Poland; Andreas Schrag of Poland; Bernhardt Boer, Heinrich Wiebe, and Jacob Peters of Bergthal. We drove on for another short distance and came to the little town of Fargo, where we remained for the night.

Tuesday, May 29. In the morning after we (sixteen of us) had rested, praise to God the Highest, we prepared at five in the morning to leave Fargo. The Red River is the boundary line between the state of Minnesota and the territory of Dakota. The land around Fargo, for a distance of 60 miles in length and 35 miles in width is extremely level and has few trees. Then it becomes more hilly and somewhat stony with numerous salt lakes, one of them being one-half mile across. This lake is spanned by a bridge. There are also streams here and there with trees along the banks. The lumber can be used only for fuel. The soil is black with a mixture of sand farther into the subsoil. At two o'clock we arrived at the James River. We were now one hundred miles from Fargo and we decided to go no farther. Funk said that he knew the land well in this region and there was no use in going any farther, since the land gets no better than that which we have already seen. The farther we go, the farther we get from Fargo and from the lumber regions, so that it would be quite difficult to settle for those reasons. The railroad continues for just another hundred miles and then ends. We took the same train back to Fargo at four o'clock in the afternoon because the land around that town looked better to us. At one o'clock, the same night we arrived at Fargo.

Wednesday, May 30. After breakfast six of us, in two wagons belonging to the railroad company, together with Funk and two agents drove out into the country to thoroughly investigate the land. We drove through many fields. The land is so extremely level, that it would be impossible for, water to be drained in a rainy season. There is much tall grass around the wet spots but the ground is not marshy. The grass is only thin, the soil is black with a sandy subsoil and further down we find a gray loam, but less sandy. One man was seeding oats. We spent the entire day roaming through the fields. We had a lunch under the open sky, which the agents provided for us, and late in the afternoon we again returned to our quarters.

Thursday, May 31. I remained in my room the entire day and wrote letters home as well as some songs. Late in the afternoon I walked down to the Red River to see the ship that was to take us to Manitoba, for we had decided to go there.

Friday, June 1. At eight o'clock in the morning we began our journey on the ship and at two o'clock in the afternoon we departed from Moorhead, down the Red River to Manitoba, twelve of his brethren from Russia. The steamship was five fathoms wide and twenty fathoms long. The Red River has a width of twenty fathoms. In the evening the ship stopped and soon the godless life of the people on deck began with music, card-playing and dancing.

Saturday, June 2. Awoke well and refreshed; praise the Lord. I composed a song of thanksgiving today.

Sunday, June 3. We traveled by ship all day today. At one time the ship was unable to move, but after four hours of repair work, we again proceeded on our way.

Monday, June 4. At eight o'clock in the morning we arrived at Fort Pembina in North Dakota. Here I saw soldiers in uniform, also many cannons. They were the first soldiers that I had seen in America and I had traveled in this country for more than a month, in different cities, etc. We proceeded a little farther to the Canadian boundary line where we all marched out of the ship and then again back into the ship in single file. We were all inspected by the English Government officials. Everyone was asked where he was from, his age, name and occupation. All was put on record. This was at ten in the morning.

Tuesday, June 5. At five in the morning we stepped from the ship and walked to the city which was one-half mile from the river. The name of the city was Winnipeg. It is only a small town. Along the river there are numerous fortresses guarded by soldiers, belonging to the English Government. The soldiers wore red uniforms. From Fargo to Winnipeg is two hundred twenty-four miles by land and somewhat farther by water, but I am not certain how much. In the after- noon we were called before the governor. He was very kind and friendly and spoke much but all in the English language. Hespeler was our interpreter. The governor spoke of all the advantages that they could give us, but of course one can not depend on that. In the afternoon twenty of us in three wagons drove out into the country to look at land and talk to the farmers. The people are lazy farmers of mixed Indian blood and are more cattlemen than agriculturalists. The land does not seem bad. The soil is a black loam with not much sand. The wheat stand was small but looked fresh and healthy. One could also see considerable un-threshed wheat left from the previous year.

Wednesday, June 6. At nine o'clock in the morning twenty-five of us again drove out into the country in five wagons with two extra wagons for tents and provisions going in advance. As we were about to leave with our wagons, we were all lined up and a man came carrying a tripod with a box and glass on top. I was wondering what he wanted and was informed that he would take a photograph of us, which was not to my taste, because I do not like to have my picture lying around in all parts of the world. But what will you do with the world? World is world and will remain world until the Lord will come and end it all. We then took the ferry boat and crossed the Red River. After we had journeyed fifteen miles we halted, fed our horses, and had dinner while it rained quite hard. In the afternoon we continued our journey through many muddy and marshy places. At one place the horses slipped and fell and we had to draw the wagons out by hand. The roads were very bad.

After we had journeyed for sixty versts, the evening drew nigh and we came to a settlement inhabited by a people of mixed Indian blood. Our tent wagons had not arrived because they had taken the wrong route. Since we did not wish to sleep under the open sky, we asked these Indians to give us lodging in their homes but they would not. Finally they consented anyway and we remained there for the night.

Thursday, June 7. After breakfast we sang a song of thanksgiving and praise to the Lord, and Brother Suderman read the nineteenth Psalm and led in prayer. At eleven o'clock the two tent wagons arrived and we had dinner and at three we continued our journey, one man on horseback accompanying us as guide to show us the land. He was a half Indian. At five o'clock we arrived at the place where we were supposed to settle. We pitched our tents, ate supper, sang a few songs of thanksgiving and retired for the night.

Friday, June 8. At ten in the morning we continued our journey and soon we came to a house where only the wife was at home and she spoke a beautiful German. They had been living in Canada for two years and we talked about many things with her and asked her many questions. She praised the country, very likely because she wanted neighbors. In America the people are all alike in that respect: everyone praises his own community because he wants it settled. "Every merchant praises his own ware." This region seemed more subject to drought. We crossed several streams and at noon had our dinner, but the mosquitoes were so bad that one could hardly defend himself. In the afternoon we drove on, crossing still other streams. On one occasion we led the horses across the stream. A little farther on we remained for the night, but the mosquitoes were terribly bad.

Saturday, June 9. After breakfast we again traveled on for fifteen versts, then had dinner and from thence proceeded on to the town of Winnipeg. The land through which we traveled that day was marshy and quite woody, but I reckoned that the lumber could be used only for fuel. At some places the land is good, but railroad facilities are poor. The town of Winnipeg is forty-five versts from this land and the roads are very bad. The lumber for building purposes must be shipped by way of the Red River from Minnesota. The half-breed Indians live on this land and it belongs to them. Grasshoppers are very plentiful. The price of stock and agricultural implements is more reasonable in the United States than in Manitoba and if the same is shipped across the boundary, a duty must be paid on it. To most of us, the Manitoba country was not to our liking, but seven of the brethren liked it and wished to journey another one hundred fifty versts to the southwest, where there was some more land for sale. The five of us, Lohrentz Tschetter, Ewert, Schrag, Tobias Unruh and myself and Brother Funk decided to return to Dakota and meet the other brethren at Moorhead, within two weeks. We took leave of the brethren and at midnight boarded our ship.

Sunday, June 10. I awoke somewhat sick. An English minister preached on board the ship. I understood nothing of the sermon. We sang German songs. This minister had his wife and two children with him who acted most vain and arrogant. It is really a pity that many of the ministers in this respect are worse than the other people. In the evening brother Funk preached in English and we sang German songs. Brother Funk explained to the audience the purpose of our journey.

Monday, June 11. At eight o'clock in the morning we stepped from the ship at Fort Pembina after journeying on the river for one hundred versts. A large wagon with four mules and one wagon with one horse were given to us to go out and see the land. At noon we started out, going westward into Dakota. On one side of the road were thick woods of oak and pine trees with the Pembina River winding its way through the woods. A short distance (three to five versts) to the north is the

Canadian boundary line. We drove on for twenty-seven versts and found very beautiful land with black soil and an excellent growth of grass. Some grasshoppers could be seen, but not so many as in Manitoba. We remained for the night at the home of a half-breed Indian. He himself was not at home. His wife and servants treated us very nicely. He had a beautiful house, the floors covered with rugs. He has about 40 head of horned cattle. The housewife gave us a good supper, for they are wealthy people. After supper we took a walk into the woods, where we found many beautiful trees such as oaks, poplars and limes, often so thick that two men could hardly reach around them. We came to a stream that flowed swiftly enough to drive a fair-sized mill. Then we again returned to our lodging place, where we sang a few songs, held a short prayer service and retired for the night.

Tuesday, June 12. We slept very well and had a good night's rest, praise to God. The lady gave us breakfast, for which we had to pay a little, but it was not much. We drove eight versts farther in the country. Here the land was quite sandy and the grass was thin. After going another twenty versts, we came to a German farmer who was very friendly to us. Here we fed our mules. The man seemed to be wealthy for he had several houses which he had purchased from the half breed Indians. His name was Emerling. He lived near the Joseph Mountains and advised us to go to the tops of these mountains for a good view of all the surrounding country. We went and found the mountains covered with a thick growth of trees. From here we got a most excellent view of all the surrounding country for miles around. We returned after a while and had dinner at his home. He told us many interesting things about the land. Barley is seeded about April 24 and cut about June 28. Wheat is seeded about April 20 and cut July 20. In the afternoon we again climbed two steep mountains. Here was a level plain, forty-five versts long and five versts wide. After driving about nine versts around this plain we again returned and had supper at Emerling's place. We sang a few songs and Brother Schrag led in prayer. After that we retired for the night.

Wednesday, June 13. In the morning Brother Ewert led us in prayer and then we had breakfast. After breakfast, we decided to look at the land on the other side of the river, but since it had rained considerably during the night, Emerling said that it would be impossible to cross with our large wagon and four mules, but he thought it might be possible to cross with one horse and small wagon. Only one of us could go along with the guide, since the wagon was so small. I was selected to go along and see the land and report in the evening. We crossed the Pembina and two other small streams. After driving for nine versts, we came upon a level plain between the Pembina and Tongue Rivers, a stretch of land eighteen versts wide. The land is at first level and the soil black, `but there is a great difference in soil at different places, here sandy and again heavier. The land seems a most excellent country for cattle-raising with plenty of water and grass. The man with whom I drove could not speak German and I could not speak English but we managed to understand each other by means of signs. I spoke to him in the Low German (*Plattdeutsch*) and he could understand quite well for there is a great similarity between the *Plattdeutsch* and English. We then returned home crossing the Tongue River which flows into the Pembina three versts away from the Red River. At six in the evening we came to the town of Pembina. I was very hungry and went to a German man named Abels, who was a butcher in the town, and he gave me something to eat. A little later the other brethren also came and Abels also gave them something to eat. We remained in Pembina for the night.

Thursday, June 14. At four o'clock in the morning we boarded the ship for Fargo to look at some land in that neighborhood. The land from Pembina to Fargo is woody on the eastern or Minnesota side of the river, but the western or the Dakota side has no trees and the land would make an excellent cattle raising country. I composed a song today while sailing on the river, to the melody, "*Barmherziger getreuer Gott.*"

Friday, June 15. At three o'clock this afternoon Brother Funk and I left the ship at a town called Grand Forks and traveled with the mail coach instead, because we could get a better view of the land. At this point the great Red River branches off to the Minnesota side. Many logs are seen floating to Manitoba. From Pembina to Grand Forks is a distance of one hundred twenty versts and from Grand Forks to Moorhead is one hundred fifteen versts. At Grand Forks there is a saw mill and a large store where almost everything can be purchased. Since we could get no horses here, we remained in Grand Forks for the night. We were invited to supper by a man named Andreas. After supper I walked out into the country and found very fine level land, black soil, and a good growth of grass. Since it got to be quite late, I again returned to the town and remained at the post office for the night. I composed a song today, "The New Jerusalem."

Saturday, June 16. We continued our journey with a two-horse mail-coach, crossing a good farming country along the Red River. The soil is black and grass is plentiful. The land along the Minnesota side has many more trees than that on the Dakota side. After going for thirty-three versts we changed coaches, now taking a four-horse coach and a different driver. We drove on for eighteen versts. Here the land was lower and there was excellent hay land. The water in the streams was clear and the land was settled with here and there a home. We then changed to another four-horse coach and went on another twenty-one versts and changed again for the next twenty-one versts. Here we found many roses blooming. For the last twenty-two versts we again changed coaches and at ten in the evening we arrived at the town of Moorhead. I walked across the Red River bridge to Fargo, a distance of one verst to my old lodging place and found a letter waiting for me from my wife and was very glad to hear from my loved ones at home. The other brethren, who had come by ship, had not yet arrived and so I remained here for the night.

Sunday, June 17. I remained in my room all day Sunday, wrote a letter home and composed a song. At noon the other brethren came from the ship. Lohrentz and Tobias had remained at Moorhead staying at the home of a German man.

Monday, June 18. At six o'clock in the morning we left Fargo for the west. After we had gone about twenty miles the train stopped. We stepped off and proceeded by wagon to our tents that had been pitched not far away. The land here is somewhat low. We took two teams and drove to the northwestward where we found numerous streams and fine level land with grass quite plentiful. At noon we returned and had dinner in our tents. After dinner the other brethren drove out to take a survey of the land. I remained at the tents, since I did not feel very well. After taking a nap I felt better. I walked six versts to the southward from the railroad and crossed numerous streams. The land seemed dry, although grass was quite plentiful. I returned home after dark and met the other brethren, who had just returned from their drive. We had supper in the tent. Tobias led us in a brief prayer service and then we retired for the night in our tents.

Tuesday, June 19. We sang a song of praise and I led the group in a short prayer service after which we had breakfast in our tents. We again drove toward the north and east to look at some lands. Herb the land was woody at some places. There were numerous streams and grass was plentiful. The land is more rolling, but the low places are not marshy. Some sections are quite stony. In the evening we returned, had supper, Brother Ewert led in prayer and, after singing a song, we retired for the night in our tents.

Wednesday, June 20. After morning services and breakfast we drove ten versts to the northwest as far as Rush River. We found tall grass. We had dinner on a spot near two trees standing close together with another lone tree standing not far away. Then we crossed the Maple River and the railroad and drove to the southward. For four versts along the Maple River the land had plenty of moisture, but the last one hundred versts the soil was dry. When we arrived at our tents in the evening we found that a heavy rain had fallen. Brother Funk led us in prayer and we remained in our tents for the night.

Thursday, June 21. After breakfast and morning service, we packed our tents and drove seven versts south through a low and grassy valley, then seven versts west and again ten versts south, across the Maple River which here has steep banks. At places one could see trees. Then we drove ten more versts southwest. Here the land was higher and grassy, trees quite plentiful and, many flowers especially along the river banks. Upon returning to our tents in the evening, we had supper and Brother Schrag led us in prayer. When we retired, a great rainstorm came with thunder and lightning, but we remained dry for our tents were well-made.

Friday, June 22. After morning services conducted by Brother Ewert, and breakfast, we drove twelve versts westward. The land was somewhat higher and quite stony. Here we crossed the railroad and we saw a large machine operated by steam, with a long arm and shovel at one end. This arm raised, bringing up the shovel with a half-load of dirt and in this manner loaded a railroad car with dirt in a few minutes. We crossed the railroad track and proceeded northward for about ten versts. The land here was still higher and also stony. Then we again returned to the same spot where we had crossed at noon, drove west two versts, left our teams at that place and boarded a train for Fargo which was thirty-seven versts east. Upon our arrival there, Lohrentz, Tobias Unruh and myself walked across the bridge to Moorhead where our baggage was stored at the home of a German man. We remained there for the night. The man seemed rather frivolous and easygoing.

Saturday, June 23. Arose well and refreshed, thank God. I did not like my new lodging place. There was a saloon in the same building and all sorts of people came in. Furthermore there was no room to write and so I told the brethren that I would take my baggage and go to Fargo to the same place where I had formerly stayed. Here I wrote three songs with pencil upon scrap paper. In the evening brother Lohrentz and Tobias also came to my room. We sang a few songs. Brother Unruh led in a prayer service and we retired for the night.

Sunday, June 24. Shortly after our usual morning services and breakfast, several of our brethren, Jacob Buller, Bernhardt Suderman and Schrag came from Manitoba. The other brethren intended to remain in Manitoba a little longer in order to look at some other lands. I remained in my room all day and wrote some.

Monday, June 25. After prayer service and breakfast, the brethren Buller and Suderman went out west to see the land along the railroad that we had gone over several days before. Lohrentz and Tobias drove out to a farmer near Fargo. They found good land and an excellent stand of grain. The wheat that had been seeded April 19 and the barley that had been seeded May 8 were now heading on June 25. They brought samples of the grain along to town. This grain was the second crop on that land, it having been broken the year before.

Tuesday, June 26. I remained in my room in the forenoon. In the afternoon a man came over to our room with Dakota and Minnesota maps and showed us where we could have access to good pine-lumber. He was an official representing the forest department and advised us to buy woodland at $1.25 per acre eighty to one hundred miles from Fargo. The wood could be floated to Fargo on the Red River. The man was not able to speak German, so he went to get a German interpreter.

He gave us Dakota and Minnesota maps. This German man invited us to his home and we accepted the offer. He lived with his father, mother and two grown sisters. They were very friendly and told us many things. They had already lived at many different places, but liked it best here in Fargo. They gave us some good beer to drink. Their house had only very thin walls, and I asked the man if it was not too cold in winter. He said it was not. We again went to our rooms and in the evening the English man called on us again bringing a letter which I was to carry and deliver to the governor of Minnesota, at St. Paul. He also gave us a jar filled with sod. Later in the evening the other brethren who had gone out west to see the land returned and told us what they had seen. They liked the land very much.

Wednesday, June 27. We left Moorhead at ten in the morning with a four-horse mail coach, seven of us brethren of the delegation and Funk. Since it was quite crowded, I sat with the driver which suited me very much for I could thereby get a much better view of the land. The land for the first eighteen versts was higher, with black soil and a fine stand of grass. We went another thirty-three versts and reached McCauleyville. Here the horses were again changed and after driving thirty-three versts farther horses were again changed. We continued fifteen versts more and arrived at Prickeritz at eight in the evening. We drove fifteen versts more and came to Breckenridge, where Seper of St. Paul and the railroad agent waited for us. We remained in Breckenridge for the night.

Thursday, June 28. We left Breckenridge at seven in the morning by train with Seper and the railroad agent. At ten we arrived at Douglas which is sixty versts from Breckenridge. Here teams were already waiting for us to take us out to the land. For the first fifteen versts from Breckenridge the land was a low plain, then the next thirty versts somewhat higher and the last fifteen versts somewhat more hilly with small lakes on both sides of the railroad line. In the distance, one mile away, one could see some forests. At eleven in the morning, we went out in two wagons to look at the land. We drove for twelve versts and then returned. We found many small lakes, a number of them every mile so that about one-third of the country is under water. Near these lakes the grass is very tall and the land near the lakeshores is quite stony. The soil is black with a mixture of shiny sand slightly beneath the surface. Still further down there is a yellowish loam. The grass is not so thick, although the wheat along the roadside looked good and was just heading. The height of the wheat came up as far as my arms. The corn also looked nice and green. The region as a whole did not appeal to me, especially for village life as we have it in Russia, because there is too much water and bottomland. In the afternoon they took another drive to the other side of the railroad line, but I did not go along because it was too crowded. The brethren came back in the evening and reported that they liked this land much better than that which we had seen in the forenoon, but it was already settled considerably. We remained for the night at the railroad station.

Friday, June 29. At ten in the morning we took the train from Douglas to St. Paul and arrived at Willmar at two in the afternoon, the distance being one hundred eight versts, just half the distance to St. Paul. The land is hilly and has many small lakes. It is quite well settled. I saw many fields of wheat, oats and barley. The stand was good and the grain was just heading. From here we went to Litchfield, a small town forty-eight versts from Willmar. At Darwin, one hundred eight versts from St. Paul, the land becomes wooded. Then we came to a small town called Delano. The land from Willmar to Delano is hilly and stony. From there we came to a large lake called Minnetonka, where two hotels are located, one of them being called the Weigalte. Then we came to Naples, a beautiful little town. We arrived there at eight o'clock in the evening and remained in the town for the night in order to look at different kinds of machinery and inquire as to the prices.

Saturday, June 30. In the morning after our usual services, we crossed the bridge over the Mississippi which is not supported as is usual by piers from beneath but is suspended from four high pillars, two on each side on the shores of the river. We saw the saw-mills of which there are seventeen in the city, some of them driven by steam and others by waterpower. A large saw-mill cuts about 22,000 feet of lumber per day. There are numerous waterfalls here, one of them having a fall of one hundred feet. We also saw factories making doors, window-sashes, and window-frames. Everything necessary for constructing a house can be procured ready-made. In another factory we saw them make furniture such as chairs, bedsteads, etc. We also saw a paper-mill, but it was not in running order that day. Then we went to a cloth factory, where many people were employed.

After I had seen all these things, that worldly wisdom had accomplished, I thought of the words in the Scripture, that after all these things shall have reached perfection, God will destroy them, for in the eyes of the Lord it is all folly. When we arrived at our rooms, we found a man waiting for us who wished to show us the sights of the city. We went along with him and he showed us the whole town. After dinner, at two o'clock, we boarded the train for St. Paul, where we were to see the governor and get information from him in regard to the lands and the matter of exemption from military service. But he could speak only English and no German and so Brother Funk acted as our interpreter. He promised us the best of everything in his power, but in regard to the matter of exemption from military service, he did not say much because it was not within his power. Then we returned to our rooms for the night.

Sunday, July 1. After our morning services I wrote a letter and a song of consolation to my wife. I remained the entire day in my little room.

Monday, July 2. I felt somewhat sick this morning because I drank too much ice-water in the great heat yesterday. At eight o'clock in the morning we went to the railway station. A special car had been attached to the rear of the train. The car had sleeping accommodations, a very convenient thing, since I felt sick. The old man Seper was with us as well as a young man by the name of Rosen, who was a Mennonite. His father is a minister in Hamburg. A railroad agent was also with us. At two in the afternoon we arrived at St. James, where we had dinner. Then we came to the little town of Worthington which is two hundred fifty versts southwest of St. Paul. The land covering these two hundred versts is mostly rolling prairie-land with black soil. We arrived at the little town of Worthington shortly before evening. Here we stepped off in order to see the land. Sixteen of us went out in four wagons driving six versts and then returned to our rooms. The land was hilly with quite a good stand of grass. The grain along the roadsides was small.

Tuesday, July 3. In the morning we proceeded by special train, thirty versts eastward to Heron Lake and from there we went out in four wagons, fifteen of us, to see the land. We drove until noon and then stopped for dinner at the home of a farmer who lived in a grove of trees. The growth of grass was quite plentiful, but the grain along the roadside was quite small, thin and of a yellowish color. In the afternoon we drove another thirty versts, following a different route. Then we returned to Heron Lake and took our train back to Worthington, where we remained for the night. **Wednesday, July 4.** I did not feel well when I arose this morning. We again took the train to Worthington and went out by wagon twenty versts to see the land. Here the wheat was also small, thin and suffered from drought. The grass was quite plentiful. The soil is sandy and mixed with saltpeter. The water is likewise mixed with saltpeter. Later in the afternoon, a hot wind came up, the same as we sometimes have at home. The land is hilly and has deep valleys here and there. We drove as far as the town of Windom, which is forty-five miles from Worthington. Here we had dinner. Then we went to Sioux City, which is located in the state of Iowa, one hundred fifty versts from Worthington. The Minnesota line is twenty versts from Worthington. We had supper in the town of LeMars. At ten in the evening we arrived at Sioux City and were met by another railroad agent. The old agent who had been with us for the last few days then took leave of us. Rosen also took leave of us and we remained for the night in Sioux City.

Thursday, July 5. The town of Sioux City is located on the Missouri River near the boundary line between Iowa and Nebraska. We left Sioux City at seven in the morning and arrived at Council Bluffs, a small town. Here we changed trains, crossed the Missouri River over a large bridge, one verst in length and came to Omaha, Nebraska. Omaha is one hundred fifty versts from Sioux City. Then we went as far west as Columbus, another small town one hundred thirty-eight versts from Omaha. Here we stopped and became acquainted with some colonists, who had recently emigrated from Odessa, one of them by the name of Hildebrand. Most of these people had purchased farms, while one of them had entered the mercantile business. We talked many things with them. The women were especially anxious to tell of their trip from Odessa to America. They were all well pleased with their new location. We remained at the home of Hildebrand for the night.

Friday, July 6. After our usual morning services, we drove twelve versts to the north of Columbus in four wagons, fourteen of us. The country is excellently fitted for wheat, oats and corn. The grass was not particularly plentiful. The land is rolling and streams are scarce. Water is found one hundred thirteen feet in the ground. Wells are made by boring, so that a narrow pail can be used for drawing the same from the well. The soil is mixed with a grayish sand and loam. There are no forests here and the lumber for building purposes must be shipped from Minnesota. The cost of this lumber, delivered is $25.00 per feet. Planed and polished lumber costs $40.00 per feet. After we had viewed the land, we again returned to Columbus, where we boarded the train at four in the afternoon for Ayr Junction, one hundred four miles from Columbus. After we had left Columbus, I found that I had forgotten my little box which contained some valuable papers, at the place where we had stayed overnight. What I was most concerned about was the fact that among the papers was also my pass. I informed the agent about it and he wired back. When we arrived at Ayr Junction the reply was already there. The agent said that by Monday I would have my box. Two other agents joined us here while the two former ones who had accompanied us so far left us. We remained here for the night.

Saturday, July 7. We traveled by rail as far as Lamel, a small town fifteen versts from Ayr Junction. Here we had breakfast and then went out in four wagons, sixteen of us in number to view the land. We drove as far as a little stream known as the Little Blue River, thirty versts from Lamel. Here we ate dinner and went on another twenty versts as far as the Red Cloud River, where we remained for the night at the home of a man. During the entire stretch of fifty versts we struck only three farm homes. The land is quite sandy and grass does not seem plentiful, hardly enough for pasture. At places one finds ruins of old mounds and ditches. Water can he found only deep in the ground and in the entire distance, we found only one small insignificant stream. The region is entirely treeless and far away from all "*Handel und Wandel.*"

Sunday, July 8. We spent Sunday in the state of Nebraska, five miles from the Kansas boundary near the Red Cloud River. We spent the day in our rooms and attended services in a church in the evening. The sermon was preached in English by a minister who traveled with us, and we sang a song in the German language.

Monday, July 9. At three in the morning we traveled back fifty versts and at three in the afternoon we arrived at the little town of Hastings. Then we went to Sutton, Fairmont and Crete. In this last-named town I received my little box of papers which I had forgotten at Columbus, the week before. Here we had supper. At midnight we arrived in Lincoln, the capital of Nebraska. From Hastings to Lincoln, the distance is one hundred eighty-six miles and we remained in Lincoln for the night.

Tuesday, July 10. In the morning eleven of us took a car to get a view of the city. The car came to our door and took us all along. My, how tired I am of all this travel and sight-seeing by this time, but I could not refuse and so I went along. When the rest wished to go another one and one-half miles to bathe in a salt spring I refused and retired to my room. We left Lincoln at eleven in the morning and arrived at Plattsniouth at three, fifty-five miles from Lincoln. Here we boarded a steamboat and crossed the Missouri River, two miles wide to the Iowa side and traveled by train fourteen versts further on, where we took leave of the other brethren, Lohrentz Tschetter, Tobias and myself going directly to Elkhart, while the other brethren went to Summerfield, Illinois. Brother Funk went to the state of Missouri to visit one of his brothers. We were all to meet at Elkhart Sunday evening. We traveled throughout the night.

Wednesday, July 11. Early in the morning we came through Galesburg where we had breakfast and then to Aurora, a large city, and at three o'clock in the afternoon we arrived in Chicago. We were met there by a German man named Resla, who had orders to meet us from the railroad agents in Nebraska. He took us to a German hotel. From Plattsmouth to Chicago is a distance of four hundred fifty miles. At five in the afternoon we boarded the train and arrived at ten that evening in Elkhart, Indiana, one hundred one miles from Chicago. We went to brother Funk's home where I expected a letter from home but was disappointed.

Thursday, July 12. At five in the afternoon Tobias Unruh and myself went with Isaac Kilmer out into the country to his farm. We had already been there before.

Friday, July 13. We remained the entire day at the home of Isaac, where we rested from our long journey. It rained all day long with much thunder and lightning.

Saturday, July 14. Felt somewhat sick when I arose in the morning. Could eat little and had constant stomach pains. At four in the afternoon Isaac took us to Holdemann, six miles away where we remained for the night.

Sunday, July 15. Felt somewhat sick when I arose in the morning. At ten we went to the church services where many people had assembled. I gave the opening sermon and Tobias Unruh gave the main sermon. After the services Isaac took us to Leatherman, one mile away, where we had dinner with some other brethren who were also ministers. In the afternoon we accompanied Isaac to another church six miles away where a service was to begin at four. There we also met Lohrentz and Schrag. They informed us that Ewert, Buller and Warkentin's son had gone to Texas, and that Suderman was in Elkhart. Tobias Unruh led in the opening sermon, and I gave the main sermon. My text was Colossians 2:1, "I would that ye knew what great conflict I have for you." The congregation was rather small, but when the sermon was over there were even less. Hardly any were left except the ministers. Very likely the sermon was not to their taste. After the service I went along with Rev. Heinrich Schaum, two miles from the church. I had such a headache that I had to lie down as soon as we reached home and did not eat anything that evening.

Monday, July 16. My headache of yesterday had ceased, but somehow I could not eat breakfast for I had no appetite. The man at whose house I stayed took us to a place two miles away where Lohrentz and Schrag stayed and from there took us to Elkhart, four miles away, where we met brother Suderman. I went to a drugstore and purchased some medicine, and went to my room. I did not eat dinner. In the afternoon we had to talk over some matters in regard to conferring with the government. Some of the brethren first wished to go to Canada before conferring with the government officials, while others had gone to Texas. So we decided that Lohrentz, Tobias Unruh and myself should make the journey alone, confer with the government officials and continue our journey homeward. We took leave of all the brethren and I led in a farewell prayer. They accompanied us as far as the railway station and we proceeded on our journey to Philadelphia.

Tuesday, July 17. This morning we were still traveling on with the train, passing through many cities and at eleven in the morning we were in Cleveland, Ohio, near Lake Erie, a large city with many hundreds of factories of various kinds. We were obliged to remain in Cleveland until four in the afternoon. At that time we departed from the city arriving at seven that evening in the city of Akron and at twelve in Pittsburgh where we changed. We stepped from the train and did not know where to find our train. Happily we found a German man who assisted us. We traveled throughout the entire night towards Philadelphia.

Wednesday, July 18. At ten we arrived at Harrisburg, at eleven at Lancaster, and at one o'clock in the large city of Philadelphia, one of the most beautiful cities in America. The distance from Elkhart to Philadelphia is eight hundred miles. Here we had the address of a certain J. Cooke, who is one of the richest men in America. We went to the office of J. Cooke which was four miles from the station. We were asked whether we had seen Hiller a German man who was to meet us at the station. We said, "No." We were given a lodging place which was paid for by the J. Cooke Co. man. Hiller then came in and informed us that Klassen and Cornelius with the three other Bergthal brethren had gone to New York City and expected to board the ship tomorrow. We asked Hiller to wire them and ask them to wait so that we might make the journey home together. We also inquired about the price of land and they informed us: $3.50 per acre. We said $3.00 is enough, and they advised us to wait until tomorrow, when we could talk with the head official. We decided to wait until the next day. We then went with Hiller to see the city waterworks which is one of the wonders of the world. The water from the river is forced one hundred feet into an elevated reservoir and then distributed through pipes all over the city.

Thursday, July 19. This morning I wrote a petition to the President of the United States. At eight o'clock Hiller came to our rooms. I showed him the petition and he said that it was very satisfactory and that he would assist us in handing it to the President personally. At ten in the morning we went to the railway offices, where we were introduced to J. Cooke. He could not speak German and Hiller was our interpreter. Cooke said that he expected to leave the city for a time on business, but there was a man in New York City, who was the highest official over the land affairs and that he would be able to inform us regarding the price of the land. Mr. Cooke treated us with some very excellent wine which we had to drink with him. When he found that we wished to see the President he gave us a letter of introduction, which may be of great assistance to us.

We were then called into another room where a group of Moravians wished to meet us and speak to us in regard to our belief and creed. We explained to them the chief principles of our confession of faith and they wrote them all down until we came to the point as to whether women could be teachers. I said, "No," and they inquired, "Why not?" I replied, "Because the apostle said, 'I suffer not a woman to teach, nor to usurp authority over the man, but to be in silence'" (1 Timothy 11:12). They said, "We like all your principles, excepting this one. We are all in Christ, men and women." And I said, "Yes, we are all equal, men and women in the eyes of the Lord, but the husband is the head of the wife and so we rather take the head than the feet." After I had said that, the discussion stopped and they took leave of us and went their way. We also retired to our rooms and at seven in the morning we boarded the train for New York City, one hundred miles from Philadelphia and arrived there at ten in the evening. We crossed a small body of water and then Hiller engaged a car to take us to his home, six miles out of the city where we remained at his home for the night.

Friday, July 20. At ten in the morning we boarded a steamship for New York City, six miles away. We were busy the entire day dealing with the land company. They did not wish to agree to points and asked us to come again the next morning at eleven o'clock when they would be ready with their decision. We returned to our rooms at the home of Hiller.

Saturday, July 1. Again went to New York City and at eleven met the land agents. They agreed to all our points but wished us to come Monday. Since we expected to have an interview with the President that day, our meeting with the agents was postponed until Tuesday. We intended to wire home and inquire as to what was best to do in regard to this land business but upon being informed that the cablegram would cost twenty-five dollars we thought it was too much and so we again returned to our rooms.

Sunday, July 22. At ten we went to New York City and attended church services at a mission where a sermon was preached in German. The minister spoke of the Cross and tribulations and faith and that we should leave all for His sake. But when I looked the congregation over, it did not seem as though they were leaving very much. There was altogether too much of this worldliness. After the service we again returned to Hiller's home and had dinner there. We remained there in the afternoon. Many guests came to see us that afternoon, and we dined with them. They were anxious to see the Russian brethren and invited us to their homes, but we excused ourselves, saying that our time was very limited.

Monday, July 23. At ten we went to New York City to see the railway agent, but he was sick and so we could do very little. In the evening we intended to go to Washington. Since this traveling back and forth was expensive, we decided that Lohrentz should stay at our room, while Tobias and myself would go to Washington with Hiller. Hiller telegraphed to the President at Washington, but received the reply that we should meet him at Long Beach. We then planned to return to our lodging place, but since there was no ship there at that hour I said that I would go to the mission and inquire whether we had received any mail. On my return I lost my way and wandered around a considerable time. When I finally found the place, neither Tobias nor Hiller was there. I waited for an entire hour and still no one appeared and so I returned to the mission and remained there for the night.

Tuesday, July 24. Received a telegram from Hiller that I should remain at the mission and that they would meet me there. At ten they arrived and we all went to the railway agent and he offered us the land for three dollars per acre. But we did not agree on a number of other points and so the deal remained open for further negotiation some time later. When we returned home we saw an oil steamer on fire in the ocean. The fire lasted throughout the day and night. That was not far from our rooms.

Wednesday, July 25. We spent the entire day in the city and returned to our quarters at Hiller's home in the evening.

Thursday, July 26. This was the day that we really intended to leave for home, for our ship was to sail today. But since we had some important work to do yet, we decided to remain longer. We had to take new courage and patience and wait until next Thursday, when another ship would leave for Hamburg. I wrote another petition to the President, for I did not particularly like the first one. At eleven in the morning we went to the city. Here I re-copied my petition and had it translated into English. Then we again returned home. Oh how I abhor life in the city. All the noise and music make me so disgusted, that I can hardly stand it.

Friday, July 27. At eight we took the steamer for New York City, walked through a part of the city and boarded another ship to Long Beach where the President spends the summer and where we were to meet him. We sailed two hours by ship and traveled one more hour by rail when we arrived at Long Beach and remained at a hotel. Hiller went to investigate when we were to appear before the President. He returned and informed us that we were to meet him at eight in the evening. Shortly before eight we left our hotel to appear before the President, which was only one and one-half miles from our lodging place. When we arrived at the President's home we were introduced to President Grant by Hiller. The President received us in the most friendly manner and we presented our petition to him personally. After reading it very carefully the President replied that we must have patience to wait for an answer to our petition. But since we are to leave New York for home on the *Cimbria* August 2, Hiller assured us that he would send us the President's reply.

Appendix B

Neu Hutterthaler Church Record Book, Narrative Sections, 1875–1919

The Church and the Register of It at Wolf Creek

TRANSLATED BY DAVID P. GROSS.
EDITED BY DAVID P. GROSS AND ROD JANZEN

Note: What follows are the first 30 pages, the narrative section, of the 841-page Neu Hutterthaler Church record book, almost all of which was written by Paul Tschetter. The remaining pages of the book are comprised of birth, death, family, marriage and other congregational records from the years 1875–1943. For the most part the translation preserves Tschetter's sometimes incorrect spelling (of names, places and non-English words), grammar and syntax.

Page 1. Introduction.

This book contains a complete collection of names, birthdays, baptisms and marriage records of all church members as well as a short biography of those deceased and a short history of our migration to America.

Paul Tschetter, 1883.

[Note: This record was first compiled in 1883 but Paul Tschetter continued to add to it during his lifetime. After his death other church leaders took on this responsibility.]

    The contents of this book are divided into four divisions: Section one lists birthdays of individual members. Section two lists the names and dates of those who were baptized. Section three lists names and dates of those who married in the congregation and the names of ministers who performed the wedding ceremonies. Section four lists the names of deceased members and the dates when they died. Page three includes the names of ministers and their dates of ordination.

Page 2. Ministerial Slate.

The Neu Hutterthaler Church is presently served by an Elder and three ministers who were elected in the old homeland of Russia to serve in their respective positions. [This sentence was written in 1883 and refers to the first three ministers named below. Tschetter or someone else added the names of other Neu Hutterthaler ministers at a later date.]

1. Martin Waldner was born on November 15, 1832 and entered the ministry on January 30, 1857.

2. Paul Tschetter was born on October 6, 1842 and entered the ministry on January 30, 1866.

3. Joseph Wipf was born on September 22, 1835 and entered the ministry in 1868.

4. Johann Hofer was born on September 12, 1848 and entered the ministry in America on February 24, 1884.

5. Michael Stahl was born on December 16, 1836. [No other information is given here.]

6. David Wipf was born on July 25, 1861 and entered the ministry on July 15, 1909.

7. Paul Tschetter was born on March 30, 1869 and entered the ministry on July 15, 1909.

Page 3. Ordination of Ministers to their Respective Positions.

Martin Waldner was ordained to the ministry by the Honorable Elder Peter Wedel of the Alexanderwohl Church of the Molotschna in 1857.

Paul Tschetter was ordained to the ministry by the Honorable Elder Peter Wedel of the Alexanderwohl Church of the Molotschna in the Hutterthal school building, in Russia in 1866.

Joseph Wipf was ordained to the ministry by the Honorable Elder Michael Stahl of the Hutterthal Church by the Taschenack (River), Government Ikatharine, in Russia, in 1869, in the village of the Neu Hutterthal, on purchased land, which is located 200 *werst* (120 miles) from Hutterthal.

During the year 1883, on January 28, the Minister Paul Tschetter was ordained to the position of Elder by the Honorable Elder Friedrich Schartner of the Silver Lake Church (America); this happened in Hutchinson County, America, in the schoolhouse near Wolf Creek.

Page 4. Ordination of Ministers by Elder Paul Tschetter in America.

Johann Hofer was ordained to his position by Elder Paul Tschetter on June 2, 1884. This happened near Wolf Creek in Hutchinson County.

Elder Joseph Hofer was ordained. [No other information is provided.]

David Wipf and Paul Tschetter were ordained to their respective positions on May 29, 1910, by Elder Paul Tschetter in the Neu Hutterthaler Church near the Wolf Creek.

Peter Stahl (Hutterdorf Church) was ordained to his position on September 9, 1917 by Elder Paul Tschetter.

Elias Wipf was ordained to his position in the Beadle County Hutterthal Church by Elder Paul Tschetter on July 14, 1912.

Joseph Hofer of Beadle County was ordained January 15, 1909.

Jacob Schartner was ordained. [No additional information is provided for Schartner or for the next three ministers listed.]

David Tiesen was ordained.

Paul Kleinsasser was ordained.

John Hofer was ordained.

Paul Gross was ordained in North Dakota on June 25, 1914.

Johann Kleinsasser was ordained on June 25, 1914.

Pages 5, 6. Record of Ministers as to Ages Attained and Years of Service to the Church.

Martin Waldner attained the age of 57 years, 4 months, and 18 days and served the Church for 33 years.

Joseph Wipf attained the age of 60 years, 9 months, and 8 days and served his church for 28 years.

Jacob Wipf attained the age of 59 years, 2 months, and 18 days and served his church for 38 years of which 20 were served as Elder. [Wipf was a minister at the Elm Spring Hutterite Colony.]

Peter Hofer attained the age of 65 years less 11 days. He served his church for 42 years and 8 months and also 3 years as Elder. [Hofer was also a minister at the Elm Spring Hutterite Colony.]

Darius Walter attained the age of 68 years, 6 months, and 15 days. He served his church for 45 years. [Walter was the Dariusleut leader at the Wolf Creek Hutterite Colony].

Paul Hofer attained the age of 67 years, 10 months, and 3 days. He served his church [the Hutterthal Church] for 30 years.

Michael Stahl attained the age of 64 years and served his church for 35 years. [Stahl was a minister at the Wolf Creek Hutterite Colony].

Schmied Michael attained the age of 57 years and served his church for 34 years. [Michael Waldner was the first Schmiedeleut leader at the Bon Homme Hutterite Colony].

Jacob Hofer attained the age of 70 years. [Hofer too was a minister at the Bon Homme Hutterite Colony.]

Jacob Waldner attained the age of 59 years and served his church for 20 years.

John Hofer attained the age of 66 years and 18 days, and served his church for 30 years

Johan Waldner attained the age of 65 years, 5 months, and 16 days.

Paul Tschetter attained the age of 77 years, 1 month, and 19 days. As minister he served 17 years less 2 days and as Elder 35 years, 8 months, and 26 days making a total of 52 years, 8 months, and 29 days of service. [This entry is an example of one added after Paul Tschetter's death.]

Jacob Walter was ordained by Elder Paul Tschetter on September 15, 1918.

Jacob W. Kleinsasser was ordained by Elder David J. Wipf on June 27, 1921.

David J. Wipf was ordained as Elder by Elder Jacob Schartner of Silver Lake on January 6, 1919.

Joseph J. Hofer and Paul J. R. Hofer were ordained to the ministry by Elder David J. Wipf on June 28, 1936.

Pages 7–17. Report of Why We Had to Leave Russia.

We lived in South Russia under privileges granted by Emperor Alexander the First, to the affect that we should be exempted from all military duties and have other privileges as well. In Petersburg the Mennonites had a special Department which dealt only with Germans and in Odessa there was a Committee for German immigrants, and so the German people had special privileges in Russia that exceeded that of other Nationalities that lived there.

Since however the German people came to Russia from various countries they still were strangers in the land. In the beginning each family received 150 acres of land but as the German people became more numerous and needed more and more land, it was not granted to them. This caused many German families to have no land at all.

However the German people knew how to cope with the situation and help themselves. They did this by developing manufacturing. Especially successful was the manufacture of wagons which were purchased by the Russians for a good price. Since this was still inadequate and things got more and more crowded in the villages, the Germans began to purchase additional land from local Noblemen. This was possible because these Noblemen had lost possession of their slaves [the Russian serfs were freed in 1861] and since they were used to living in luxury and having a lot of festivities, they for the most part soon became poor and found it necessary to sell their land. This indeed was the main reason for jealousy against the German people which caused the Russians to say, "Why are the German people enjoying so many privileges? That is why they are getting rich."

The Mennonites did not continue to adhere to their traditions, however, but became proud, presumptuous, and crowded themselves into holding any office they possibly could. They came as far as Petersburg with their business deals. Their pride had risen to a point where it could not rise any higher and at its highest point became an abomination before God. Those of us who called ourselves Hutterites had also departed far from the path of our forefathers.

We Hutterites did not permit the spirit of God to direct us but rather much more the spirit of the world. All effort was only for material things rather than the Heavenly Treasurer of Salvation which of course is the most important. We claimed to be defenseless Christians but we had already failed in our defenselessness in 1853 in the Crimean War when we had association with a War Lord and made a bad reputation for ourselves. Not only that; we had simply not remained humble and meek as our faith calls for and as behooves God's people. Then suddenly God instituted something that was indeed entirely strange to us. I interpret it as an awakening for us. It was the love of our Heavenly Father that wanted to bring us closer to Him and rouse us from our sleep.

It was in 1870 that a new law was passed in Russia that required that within the next ten years we must decide to obey the new conscription law or leave Russia. It concerned not only military duty but all other privileges that we had enjoyed. They were to be suddenly taken away and we were to be placed on an equal basis with all other farmers of Russia. That was something strange for us. The privileges were the very foundation for Mennonites.

Now was the time for meetings in order to decide what to do. We Hutterites also had a meeting which Elder Michael Stahl ordered and he also invited me even though I lived 200 *werst* distance from the Hutterthal Church on newly purchased land. Without delay Jacob Mendel and I made the trip to attend the meeting which was held in the Hutterthal School building. Here the discussion centered on the question of what we could do and what would be the best move. The following ministers were present, namely: John Waldner, Martin Waldner, Jacob Wipf, Peter Hofer, and Paul Tschetter.

Conditions seemed to be getting serious; everyone was excited and everyone feared the news. After much discussion it was finally decided that we send delegates to Petersburg to investigate the matter. Three men were appointed to make the trip, namely: Elder Michael Stahl, Jacob Wipf, and Paul Tschetter. So on February 7, 1872 we three with God's help departed on our gigantic city of Petersburg and in three times twenty-four hours travel, one evening we arrived at the splendid city which was 2,000 *versts* distant from home.

There we met with an official who earlier had been head of a Committee in our region but now held a highly respected position in Petersburg. We explained our problem to him. He said, "I cannot help you with your problem. It is not under my jurisdiction. I have nothing to do with it." He was however very friendly and asked where we were from and where we lived. When Brother Jacob Wipf explained to him it appeared that he was acquainted with the place because he had visited Hutterthal in his younger years because at that time he had some jurisdiction over the German people. He informed us that we must meet with the man that is president of the commission from which the new law originated. He lived in the same building and his name was Mister Gross. With this information he bowed before us and departed. Now we went to call on Mister Gross. Before his office door stood a servant. We informed him that we wished to speak to his master. He explained to us that we would have to wait a little (after he had informed the official about us). After waiting about a half hour he invited us into his office and asked in a grim tone, "What is your wish?" We explained our problem to him and he replied, "The Mennonites are not drafted to shed blood but are expected to serve with the sanitary service but the whole matter has not yet been put before the High Court. This fall the law will first come before the High Court and then you can appeal to them." With this he bowed and departed.

After we had been in Petersburg for seven days we left for home and with God's help arrived safely. The only thing we accomplished with this long trip was that we now knew how matters stood with us. We would be drafted to serve in the Sanitation Department of the military. Now good judgment was needed.

In the fall of the same year Brother Paul Gross, Minister Peter Hofer, and Elder Michael Stahl made another trip to Petersburg. But it was of no advantage and matters remained as we had been informed on the first trip. Now we were obliged to find another plan. Many Mennonites had decided to migrate to America and had appointed deputies to investigate if in America we could enjoy freedom of religion. So we sold our land to a nobleman and joined the Mennonites in order to travel with their delegates on their trip to America. [Note: Tschetter did not actually sell any land at this time. Why he implies that this was case is a mystery.]

Since the Hutterthal Church would not agree with us that they too should send a delegate with the Mennonite delegates, we out of our Church (Neu Hutterthal) which consisted of only 20 families elected two delegates, namely Lohrentz Tschetter and Minister Paul Tschetter, to also make the trip to America. So with prayer, sighing, and weeping we began this distant voyage with much faith in our Heavenly Father that He would bring us back home in good health. This was on the 14th of April 1873. Since two Kleine Gemeinde members were to travel with us, we met in Nikipol. The next day we left on a steamer on the Dnieper River.

First we arrived in Kherson and then left for the great city of Odessa. There we met with a German man named Toews who advised us how to travel. Then we crossed Russian Poland to the Russian border. The city on the border is named Molotscheska. From there we crossed Austrian Poland, Galizian, as far as Prussian Poland. The city on the border is named Oswiecim. From there we crossed Prussian Poznan and Lemburg to the capitol and giant city of Berlin and then to Hamburg. The entire trip on land was made in six days. After this there was no more travel on land. Now we traveled on water until America but we had to wait three days before the ship Silesia left for America.

After three days, amid prayer and sighing and fully depending on God, we entered the ship which floated on the Elbe. We were four in our company. The other two travel companions were David Klassen and Cornelius Toews. Now our little ship approached the splendid Silesia which floated on the North Sea. Arriving we departed from the smaller vessel and embarked on the giant ship, and with loud music the Silesia departed. After two days we came to the harbor city in France (Le Havre). Here after a lapse of 24 hours we entered the great and wild Atlantic

Ocean. But ocean travel did not agree with me; I got seasick and often had to throw up. With Lohrentz, things were somewhat better; with Klassen all was well, but with Toews it was worse than with me.

After 13 days of swimming around on the stormy ocean we arrived at the giant city of New York. How happy we were to tread on solid ground again. From New York we traveled by train to Elkhart, Indiana where we arrived at the home of a Mennonite minister with the name of Funk. However since he was not at home we had to wait for his arrival and when he arrived he greeted us with friendliness. He also became our travel companion after we had spent a few days in Elkhart with brothers of our faith. Now we traveled on by train. First we arrived in the great city of Chicago and then on westward to the city of St. Paul which lies in the state of Minnesota where we were to meet with other brethren from the Molotschna.

However since we could not await their arrival we traveled on from St. Paul to a small town called Duluth. This little town of Duluth is 156 miles distant from St. Paul. From there we traveled 256 miles until Glendon where we tarried one day until all the Deputies arrived, namely Jacob Wolle, Elder Leonard Suderman, Elder Wilhelm Ewert from Prussia and Elder Tobias Unruh from Poland, Andreas Schrag also from Poland, Lenhardt Boer, Heinrich Wiebe and Jacob Peters from Bergthal. Now with Funk we numbered twelve people all together.

From Glendon we moved on to Fargo which is located on the Red River in Dakota Territory. Since we also agreed to also see the land in Manitoba which is under English control, we boarded a ship which was sailing to Winnipeg which is located in Manitoba. After four days of travel on water we arrived at Winnipeg which is 294 miles distant from Fargo. We viewed some of the land in Manitoba which appealed to some of us but not to others because it appeared to be a totally wild region. It appealed to the two Kleine Gemeinde delegates and the three Bergthaler delegates but to me and the other delegates it did not appeal because it was too far north and too cold.

So we departed from the other brethren and turned back to Fargo in Dakota which we viewed the land carefully and it appealed to us quite well. From here we traveled back to St. Paul in Minnesota. From St. Paul we traveled 259 miles southwest and viewed the land there but it did not appeal to us; so from there we traveled to Iowa and came to Sioux City. But since there was no free government land left in Iowa we went into the state of Nebraska instead and arrived in the city named Omaha which lies on the Missouri River. The land in Nebraska didn't appeal to us either. Dakota appealed to us more so we decided to settle in Dakota. Viewing land with the help of God now ended and we returned to Elkhart, Indiana. We had spent 52 days viewing land.

From Elkhart we traveled to the large city of Philadelphia because that was the place where the owner of the land along the North Pacific lived. [Tschetter is referring to Jay Cooke.] We wanted to know exactly what price he wanted per acre. It is to be noted that at all times a man who represented the railroad company, whose name was Michel Hiller, was with us. We were sent, with Michael Hiller, to New York where the land office was located; so we journeyed to New York. New York is 100 miles from Philadelphia. Hiller took us there and brought us to his home which was located two miles distant from New York City. Faint and tired we rested somewhat here.

Now there were only three in our company, namely Lohrentz and Tobias and myself. The rest had traveled on to Kansas. By now we had noticed that there was plenty of land available and no shortage of it in America. Due to much investigation we had learned that in peacetime no soldiers were drafted from among the citizens but all soldiers were instead hired. However in time of war nothing was assured. Since however we wanted something specific, we had to turn to President Grant for more complete information. The man Hiller was helpful to us in making it possible to appear before President Grant who at this time was located on the island of Lanbrints. So we presented him with a petition which reads as follows: [This petition is published in full in Appendix C.]

On July 27, led by Hiller, we traveled to the Island of Lanbrants. We traveled from New York on water and for one hour by train and arrived safely and well on the Island Lanbrants where with Hiller's arrangements we were able to appear before the President at 8 o'clock in the evening. He accepted us very cordially and we presented our petition. He examined it and said that he could not give a response that very evening because he could not speak German. Mr. Hiller was there to interpret for us. We had to have patience until there was a reply. However since it took too long for us, we took our departure from the United States on August 2 on the vessel *Cimbria* and sailed for home with the understanding that a reply would be forwarded to us by means of Mr. Hiller.

After 11 days on the stormy ocean we arrived at Hamburg. We thanked God for His Fatherly provision and that He had so graciously protected us. We were happy to once more step foot on solid ground. After a few days delay in Hamburg we came home happy and in good health on August 22. We thanked God for fatherly protection preserving us during that far journey. The entire trip lasted 132 days.

We found all our loved ones safe and in good health except for 7 year-old Jacob who had died during our absence. We don't begrudge him the rest but instead entreat him to the Lord our God, and I am assured that he will be a little angel in heaven. Now our trip was completed with God's help.

We called for a church meeting and reported everything word for word regarding how we found things in America. However since we had not yet received an answer to our petition, we could only tell people verbally about religious freedom in America and had to wait patiently until we would get a written reply.

Now the time had not yet arrived for us to sign the contract that closed our land deal with the nobleman; November 1st had been the date set for the closing. When the first of November arrived and the deal was to be closed we all met at the government city Ekaterinoslav. But now the nobleman began to find excuses for not closing the deal. His excuse was that he did not yet have the money because it amounted to 150,000 rubles. So after spending 16 days in the city we departed for home not having finished our business. Now we were in a bad situation because the nobleman had already taken possession of all of our cattle, horses and agricultural implements and had sold them at a public auction.

Some of the brethren [at Neu Hutterthal village] began to purchase horses in order to plow in spring. However I did not have ambition to start plowing again because I thought that if I would began to farm again, we would all remain in Russia and our young men would be drafted. While everything was so mixed up, Mr. Hiller suddenly arrived with the written reply to our petition which read as follows: [This text is published in full in Appendix D.]

This information, which contained no special privileges, was read before the Church. Now one could say "Here it is and there it can happen" [i.e. here (in Russia) the Hutterites knew that soon they would lose their privileges; there (in the United States) they might still attain them.] Now we must immigrate only with good hope. And of what value is it to make an agreement with men? They can also break the same. This we had already experienced with our privileges in Russia. Where there was no great ambition to migrate before, this had made a great impression. Now good counsel came with a price. I had however decided to migrate and so I began to work to secure a migration pass. Five families wished to depart immediately. All that happened during the time I was acquiring a pass will be left inside the pen.

Page 17, 18. Description of the First Migration.

In order to avoid the awakening of envy later among our descendents, and since we had already received our pass to migrate in Simferopol, we left Russia on September 22, 1874. We were five families total, including the following people: Joseph Tschetter, Jacob Tschetter, Joseph Hofer, Joshua Hofer, two Sons of Lohrentz, namely, Lohrentz Tschetter and Paul Tschetter and the two sons of George Gross, namely, George Gross and William Gross.

After six weeks of travel, namely 18 days on the ocean and the rest of the days on land, we arrived at Elkhart, Indiana on November 11, according to the Hiesiger calculation. We arrived healthy and well with God's blessing and help but since it was already late, winter having already set in, we arranged for temporary winter quarters. We rented a house where we all had one room. After a stay of four months we traveled on to Dakota Territory to the town of Yankton where we stayed another month after which we traveled to a location 45 miles from Yankton which lies on the Wolf Creek. The Hutterdorfers had settled there along with the colonies.

On August 23, 1875, Reverend Joseph Wipf arrived with the other brethren, also well-kept under God's blessing and protection. Now the Church [Neu Hutterthal] was together again. Later other brethren came from Hutterthal and Johannesruh and joined the church. Also Reverend Martin Waldner came with Elder Michel Stahl. The Elder joined the Darius Walter Colony [the Wolf Creek Colony] and Martin Waldner joined our fellowship.

Now I want to report how we fared with non-resistance while we still lived in Neu Hutterthal in Russia.

Pages 19, 20. Report Regarding Our Non-Resistance.

In Russia we received a written command from our Elder that the weapons that were found among us were to be totally annihilated. As it was ordered the two guns that were found were immediately destroyed. However when we came to America the spirit of gun ownership reappeared. Many of our Church members purchased guns and they used Sunday as day for travel in order to hunt and provide food. It wasn't the case, however, that there wasn't food to eat because God had blessed us so that we always had bread. The longer we waited the worse it got.

When Johann Waldner also came to America, Joseph Wipf and I thought that we would form an alliance with Johann Waldner and Paul Hofer and Johann Wipf, all three ministers [at the Hutterthal Church] to organize into one Church and again elect an Elder, and then together to put away all guns. Even though we tried ever so hard, all attempts failed and guns were the reason, because Johann Waldner saw it unnecessary to put away all guns [in his congregation]. So we couldn't become united and we remained a separate congregation and put away weapons in our congregation. In order to have no members with weapons [at Neu Hutterthaler] the following church regulation was established:

Church Regulation

Because we claim to be a non-resistant people who carry no weapons according to our Confession of Faith, and since we left Russia for that very reason, it appears inappropriate for us to carry guns because it contradicts our Articles of Faith; also because our youth could easily be led astray if they become accustomed to carry a weapon, and if it would happen that they would be drafted into military duty, it would be easier for them to comply. For this reason we have come to see it a great mistake in the Church and we Church leaders are responsible due to our solemn promise to order such evil to be abandoned in the Church. All who do not agree with us, but consider it a right and a privilege to own a gun will be separated from the Church until they admit they are in error. The parents of such children who are not yet Church members but own or carry a gun will be held responsible because as Christian parents they have not kept their children in better order.

All those Church members who agree with us should sign the above Church Regulation in their own handwriting without being forced.

[Names of those who signed the Church Regulation follow.]

Paul Tschetter, Joseph Wipf, Martin Waldner, Jacob Tschetter, Joseph Tschetter, Joseph Hofer, David Tschetter, Jacob Tschetter, Paul Walter, Jacob Mendel, Paul Stahl, Andrew Gross, Lohrentz Tschetter, Jacob Tschetter, Joshua Hofer, Paul Tschetter, Andreas Hofer, Samuel Glanzer, Samuel Glanzer, Johann Tschetter, Andreas Wipf, Joshua Hofer, Zacharias Wipf, Joseph Hofer, Franz Walter, Elias Kleinsasser, Elias Wipf, Peter Tschetter, Isaac Walter, Joseph Glanzer, Johann Hofer, Joseph Walter, Jacob Hofer, Samuel Hofer, Paul Hofer, Paul Mendel, Joseph Hofer, Wilhelm Gross, Joseph Walter, Daniel Wurz, Jacob Dekker, Joseph Pullman, Johann Wollman, Michael Hofer, Michael Hofer, Paul Tschetter, Jacob Wurz, David Hofer, George Gross, Jacob Walter, Jacob Knels, Paul Gross, Joseph Hofer, David Wollman, Johann Tschetter, Johann Tschetter, David Wipf, Paul Kleinsasser, Jacob Hofer, Elias Walter, Jacob Knels, David Tschetter, Joseph Wipf, Joseph Wipf, Paul Gross, Joseph Pollman, Joshua Stahl, David Tschetter, Peter Hofer, Wilhelm Gross, Mathias Kleinsasser, Jacob Hofer, Joseph Pollman, Michael Wollman

Page 21. Report of an Event in the Church.

In 1884 a great evil and black spot tried to enter the Church in that some members engaged in playing pool, and since we as guardians had noticed that it became more and more common, we considered it necessary to abandon such an evil; so we assembled the Church and presented the matter to them. The Church acknowledged that such an evil should be abandoned; so it was decided that should anyone play the game, he should apologize before the church for the first offence; for the second offence, another apology; but for the third offence he should be separated from the Church. This happened on January 26, 1884 in America at Wolf Creek.

Pages 21–24. Church Orphan Ordinance.

On January 2, 1886, the Church of Elder Paul Tschetter had a special meeting and after much consideration it was agreed to establish an Orphan Ordinance which was to be in effect in case of a death. The following rules should apply. First of all anyone who wished to have his division [inheritance and child placement decisions] made according to the Church Orphan Ordinance must report within ten days to the head of the organization. Anyone who does not report to this head within ten days signifies by this that he does not wish to permit his division by our organization. It is to be understood however that everyone has the freedom of choice about where he wants his division to occur. It should also be understood that if anyone decided to have his division made by our organization and later wishes to nullify that decision and then permit his division by the worldly organization [the state], he shall be considered disobedient and will not be considered a member of the Church.

It is also to be understood that a man and woman, when they want to be joined in marriage must bring a copy of the division certificate from the head of Orphan Organization to the Elder. Likewise, those who have permitted their division by a worldly organization must not only bring a certificate from our Organization head but also a copy of their division to the Elder. Thus our Organization will function as it did among the Mennonites in Russia. These Orphan Regulations are in the hands of the Organization's director.

For his work the director shall receive from the Church one quarter cent for every dollar he administers. The person elected to be the director was Michel Hofer and the term of office is four years.

Herewith we commit ourselves with our own handwritten signature. [The signatures of those that agreed to follow the ordinance are printed below.]

Johann Tschetter, Jacob Tschetter, David Tschetter, Daniel Wurz, Joseph Pollman, Joseph Hofer, Michel Hofer, Paul Gross, David Wipf, Mathias Kleinsasser, Joseph Pollman, David Hofer, Paul Kleinsasser, Jacob Knels, Johan Hofer, Jacob Mendel, Franz Walter, Wilhelm Gross, Wilhelm Gross, Johan Wollman, Andreas Hofer, Andreas Gross, Paul Stahl, Jacob Hofer, Joshua Hofer, Isaac Walter, Johan Tschetter, Paul Tschetter, Joshua Hofer, Jacob Wurz, Elias Walter, Jacob Hofer, Samuel

Hofer, Paul Mendel, Michael Hofer, Johan Tschetter, Joseph Walter, George Gross, Paul Gross, Michael Hofer

Page 25. A New Church Building.

On November 11, 1888 we had the first preaching service in our new church building. The Church cost $1,300. The funds were raised by free will contributions from the members of the Church. The next time the Church was improved it cost $600.

Page 25–30. What Happened in our Church during the So-Called World War.

After our Church had practiced its faith in peace and quiet for 40 years, the so-called World War broke out in Europe on August 4, 1914 which here and there caused much anxiety among the brethren because the older brethren knew from experience that God would punish his people. The war in Europe became more and more severe; the murder and slaughter of people became more gruesome; one nation after another became involved. Germany and France were the ones that started the war.

The need and grief became ever greater due to the war until finally on April 6, 1917 even the United States declared war on Germany which meant troublesome times for the Mennonites of our land.

Now was the time to hold high the sword of the Spirit and the Shield of Faith. Here and there meetings were held, counseling done, decisions made, and petitions were sent to the President by which our government learned that here and there there are still some citizens who do not accept the sword.

And so the woes of this, God's judgment, became ever mightier until on June 5, 1917, the call came for young men aged 21 to 31 to register for the draft, which caused the woes to turn to grief. This grief brought both young and old upon their knees and many tears were shed.

The grief first became real when on September 22, 1917, the first young men were drafted, which included two of our brethren, namely, Joseph Gross and Jacob Hofer. These were experiences which our people had never before experienced. So our young men were ordered, one after another, to come to Parkston, South Dakota, where on a certain day they had to board a military train to travel to various military camps.

Our Church as well as other Churches in the neighborhood held earnest prayer meetings so that all Mennonites were awakened and learned to trust God more.

The hatred toward the German people became ever greater so that even the use of the German language was forbidden in churches and schools. This ruling was to go in effect on July 18, 1918. In spite of the fact that this ordinance gave us much grief, we never abided by it in our Church, even though the minister of the day approached the pulpit with a heavy heart. The Spirit of the Lord reminded us that we must obey God more than man.

When on October 12, 1918, all males between the ages of 18–45 were required to register, the pressure of the war became so heavy that some of our people fled to Canada hoping to find refuge there under the privileges granted to Mennonites

This migration together with the drafting of our young men for military duty brought fathers and mothers almost to despair. Much comfort had to be extended. Now the Scriptures became more clear where it says, "Rachel wept for her children and would not be comforted" (Jeremiah 31:14).

Heartbreaking were the scenes of departure at indeterminate times. The sons of widows were torn from their motherly embrace; fathers had to carry their sons out of the house because the loved ones did not want to leave home.

Having arrived in the camps the beloved brethren of faith were subjected to all possible temptations attempting to persuade them to accept the weapons or sword. Most of them remained steadfast and then were assigned to other work.

Most of them were assigned to farm work and others were taken from one camp to another and some of them were even transported across the ocean to France.

Finally on November 11, 1918 an Armistice was declared and peace negotiations began.

The young men returned home one by one and the joy of the parents was indescribable. On July 29, 1919, the last young men came home and the dark cloud seemed to have disappeared except for the wound that brought it back: Brother Jacob Hofer fell as an offering to the war. This dear, young, handsome and strong brother fell on the slaughter field on October 16, 1918 and is buried somewhere in France.

Added to all of this grief, in September 1918, a pestilence covered the whole earth. It was called the Spanish Influenza and took a toll of some 6,000,000 lives. In our Church the only offering was the young and only son, Andreas, of the Jacob Walter family.

Since that time war and epidemic are in the past in spite of war clouds which will no doubt continue for a long time to come. We are all thankful to God for his gracious protection. For this reason the Church assembled on the evening of October 19, 1919, in order to celebrate a special service of thanksgiving to God.

The following men were drafted. First is the name of the young man; next to the name, the date when he was drafted; and last, the date when he was released, if at all.

Name	*Date Drafted*	*Date Released*
Jacob J. Hofer	September 22, 1917	Never returned
Joe A. Gross	September 22, 1917	May 1, 1919
Joseph L. Hofer	April 29, 1918	July 29, 1919
Joseph S. Wipf	June 25, 1918	December 25, 1918
David L. Tschetter	June 16, 1918	June 22, 1918
Joseph S. Walter	June 25, 1918	June 15, 1919
Lorenz Tschetter	June 22, 1918	December 23, 1918
Andrew P. Gross	July 23, 1918	December 14, 1918
Samuel P. Gross	August 28, 1918	December 28, 1918
Jacob M. Walter	August 28, 1918	June 25, 1919
Joseph M. Walter	August 28, 1918	March 3, 1919

Appendix C

Paul Tschetter's Letter of Petition to President Ullysses S. Grant, August 8, 1873

To his Excellency, the President of the United States:

Whereas, we the undersigned having lost by the new military law of Russia the privileges granted to us by the Emperor Paul, for Evermore, that we Mennonites should be exempt from military service, it being against our conscience and religious faith; and whereas, having heard and read in many books of our brethren that exemptions from military service exist in the United States of America, we have been chosen to visit America to investigate this matter.

The result of these investigations is that, as far as understood our Mennonite brethren already settled in this country have been called upon to serve during the late civil war; although they declared it was against their conscience and religious faith, and that they could get a release only by the payment of three hundred dollars each.

We therefore fear that in leaving and selling our homesteads and lands in Russia for a low price spending almost all our money to make the long voyage to this country and to reach our destination, it might be the case that should a war break out and we should be asked to pay three hundred dollars (or any other sum of money) for exemption from liability to serve, it would have been in vain for us to emigrate and leave behind us our cherished memories; and we would be no better off than in Russia.

We the undersigned deputies therefore most respectfully beg to ask of Your Excellency to allow to us and all our brethren exemption from military service for the next fifty years, without payment of money on our part for such exemption. We also desire to be allowed to keep our German schools in our colonies, and to administer them according to our own rules as we have done in Russia.

We further beg to ask of your Excellency whether we shall be allowed *not* to serve as judges or jurymen; this being likewise contrary to our religious faith and leaving it a matter of option with us to exercise the privilege of voting, or not as the case may be, at Elections—after we have been duly naturalized as American citizens.

When we shall be able to show a written grant of these privileges on returning to our brethren in Russia, an immense emigration from that country will take place; while in the contrary case only a comparatively small number will leave, the greater portion being unwilling to emigrate on uncertain hopes and run the risk of arriving here as poor men without having bettered their condition in any way.

We most respectfully ask your Excellency's consideration of this our petition, and as early a response in writing as the case will admit of meanwhile subscribing ourselves.

Your obedient servants,

Paul Tschetter
Lohrentz Tschetter
Tobias Unruh

Appendix D

Ulysses S. Grant's Response to Paul Tschetter's Petition, September 5, 1873

Written by Hamilton Fish and Addressed to Michael Hiller

The President sent to me the petition of the Mennonite delegates, and the reason for the delay in the answer is this: At the time of the meeting of Mennonites with the president he was told that they wished to depart in a few days. The only answer that could be given was that the President could not guarantee them the assurances they desired.

They wished guarantees of exemption from military service, and also jury service. They desire also to be free from the payment of substitute money in case of draft; and the right to govern their own schools.

Since personal military service, citizenship obligations, jury service, and control over schools are all matters that fall under the jurisdiction of the various states in which they wish to settle, the President says he cannot exempt them from the laws of the states and the laws to which other citizens are subject. As to the exemption from paying substitute money for fifty years, that, too, is beyond his power of promising. It is true, however, that for the next fifty years we will not be entangled in another war in which military service will be necessary. But should it be necessary there is little likelihood that Congress would find justification in freeing them from duties which are asked of other citizens.

It was impossible therefore to grant the answer which you [Michael Hiller] and the delegates wished before their departure. I had to withhold the answer until I had opportunity to see the President.

With greatest obedience
Your Humble Servant
HAMILTON FISH

Appendix E

Hutterite Memorial, 1874–1974, Bridgewater, South Dakota

Note: *The following is the narrative etched onto the "Hutterite Memorial" stone, which was dedicated on September 22, 1974, and placed in the Neu Hutterthaler Church cemetery, Bridgewater, South Dakota. We have not included the inscription's list of six local Prairieleut congregations since it contains out-of-date information.*

In humble thanksgiving to Christ Our Savior, in Grateful remembrance of our early Church leaders,

In deep appreciation of our country America and as a Challenge to our posterity,

We dedicate this memorial Jesus Christ the same yesterday and today and forever. Heb. 13:8.

The Hutterites, named after Jacob Hutter, an Early Church leader, are a branch of the Anabaptist Movement that began in Switzerland In 1525. The Hutterite Church with the communal way of living began in Moravia, Austria in 1528.

After centuries of religious persecution in various parts of Europe God's providence, through the leadership of Rev. Paul Tschetter 1842–1919 and Lorenz Tschetter 1819–1879, brought them to America between 1874–1879. Rev. Paul Tschetter settled near this site and His grave is near by. Lorenz Tschetter settled Near Olivet, So. Dak. where a simple slab marks his grave on a lonely hill one mile southeast Of Olivet.

Two main branches of the Hutterites exist today: Those who live in Bruderhofs and have all Property in common and those who believe in Individual ownership and identify with the Mennonites. The Latter, after meeting in homes for Worship and later in schoolhouses eventually established the following churches ...

Bibliography

American Industrial Committee, editors. *Crucifixions in the 20th Century: The Cases of Jacob Wipf and the three Hofer Brothers.* Chicago: American Industrial Committee, 1919.
Anderson, James. "The Pentecost Preaching of Acts 2: An Aspect of Hutterite Theology." PhD dissertation, University of Iowa, 1972.
Anderson, Lawrence. "Hutterite Names with an Emphasis on the Knels Family Name." Unpublished paper (January, 1985). Tony Waldner Collection, Fordville, North Dakota.
———. "The Hutterites." Unpublished presentation. Madison, SD, 1983.
Aries, Phillippe. *The Hour of Our Death.* Translated by Helen Weaver. New York: Oxford University Press, 1991.
Arndt, Karl J. *George Rapp's Successors and Material Heirs, 1847–1916.* Cranbury, NJ: Associated University Presses, 1971.
———. "The Harmonists and the Hutterites." *The American-German Review* (August 1944) 24–27.
Beadle, William. *Autobiography of William Henry Harrison Beadle.* Pierre, SD: State Historical Society, 1906.
Bender, Elizabeth, editor. "The Last Words of Michael Waldner." In John A. Hostetler, *Hutterite Society*, 355–57.
Bender, Harold S., editor. "A Hutterite School Discipline of 1578 and Peter Schorer's Address of 1568 to the Schoolmasters." *MQR* (October 1931) 231–44.
———. "Lot." In *MennEncy*, 3:443.
Bennett, John C. *Hutterian Brethren: The Agricultural Economy and Social Organization of a Communal People.* Stanford, CA: Stanford University Press, 1967.
Bestor, *Backwoods Utopias: The Sectarian Origins and the Owenite Phase of Communitarian Socialism in America, 1663–1829.* Philadelphia: University of Pennsylvania Press, 1970.
Boese, J.A. *The Prussian-Polish Mennonites Settling in South Dakota.* Freeman, SD: Pine Hill, 1967).
Brock, Peter. *Pacifism in Europe to 1914.* Princeton: Princeton University Press, 1972.
Centennial Book Committee, editor. *A Tale of Three Cities.* Freeman, SD: Pine Hill, 1979.
Christopher, Stefan C., editor. "A Description of the Beginning of True Christian Community among the Schmiedeleut Hutterians: As It Began by the Power of the Spirit." Unpublished paper, 1972. Heritage Hall Museum and Archives, Freeman, South Dakota.
Clark, Peter Gordon. "Leadership Succession Among the Hutterites." *Canadian Review of Sociology and Anthropology* (Summer 1977) 294–302.

Constitution for the Neu Hutterthaler Mennonite Church. Freeman SD: no publisher, 1948. Heritage Hall Museum and Archives, Freeman, South Dakota.

Constitution for the Neu Hutterthaler Mennonite Church. Freeman, SD: n.p., 1974. Heritage Hall Museum and Archives.

Correll, Ernst, editor. "Mennonite Immigration into Manitoba: Sources and Documents, 1872, 1873." *MQR* (July, 1937) 196–227; (October, 1937) 267–83.

———. "President Grant and the Mennonite Immigration from Russia." *MQR* (April 1935) 144–52.

Cross, David. *Hutterite CO's in World War One*. Hawley, MN: Spring Prairie Printing, 1998.

Dakota Territory Centennial Committee, editors. *Dakota Panorama*. Freeman, SD: Pine Hill, 1961.

Donner, Heinrich. "Report of the Anabaptist Brethren at Wishink in the Ukraine." In *Hutterite Roots*, edited by Hutterite Mennonite Centennial Committee, 119–27. Freeman, SD: Hutterite Mennonite Centennial Committee, 1985.

Dyck, Cornelius J. *An Introduction to Mennonite History*. Scottdale, PA: Herald, 1980.

———, and Dennis D. Martin, eds. *Mennonite Encyclopedia*. 5 vols. Hillsboro, KS: Mennonite Brethren Publishing, 1955–1990.

Ehrenpreis, Andreas. *An Epistle on Brotherly Community: The Highest Command of Love*. Rifton, NY: Plough, 1978.

Eichler, Evan. "Hutterian Surnames." Unpublished paper, 1998. Rod Janzen Collection.

———. *Hutterite Genealogy: Surnames of Founding Families: Church Book Extractions*. http://feefhs.org/hut/h-surnam.html, 1997.

Engels, Friedrich. *The Peasant's War in Germany*. Moscow: Foreign Languages Publishing House, 1956.

Epp, D. H. *Johann Cornies: Züge aus seinem Leben und Wirken*. Rosthern, SK: Echo, 1946.

Fischer, Hans. *Jakob Huter: Leben, Froemmigkeit, Briefe*. Newton: Mennonite Publication Office, 1956.

Flint, David. *The Hutterites: A Study in Prejudice*. Toronto: Oxford University Press, 1975.

Friedmann, Robert. "The Epistles of the Hutterian Brethren." *MQR* (July 1946) 1–31.

———. "Hutterite Worship and Preaching." *MQR* (January 1966) 5–26.

———. *Hutterite Studies*. Goshen, IN: Mennonite Historical Society, 1961.

———. "Introduction." In "Article Three of the Great Article Book: A Notable Hutterite Document Concerning True Surrender and Christian Community of Goods." Translated by Kathleen Hasenberg, *MQR* (January 1957) 22–62.

———, editor. "Michael Waldner's *The Reestablishment of Communal Life among the Hutterites in Russia* (1858)." *MQR* (April 1965) 147–52.

———. "Peter Riedemann: Early Anabaptist Leader." *MQR* (January 1970) 5–44.

Friesen, John J., editor. *Peter Riedemann's Hutterite Confession of Faith*. Scottdale, PA: Herald, 1999.

Funk, Merle J. F. "Divided Loyalties: Mennonite and Hutterite Responses to the United States at War, Hutchinson County, South Dakota, 1917, 1918." *MennLife* (December 1997) 24–32.

Gering, John J. *After Fifty Years: A Brief Discussion of the History and Activities of the Swiss-German Mennonites from Russia Who Settled in South Dakota in 1874.* Freeman, SD: Pine Hill Printery, 1924.

Gesangbuch: Eine Sammlung Geistlicher Lieder zur Allgemeinen Erbauung und zum Lobe Gottes. Elkhart, IN: Mennonitischen Verlagshandlung, 1895.

Giesinger, Adam. *From Catherine to Khruschchev: The Story of Russia's Germans.* Lincoln, NE: Society of Germans from Russia, 1981.

Glanzer, Justina S. W. *Life Story of S. W. Glanzer and Justina W. Glanzer.* Freeman, SD: Pine Hill, 1971.

Glanzer, Paul E., Marilyn Wipf, and Jeanette Hofer, editors. *A Century of God's Blessing: Neu Hutterthaler Mennonite Church, 1888-1988.* Freeman, SD: Pine Hill, 1988.

Goertz, Reuben. "The Legacy of the First American Tornado Ever Photographed in Dakota Territory, 1884." Unpublished paper, n.d. Center for Western Studies, Sioux Falls, South Dakota.

———. *Princes, Potentates and Plain People.* Sioux Falls, SD: Center for Western Studies, 1994.

Grant, Ulysses S. *Personal Memoirs* (Old Saybrook, CT: Konecky & Konecky, n.d. [ED: check]

Gross, David, editor. *Schmiedeleut Family Record.* High Bluff, MB: Sommerfield Colony, 2003.

Gross, David P., and Arnold M. Hofer, editors. "The Neu Hutterthaler Church Record Book." Unpublished document, 1997. Heritage Hall Museum and Archives, Freeman, South Dakota.

Gross, Leonard. *The Golden Years of the Hutterites.* Scottdale, PA: Herald, 1997.

Gross, Paul S. *The Hutterite Way.* Saskatoon, SK: Freeman, 1965.

Gross, Paul S. and Elizabeth Bender, translators. "A Hutterite Sermon of the 17th Century." *MQR* (January 1970) 59–71.

Gross, Mrs. Paul S. *A History of the Salem MB Church, 1886-1986.* Freeman, SD: Pine Hill, 1986.

Guericke, Justina. *Precious Memories of a Historical House.* Freeman, SD: self published, 1985.

Harder, Leland. "The Russian Mennonites and American Democracy under Grant." In *From the Steppes to the Prairies (1874-1949),* edited by Cornelius Krahn, 48–64. Newton, KS: Mennonite Publication Office, 1949.

Hasselstrom, Linda. *Roadside History of South Dakota.* Missoula, MT: Montana Press, 1994.

Hiebert, Clarence. *Brothers in Deed to Brothers in Need: A Scrapbook About Mennonite Immigrants from Russia, 1870-1885.* North Newton, KS: Faith and Life Press, 1974.

Hiebert, Jerald. *The Hutterite Story of a Pure Church: A Story of Dariusleut Alberta Hutterites, 1918-2000.* Raymond, AB: self-published, 2006.

Historical Committee, editors. *History of the Neu Hutterthaler Church.* Freeman, SD: Pine Hill, 1968.

———, editors. *Menno: The First 100 Years, 1879-1979.* Freeman, SD: Pine Hill, 1979.

Hoehnle, Peter. "Michael Hofer: A Communitarian in Two Worlds." *Communal Societies* (2002) 83–86.

Hofer, Arnold M., editor. *The Diaries of Joseph "Yos" Hofer.* Freeman, SD: Hutterite Mennonite Centennial Committee, 1997.

———, and Pauline Becker, *The John Hofer and Anna Wurtz Family Record.* Freeman, SD: self-published, 1991.

Hofer, D. M. *Die Hungersnot in Russland und Unsere Reise um die Welt.* Chicago: K.M.B. Publishing, 1924.

Hofer, Jacob E. "A History of the Neu Hutterthaler Church, including the European Background." BA senior seminar paper, Goshen College, Goshen, Indiana, 1953. Heritage Museum and Archives, Freeman, South Dakota.

Hofer, Jacob M. editor. "The Diary of Paul Tschetter." MQR (July, 1931) 112–27; (October, 1931) 198–219.

Hofer, John S., editor. *1 John 5:1-3: The Victory of Faith Sermon.* Elie, MB: James Valley Colony, n.d.

———. *A History of the Hutterites.* Winnipeg: W. K. Printers, 1982.

Hofer, Samuel. *The Hutterites: Lives and Images of a Communal People.* Saskatoon, SK: Hofer, 1998.

Holzach, Michael. *The Forgotten People: A year among the Hutterites.* Sioux Falls, SD: Ex Machina, 1993.

Homan, Gerlof D. "Mennonites and Military Justice in World War I." MQR (July 1992) 365–75.

Hoover, Walter. *Hutterian-English Dictionary.* Saskatoon, SK: Walter Hoover, 1997.

———. *The Hutterian Language.* Saskatoon, SK: Walter Hoover, 1997.

Hostetler, John A. *Hutterite Society.* Baltimore: Johns Hopkins University Press, 1974.

———, Leonard Gross, and Elizabeth Bender, editors. *Selected Hutterian Documents in Translation.* Philadelphia: Temple University Press, 1975.

Hostetler, John A., and Gertrude Huntington. *The Hutterites in North America.* New York: Harcourt Brace, 1996.

Huntington, Gertrude. "Living the Ark: Four Centuries of Hutterite Faith and Community." In *America's Communal Utopias*, edited by Donald Pitzer, 319–51. Chapel Hill: University of North Carolina Press, 1997.

Hutter, Jacob. *Brotherly Faithfullness: Epistles from a Time of Persecution.* Rifton, NY: Plough, 1979.

Hutterian Brethren. *Constitution of the Hutterian Brethren Church and Rules as to Community of Property.* Winnipeg: E.A. Fletcher Barristers and Solicitors, 1950.

———. *The Chronicle of the Hutterian Brethren I.* St. Agathe, MB: Crystal Spring Colony, 1987.

———. *The Chronicle of the Hutterian Brethren II.* St. Agathe, MB: Crystal Spring Colony, 1996.

———. *Gesang Buchlein.* Hawley, MN: Spring Prairie Printing, 1998.

———. *Das Kleine Gesang Buch für Allgemein Gebrauch.* MacGregor, MB: Baker Colony, 1995.

———, editor. *Die Lieder der Hutterischen Bruder Gesangbuch.* Scottdale, PA: Herald, 1914.

Hutterian Educational Committee, editors. *The Hutterian Church Responds to Questions of Faith.* Elie, MB: James Valley Book Centre, 2000.

Hutterite Mennonite Centennial Committee, editors. *A History of the Hutterite Mennonites.* Freeman, SD: Hutterite Mennonite Centennial Committee, 1974.

———. *Hutterite Roots*. Freeman, SD: Hutterite Mennonite Centennial Committee, 1985.
Jansen, Peter. "Diary." In Frances Janzen Voth, *The House of Jacob: The Story of Jacob Janzen, 1822–1885, and His Descendents*, 67. Tucson, AZ: self-published, 1984.
———. *Memoirs of Peter Jansen: The Record of a Busy Life, an Autobiography*. Beatrice, NE: self-published, 1921.
———. "Reise Nach Amerika." In Marion Kleinsasser Towne, *Jacob Hutter's Friends: Twelve Narrative Voices from Switzerland to South Dakota over Four Centuries*. Freeman, SD: Pine Hill, 1999.
Janzen, Peter. "Reise nach Amerika." In Frances Janzen Voth, *The House of Jacob: The Story of Jacob Janzen and His Descendents*, 64–65. Tucson, AZ: self-published, 1984.
Janzen, Rod, editor. *God's Salvation Plan*. Hawley, MN: Spring Prairie Colony, 1988.
———. "The Hutterite High School Experience: Boundary Maintenance on the Prairies." *Szygy: Journal of Alternative Religion and Culture* (July 1993) 339–48.
———. "The Hutterites and the Bruderhof: The Relationship between an Old Order Religious Society and a 20th Century Communal Group." *MQR* (October 2005) 505–44.
———. "Jacob D. Hofer, Evangelist, Minister and Carpenter." *California Mennonite Historical Society Newsletter* (May 1994) 1–8.
———. *Perceptions of the South Dakota Hutterites in the 1980s*. Freeman, SD: Freeman Publishing, 1984.
———. *The Prairie People: Forgotten Anabaptists*. Hanover, NH: University Press of New England, 1999.
———. "The Prairieleut: A Forgotten Hutterite People." *Communal Societies* (1994) 67–89.
———. *Terry Miller: The Pacifist Politician, From Hutterite Colony to State Capitol*. Freeman, SD: Freeman Publishing, 1986.
———, and Jean Janzen. "Paul Tschetter's Chicago Fire Hymn." *MQR* (April 2007) 261–72.
Kaplan, Bert, and Thomas F. A. Plaut. *Personality and Communal Society* (Lawrence, KS: University of Kansas Press, 1956).
Karolevitz, Robert. *Yankton: A Pioneer Past*. Aberdeen: Northern Dakota State College Press, 1972.
Kaufman, Edmund G., editor. *General Conference Mennonite Pioneers*. North Newton, KS: Bethel College, 1973.
Kienzler, Hanna. *Gender and Communal Longevity among Hutterites*. Aachen: Shaker Verlag, 2005.
Kirkby, Mary-Ann. *I Am Hutterite*. Prince Albert, SK: Polka Dot, 2007.
Klassen, N. J. "Mennonite Intelligentsia in Russia." *MennLife* (April 1969) 51–60.
Klassen, Peter J. *The Economics of Anabaptism*. London: Mouton, 1964.
Kleinsasser, Amos, editor. *Our Journey of Faith: Hutterthal Mennonite Church, 1879–2004*. Freeman, SD: Hutterthal Mennonite Church, 2004.
Kleinsasser, Jacob, editor. *A Hutterite Sermon on Luke 23:24–26*. St. Agathe, MB: Crystal Spring Colony, 1982.
———. *Book 2: Hutterite Teachings*. St. Agathe, MB: Crystal Spring Colony, 1996.
———. *Teachings for the Celebration of Easter and the Lord's Supper*. St. Agathe, MB: Crystal Spring Colony, 1999.

Kleinsasser, Joseph A. *A History of the Bethel Mennonite Church, 1919-1979*. Freeman, SD: Pine Hill, 1979.

Krahn, Cornelius, editor. *From the Steppes to the Prairies*. Newton, KS: The Historical Committee of the General Conference of the Mennonite Church of North America, 1949.

Krause, Bertha Laura Schmidt. *Tschetter-Waldner Families*. Ridgefield, WA: self-published, 1999.

Kraybill, Donald B., and Carl F. Bowman. *On the Backroad to Heaven: Old Order Hutterites, Mennonites, Amish and Brethren*. Baltimore: Johns Hopkins University Press, 2001.

Krieger, Leonard, editor. *The German Revolution: The Peasant's War in Germany*. Chicago: University of Chicago Press, 1967.

Krisztinkovich, Bela. *Haban Pottery*. Budapest: Corvina, 1962.

Krisztinkovich, Maria. "Some Further Notes on the Hutterites in Transylvania." *MQR* (April 1963) 203-13.

———, compiler. *An Annotated Hutterite Bibliography*. Edited by Peter C. Erb. Kitchener, ON: Pandora, 1998.

Kuentsche, Hans Friedrich. "The Pentecost Lehren." In James Anderson, "The Pentecost Preaching of Acts 2: An Aspect of Hutterite Theology." PhD diss., University of Iowa (1972.

Kuleshov, Maxim, editor. *History of Raditschewa*. N.p., 1999. WTC.

Laskin, David. *The Children's Blizzard*. New York: HarperCollins, 2004.

Lehrerleut Hutterian Brethren, editors. *Lehrerleut Hutterian Brethren Family Records, 1771-2006*. Sunburst, MT: Rimrock Colony, 2007.

Letkemann, Peter. "Molochna 2004: Mennonites and their Neighbors, 1804-2001." *MQR* (January 2005) 109-20.

Liebrandt, George. "The Emigration of the German Mennonites from Russia to the United States and Canada, 1873-1880." *MQR* (January 1933) 5-41.

Maendel, Jonathan. "Historical Guidelines for the Hutterian School System." Unpublished manuscript, 2002.

Manfred, Frederick. *The Chokecherry Tree*. Albuquerque: University of New Mexico Press, 1975.

———. *Sons of Adam: A Novel*. New York: Crown, 1980.

Martens, Helen. *Hutterite Songs*. Kitchener, ON: Pandora, 2001.

Martens, Larry. "Musical Thought and Practice in the Hutterite Community." MA thesis, University of Kansas, 1960.

Martin, Alice O. "The Founder Effect in a Human Isolate: Evolutionary Implications." *American Journal of Physical Anthropology 32* (1970) 351-68.

Masuk, Lesley. "Patriarch, Technology and the Lives of Hutterite Women: a Field Study." MA thesis, University of Saskatchewan, 1998.

McFeely, William S. *Grant: A Biography*. New York: Norton, 1982.

Mendel, Jacob J. *A History of the People of East Freeman, Silver Lake and West Freeman*. Freeman, SD: Pine Hill, 1961.

Miller, Ann, and Peter H. Stephenson. "Jacob Hutter: An Interpretaion of the Individual Man and His People." *Ethos* (April 1980) 229-52.

Miller, Ross. *The Great Chicago Fire*. Chicago: University of Illinois Press, 2000.

Milton, John. *South Dakota: A History*. New York: Norton, 2003.

Morgan Kenneth, and Mary T. Holmes et. al., "Population Structure of a Religious Isolate: The Darisuleut Hutterites of Alberta." In *Current Developments in Anthropological Genetics*. Vol. 2, *Ecology and Population Structure*, edited by M. H. Crawford and J. H. Mielke, 429ñ48. New York: Plenum, 1983.

Murphy, Patrick, editor. *2008 Hutterite Directory*. Elie, MB: James Valley Colony, 2008.

Packull, Werner C. *Hutterite Beginnings: Communitarian Experiments during the Reformation*. Baltimore: Johns Hopkins University Press, 1995.

———. *Mysticism and the Early South German-Austrian Anabaptist Movement, 1525-1531*. Scottdale, PA: Herald, 1977.

———. *Peter Riedemann: Shaper of the Hutterite Tradition*. Kitchener, ON: Pandora, 2007.

Penner, *Die Ost und Westpreussischen Mennoniten in ihrem religiosen und sozialen Leben in ihren Kulturellen und wirtschaftichen Leistungen*. Vol. 1. Weierhof, Germany: Mennonitischen Geschictsverein, 1978.

Peter, Karl A. *The Dynamics of Hutterite Society: An Analytical Approach*. Edmonton: University of Alberta Press, 1987.

Peter, Karl A., Edward D. Boldt, Ian Whitaker, Lance W. Roberts, editors. "The Dynamics of Religious Defection among Hutterites." *Journal for the Scientific Study of Religion* (1982) 327-37.

Peter, Karl A. and Franziska Peter, editors. *Hutterite C.O.'s and their Treatment in the U.S. Army during World War I*. Cranford, MB: Lakeside Colony, 1982.

Peter, Karl A. and Ian Whitaker. "Hutterite Perceptions of Psychophysiological Characteristics." *Journal of Social Biological Structures* 7 (January 1984) 1-8.

Peters, Alan. "Unraveling the Origins: How Much Dutch?" *California Mennonite Historical Society Newsletter* (May 1995) 3-4.

Peters, Victor. *All Things Common*. Minneapolis: University of Minnesota Press, 1965.

Peterson, Nancy M., editor. *People of the Old Missury: Years of Conflict*. Frederick, CO: Renaissance, 1989.

Plett, C. F. *The Story of the Krimmer Mennonite Brethren Church*. Winnipeg: Kindred, 1985.

Rath, George. *The Black Sea Germans in the Dakotas*. Freeman, SD: Pine Hill, 1977.

Redekop, Calvin and John A. Hostetler, "The Plain People: An Interpretation." *MQR* (October 1977) 266-77.

Rempel, David G. "The Mennonite Commonwealth in Russia." *MQR* (January 1974) 17-22.

Riedemann, Peter. *An Account of Our Religion, Doctrine and Faith*. Rifton, NY: Plough, 1970.

———. *Confession of Faith*. Rifton, NY: Plough, 1970.

Ruth, John L. *The Earth is the Lord's: A Narrative History of the Lancaster Mennonite Conference*. Scottdale, PA: Herald, 2001.

Sapir, Edward. *Culture, Language and Personality*. Berkeley: University of California Press, 1958.

Sawislak, Karen. *Smoldering City: Chicagoans and the Great Fire, 1871-1874*. Chicago: University of Chicago Press, 1995

Scheer, "The Hutterian German Dialect." *MQR* (July 1980) 229-43.

Schell, Herbert S. *History of South Dakota*. Pierre: South Dakota State Historical Society Press, 2004.

Scheuner, Gottfried. *Inspiration Historie, 1867–1876*. Amana, IA: self-published, 1900. Amana Historical Society Archives, Amana, Iowa.

Schlabach, Theron, editor. "An Account by Jakob Waldner: Diary of a Conscientious Objector in World War I." *MQR* (January 1974) 73–111.

Schlachta, Astrid von. "'Against Selfishness': Community of Goods as Life Choice." In *Commoners and Community*, edited by C. Arnold Snyder, 257–79. Kitchener, ON: Pandora, 2002.

———. *Die Hutterer zwischen Tirol und Nord Amerika: Eine Reise durch die Jahrhunderte*. Innsbruck: Universitatsverlag Wagner, 2006.

———. "'Searching Through the Nations': Tasks and problems of Sixteenth-century Hutterian missions." *MQR* (January 2000) 27–49.

Schmidt, John F. "The Immigrants and the Railroads." *MennLife* (mid-year issue, 1974) 14.

Schnell, Kempes. "John F. Funk and the Mennonite Migrations of 1873–1885." In *From the Steppes to the Prairies*, edited by Cornelius Krahn, 69–91. Newton, KS: The Historical Committee of the General Conference of the Mennonite Church of North America, 1949.

———. "John F. Funk's Land Inspection Trips as Recorded in his Diary, 1872, 1873." *MQR* (October 1950) 295–311.

Shenk, Wilbert, editor. *Samuel S. Haury: Letters concerning the Spread of the Gospel*. Scottdale, PA: Herlad, 1981.

Smith, C. Henry. *The Coming of the Russian Mennonites: An Episode in the Settling of the Last Frontier*. Berne, IN: Mennonite Book Concern, 1927.

———. *The Story of the Mennonites*. Newton, KS: Faith and Life Press, 1957.

Snyder, Arnold. *Anabaptist History and Theology*. Kitchener, ON: Pandora, 1995.

Stahl, Lisa Marie. *My Hutterite Life*. Helena, MT: Farcountry 2003.

Stayer, James M. *The German Peasant's War and Anabaptist Community of Goods*. McGill-Queens Studies in Religion 6. Montreal: McGill-Queens University Press, 1991.

Stephenson, Peter H. *The Hutterian People: Ritual and Rebirth in the Evolution of Communal Life*. Lanham, MD: University Press of America, 1991.

Suderman, Leonhard. *From Rusia to America: In Search of Freedom*. Steinbach, MB: Derksen, 1974.

Swiss-German Centennial Committee, editors. *The Swiss Germans in South Dakota*. Freeman, SD: Pine Hill, 1974.

Tindall, George Brown. *America: A Narrative History*. New York: Norton, 1984.

Toews, John B. "Non-resistance Re-examined: Why did Mennonites leave Russia in 1874?" *MennLife* (Mid-Year Issue, 1974) 8–14.

Towne, Marion Kleinsasser. *Jacob Hutter's Friends: Twelve Narrative Voices from Switzerland to South Dakota over Four Centuries*. Freeman, SD: Pine Hill, 1999.

———. *The Onliest One Alive: Surviving Jonestown, Guyana*. Marion K. Towne, self-published, 1995.

Traveler's Official Guide of the Railway and Steam Navigation Lines in the United States and Canada. Philadelphia: National Railway Publication Company, 1874.

Tschetter, David J. "The Paul Tschetter Family." Unpublished document, n.d. (circa 1980).

Tschetter, Jacob A. "Family History." Unpublished document. WTC, n.d.
Tschetter, Joseph W. "A Brief Biography of Paul Tschetter 1842-1919." In Jacob M. Hofer, editor, "The Diary of Paul Tschetter." *MQR* (July 1931) 112-27; (October 1931) 198-219.
Tschetter, Mrs. Joseph W. *My Life's Story, 1880-1945*. Chicago: self-published, 1945.
Tschetter, Larry, and Edith Tschetter, editors. *Jacob W. Tschetter Family Record*. Freeman, SD: Pine Hill, 1977.
Tschetter, Paul G. "Anecdotes as I Remember Them Being Told to Me by My Grandfather, Paul P. Tschetter." Handwritten notes, Nancy M. Peterson Collection.
———. "Die Auswanderer." In *People of the Old Missoury*, edited by Nancy M. Peterson, 89-98. Frederick, CO: Renaissance House, 1989.
———. "A Legacy of Paul Tschetter." unpublished manuscript, 1987. Nancy M. Peterson Collection.
Tschetter, Peter, editor. *Hutterite Sermon, Acts 2:43-44*. Flandreau, SD: Pleasant Valley Colony, 1981.
———. "Hutterite Sermon Collection." Unpublished. Flandreau, SD: Pleasant Valley Colony, 1984.
Tschetter, Wesley. "Biography of Rev. Joseph W. Tschetter (1876-1955)." Unpublished manuscript, 2007.
———. "Reflections on the Life of Paul Tschetter." Presentation at the dedication of a memorial at the Neu Hutterthaler Church. Unpublished manuscript, 1995. WTC.
Unruh, John D. *A Century of Mennonites in Dakota*. Pierre, SD: South Dakota Historical Collections, 1972.
Urry, James. *None but Saints: The Transformation of Mennonite Life in Russia, 1789-1889*. Winnipeg: Hyperion, 1988.
Van Den Berghe, Pierre L. And Karl A. Peter, "Hutterites and Kibbutzniks: A Tale of Nepotistic Communism." *Man* (1988) 522-39.
Waldner, Gary. "Among the Habaner of Czechoslovakia." *MennLife* (April 1966) 84-91.
Waldner, Marie J., and Marnette D. Hofer. *Many Hands, Minds and Hearts: A History of Freeman Junior College and Freeman Academy, 1900-2000*. Sioux Falls, SD: Freeman Academy, 2000.
Waldner, Tony, editor. *Russian Record: Hutterite Family Records from the early 1700s to 1874*. Fordville, ND: Forest River Colony, 2003.
Walter, Elias, trans. *Preface and Teaching: Acts 2*. Winnipeg, MB: Hutterian Brethren, 1901.
Walter, Kenneth J. *Matthias M. Hofer Family Record*. Freeman, SD: Pine Hill, 1971.
Waltner, Emil J. *Banished For Faith*. Freeman, SD: Pine Hill, 1968.
Waltner, Gary. "Among the Habaner of Czechoslovakia." *Mennonite Life* (April 1966) 89.
Weaver, Denny. *Becoming Anabaptist: The Origins and Significance of Sixteenth Century Anabaptism*. Scottdale, PA: Herald, 2005.
Whorf, Benjamin. *Language and Thought, and Reality*. Cambridge: MIT Press, 1956.
Wilder, Laura Ingalls. *On the Way Home: The Diary of a Trip from South Dakota to Mansfield, Missouri, in 1894*. New York: Harper & Row, 1962.

Wipf, Joseph K., and Dave S. Wipf, editors. *Dariusleut Family Record List*. Cranford, AB: Lakeside Colony, 2006.

Wurtz Edna, and Catherine Masuk. *Rooted and Grounded in Love: The History and Family Records of the Langham Prairie People*. Saskatoon, SK: self-published, 2000.

Young, James A. "Tumbleweed." *Scientific American* (March 1991) 82–87.

Young, Pauline. *Pilgrims of Russia-Town*. Chicago: University of Chicago Press, 1932.

Zeman, Jerald. *The Anabaptists and the Czech Brethren in Moravia, 1526–1628*. The Hague: Mouton, 1969.

Zempel, Solveig, editor. *When the Wind is in the South and Other Stories*. Sioux Falls, SD: Center for Western Studies, 1984.

Zieglschmid, A. J. F. *Die älteste Chronik der Hutterischen Bruder: Ein Sprachdenkmal aus frühneuhochdeutscher Zeit*. Philadelphia: Carl Schurz Memorial Foundation, 1943.

———. *Das Klein-Geschichtsbuch der Hutterischen Bruder*. Philadelphia: Carl Schurz Memorial Foundation, 1947.

Index

Agriculture, 23, 34, 73, 118–24
Alcatraz, 19
Alwinz (Transylvania), 15, 25, 26
Amana Society, 111
Amish Mennonites, 240
Anabaptists and Anabaptism, 9–11, 15, 50, 53, 57, 73, 99, 144, 221, 223, 288
Anfechtung, 182–83
Assurance of salvation, 181–85

Beadle, William, 76, 114, 126, 128
Berg, Albert, 57, 59
Bertsch, Gideon, 161
Blizzard of 1888 (Dakota Territory), 126–27
Blumenort (Ukraine), 29, 35
Boese, J. A., 99
Bon Homme Colony, 46, 102, 108, 1120, 136, 127, 139, 144, 270
Brauch, Jacob, 100
Brennemann, Daniel, 238, 241, 242
Bridgewater (South Dakota), 143, 186, 207, 220, 222, 288

Casting of lots, 41–42, 149
Chicago Fire (1873), 69–72, 243
Chicago Milwaukee and St. Paul Railroad, 96, 97, 98, 105
Chortitza Colony (Ukraine), 18, 23, 33, 46, 51, 216
Chronicle of the Hutterian Brethren, 13, 26, 27, 32, 43, 134, 139, 154, 185
Clark, Peter Gordon, 213
Clark Colony, 140–41

Cooke, Jay, 3, 78, 79, 82, 90–91, 219, 263, 276
Cornies, Johann, 22, 23, 29–32, 36, 40, 94, 165, 170
Correll, Ernst, 98
Custer, George, 79–80

Dakota Immigration Bureau, 100
Dakota Territory, 3, 4, 35, 73–74, 76, 89–90, 97–99, 102, 105–6, 109–10, 113–30, 134, 143–45, 150, 160, 218, 278
Dariusleut, 108, 136, 140, 154, 213, 270
Decker, Hans, 134
Decker, Katherina Wollman, 168
Decker, Paul, 126, 206, 215
Decker, Susanna Tschetter, 103, 197, 204–5
Dyck, Cornelius J., 173

Education, 14, 21, 31, 36, 49, 129–30
Ehrenpreis, Andreas, 5, 12, 135, 154
Elmspring Colony, 5, 108, 137–39, 144
Engels, Friedrich, 11
Evangelical Protestantism, 43, 144, 171–88, 201–2, 224
Ewert, Albert, 202
Ewert, Wilhelm, 54, 74, 76, 246, 251, 154, 275

Fish, Hamilton, 79, 82, 86, 90, 287
Fisher, Anna Hofman, 170, 185, 197–201, 224

Freeman (South Dakota), 102, 107, 136, 138, 157, 195, 210
Freeman College and Academy, 130
Freeman *Courier*, 117, 156, 191, 193, 197
Funk, Francis, 111
Funk, John F., 51, 65–66, 68, 75, 85–86, 90, 93, 98–100, 103–5, 111, 112, 127, 236, 239, 247, 261, 275

Gelassenheit, 5, 11, 133–34, 183
Gering, John J., 99
Glanzer, Jacob, 194
Glanzer, Justina S. W., 121, 178, 191–92
Glanzer, Samuel S. W., 178, 179, 194
Glanzer, Tim, 185
Goertz, Reuben, 127
Goossen, Dietrich, 177, 211
Goossen, Henry, 177
Grant, Ulysses S., 2, 3, 64, 77–82, 85–88, 90, 93, 192, 219, 263, 265–66, 276, 285–86, 287
Gross, David P., 267
Gross, Leonard, 11
Gross, Macy, 141
Gross, Mrs. Paul S., 172
Guericke, Justina, 37, 121–24, 129, 141, 165, 170, 198, 212

Habaner, 16, 87, 191
Harmony Society, 110, 111
Hasselstrom, Linda, 114
Haury, Samuel S., 144–46
Heritage Hall Museum and Archives (Freeman, South Dakota), 57
Hiebert, Clarence, 66
Hiller, Michael, 69, 78, 80, 86–88, 90, 95, 97–98, 263, 264–66, 276, 277, 287

Hofer, Arnold M., 20, 23, 53, 92, 95, 185–86, 195, 216
Hofer, Ben, 205
Hofer, David M., 148, 180, 215–26
Hofer, Egon, 186
Hofer, Jacob E., 149, 153, 158, 160, 165, 167, 171, 191, 202, 203
Hofer, Jacob J., 139, 176, 183
Hofer, Jacob M., 60, 224
Hofer, Johann, 150, 151, 177, 192, 268
Hofer, Joseph, 127–28, 178–79
Hofer, Joseph (World War I martyr), 139, 194
Hofer, Joseph ("Yos"), 53, 63, 109, 126, 135, 137, 150, 157–58, 166, 170
Hofer, Joshua M., 207
Hofer, Maria Tschetter, 46, 103, 143, 207
Hofer, Michael, 139
Hofer, Paul L., 195
Hofman, Christian, 125, 195, 196, 199, 209, 210, 211, 212, 218, 219
Hofman, Justina Tschetter, 7, 125, 127, 136, 137, 143, 200, 210, 211, 212, 218, 219, 224
Holdemann, Joseph, 240–41, 261
Homestead Act of 1862, 89–90, 115, 117
Hostetler, John A., 85, 101
Huntington, Gertrude, 14, 35
Hut, Hans, 13, 15
Hutter, Jacob, 11–12, 135, 288
Hutterdorf Church (South Dakota), 138, 150, 154, 220, 269
Hutterdorf village (Ukraine), 33, 35, 103, 107, 227, 278
Hutterisch, 5, 19, 148, 159
Hutterite Mennonite Centennial Committee [AQ]

Hutterites
  Ark metaphor, 12, 181, 222
  Carinthian converts, 15–16, 25, 27
  Community of goods, 1, 5, 6, 10–11, 33–35, 131–35
  Crafts, 13, 15, 21
  Dress, 15, 19, 33
  History, 9–24
  Marriage, 31–33, 40
  Missions, 13, 144
  Moravia, 11–14, 87, 216, 288
  Persecution, 12, 26–27
  Slovakia, 12–15, 87, 216
Hutterthal Church (South Dakota), 114, 137, 138, 150, 154, 180, 220, 270, 279
Hutterthal village (Ukraine), 23, 29–32, 34–35, 37, 41, 44, 46, 53, 94, 136, 218, 268, 269, 273

Immigration, 84–112, 223, 271–72, 278–79

Jansen, Cornelius, 51, 79
Jansen, Peter, 79, 113, 183
Janzen, Chris, 81
Janzen, Peter, 30
Johannesruh (Ukraine), 23, 33, 35, 94, 109, 144, 217
Jones, Jim, 215

Kaplan, Bert, 182–83
Krehbiel, Christian, 51, 112
Klassen, David, 54, 60, 63, 66, 68, 228, 230, 236, 263, 275
Kleinsasser, Barbara Tschetter, 143
Kreuz (Transylvania), 15
Krimmer Mennonite Brethren, 5, 6, 52, 130, 144, 159, 171–88, 200, 204, 221, 222, 224
Ku Klux Klan, 210
Kutter Colony, 136, 195

Lehrerleut, 108, 137, 139, 140, 159
Lehren (Hutterian sermons), 6, 15, 19, 20, 34, 45, 68, 104, 131, 133–34, 145–46, 160–64, 166, 175, 179, 186–87, 202, 220, 224
Letkemann, Peter, 34, 36
Liberty Bonds, 194, 223
Lieder (Hutterian hymns), 15, 20, 141, 160, 164, 165, 187, 220

Marx, Karl, 77
Masuk, Catherine, 120
Mendel, Jacob J., 60, 99, 117, 138, 139, 156, 191, 193
Mennonite Board of Guardians, 66, 88, 98, 111
Mennonite Brethren Church, 52, 204, 222
Mennonite Executive Aid Committee, 88, 98
Molotschna Colony (Ukraine), 22, 23 30, 36, 45, 46, 51, 150, 244, 268, 275
Moravian Church, 78, 263–64
Murphy, Patrick, 163

Native Americans, 9, 104, 113
Neu Hutterthal village (Ukraine), 33, 46, 53–54, 64, 83–84, 88, 94–95, 105–9, 112, 143, 147, 215–16, 218, 269, 274, 277, 278, 279
Neu Hutterthaler Church (South Dakota), 4, 7, 53, 54, 83, 88, 127–28, 139, 142–71, 173–95, 200–206, 210, 215, 219, 220, 224, 267–71, 279–84, 288
Nicknames, 128–29
North Carolina KMB Mission Church, 209–10

Northern Pacific Railroad, 3, 66, 72–74, 77–78, 87, 89, 91, 95–98, 105, 226
Old Mennonites, 235–43
Old Order Amish, 67
Olivet (South Dakota), 144, 149, 157–58, 199, 288
Ontjes, Alice Wipf, 203
Ontjes, Kenneth, 160, 176, 203

Panic of 1873, 5, 91, 92
Peace Corps, 215
Pentecost, 10, 15, 131, 157, 166, 246
People's Temple, 215
Peterson, Nancy, 106, 107
Plaut, Thomas, 182–83
Prairieleut, 4, 8, 92, 108, 114, 121, 128–30, 134–51, 154, 156, 159, 165, 167, 169, 171–74, 182, 189, 192–94, 204, 207, 216, 220–21, 224

Raditschewa (Ukraine), 2, 18–22, 29, 30, 43, 216, 217
Rath, George, 190
Red River valley, 74, 76, 89, 90, 97, 98, 100, 252–53
Riedemann, Peter, 12, 15, 41
Rockport Colony, 139, 140
Rolvaag, O. E., 115
Roman Catholic Church, 10, 14, 16, 43, 87, 132
Ruth, John, 112

Sabatisch (Slovakia), 15, 25
Salem Krimmer Mennonite Brethren Church, 176–88, 205, 208, 210, 222
Schartner, Friedrich, 150, 269
Schartner, Jacob, 150, 151, 269
Schell, Herbert, 119, 126, 190
Scheromet (Ukraine), 95, 144
Schlachta, Astrid von, 41
Schmiedeleut, 108, 140, 163, 270

Schrag, Andreas, 54, 74, 76, 99, 150, 255, 262
Simons, Menno, 44, 62, 231
South Dakota Council on Defense, 191
Stahl, A. A., 198, 210, 211
Stahl, Barbara Tschetter, 198, 210, 211
Stahl, David, 136–37
Stahl, Michael, 45, 46, 50, 51, 109, 137, 139, 150, 268, 272, 273, 274, 278
Stahl, Peter, 150, 151, 269
Suderman, Leonhard, 54, 94, 239, 249, 22, 275

Thirty Years War, 14, 158
Thrash, Catherine, 215
Tidioute (Pennsylvania), 110–11
Toews, Cornelius, 54, 60, 63, 66, 68, 228, 230, 236, 263, 275
Tschetter (surname), 25–27
Tschetter, Albert, 210, 211–14
Tschetter, Alfred, 215
Tschetter, Anna Glanzer, 195, 211
Tschetter, Barbara, 142, 163, 207–8
Tschetter, Barbara Kleinsasser, 27–29, 35, 117, 174–76
Tschetter, David W., 143, 164, 176, 180, 195, 196, 211
Tschetter, Emil, 77, 122, 170
Tschetter, Jacob J., 27–29, 35, 117, 147, 177
Tschetter, Jacob A., 20, 29, 117, 124
Tschetter, Jacob M., 176
Tschetter, Jacob W., 47, 120, 121, 127, 128, 135, 143, 167, 170, 176, 180, 197, 208
Tschetter, Jean, 214–15
Tschetter, Johannes, 136
Tschetter, John, 108, 172–75, 179–80, 183

Tschetter, Joseph W., 126, 130, 139, 143, 148, 176–78, 180, 184, 193–94, 197–98, 200, 208–10
Tschetter, Katherina Hofer, 138, 142, 177–78, 180, 182, 184, 197–98, 200, 208–9
Tschetter, Kris, 215
Tschetter, Lohrentz, 2, 51–54, 60, 64, 76, 80–83, 99, 101, 103, 126, 201, 227–28, 253, 255, 262, 274, 278, 280, 286, 288
Tschetter, Lohrentz Jr., 126, 278
Tschetter, Loren, 214–15
Tschetter, Maria (Paul Tschetter's wife), 35–40, 46–47, 85, 103, 115, 122–26, 142–43, 170, 177, 184, 195–97, 201, 205–8, 210, 214, 216, 218
Tschetter, Paul
   Alcohol, 126, 146, 166, 185–86
   Chicago, 69–72, 105, 243, 275
   Childhood, 37
   Church discipline, 169–71
   Church services, 160–66
   Delegate to North America, 51–83, 218–19
   Diary, 2, 44, 54–83, 218, 227–66
   Dress restrictions, 167–68, 170, 237
   Elkhart (Indiana), 66–68, 77–78, 103–5, 160, 235–43, 261–62, 263, 275, 276, 278
   Final years, 192–220
   Gun ownership, 8, 68, 153–55
   Hutterite colonies, 121–41
   Hymns, 59–62, 69–71, 74–76
   Joshua image, 1, 2, 7
   Legacy, 221–28
   Ministerial selection and responsibilities, 43–45, 144–71, 223
   Missions and evangelism, 159
   Music and musical instruments, 164–65, 169–71, 202–3, 219

   New York City, 63, 66, 80–81, 104, 168–69, 219, 235, 264, 265, 275, 276
   Non-resistance and pacifism, 50–51, 67–68, 155, 204, 210, 221, 223, 241, 272, 279
   Photographs, 37–38, 63–64
   Sermon books, 160–62
   Settlement years, 113–31
   Sunday School, 158–59
   Tobacco and smoking, 7, 66, 149, 156, 170, 219, 237, 240
   Weddings, 165, 166
   World War I, 8, 138–41, 185, 189–95, 223, 282–83
Tschetter, Paul W. ("Big Paul"), 46, 143, 156, 176, 196–97, 206–7
Tschetter, Paul G., 37, 64, 103, 105, 130, 160, 181, 183–84, 196, 200–201
Tschetter, Paul J., 178, 268
Tschetter, Peter, 135–36
Tschetter, Ronald A., 215
Tschetter, Susanna Decker, 167, 180, 208
Tschetter, Susanna Mendel, 173–74, 179–80
Tschetter, Wesley, 19, 21, 120, 128, 215–18

Unruh, Daniel, 98–100
Unruh, John D., 99, 100, 101, 145, 158
Unruh, Tobias, 2, 54, 76–78, 86–87, 99, 150, 246, 253, 255, 261, 262, 275, 286
Ukase (edict from Tsar, 1870), 48–49, 91, 94, 272

Waisenordnung (Church Orphan Ordinance), 152, 281–82
Waldner, David, 95, 103
Waldner, Johannes (Hutterite elder and chronicler), 18

Waldner, John, 137–38, 279
Waldner, Martin, 44, 109, 149, 268, 270, 273, 278, 280
Waldner, Michael, 33–35, 95, 102, 103, 109, 111, 139, 181, 270
Walpot, Peter, 12, 135, 181
Walter, Clifford, 107, 161
Walter, Darius, 53, 95, 102, 107, 139, 278
Walter, Jacob, 18, 37
Walter, Jacob J., 181
Wedel Peter, 45, 46, 268
Wiebe, Heinrich, 180
Wiebe, Jacob A., 173, 183
Wilson, Woodrow, 110, 192
Wipf, Jacob, 35, 44, 50, 270, 273
Wipf, Mike, 163
Wishenka (Ukraine), 17, 18, 26, 27, 217
Wolf Creek Colony, 5, 102, 103, 107, 117, 135, 137–39, 270, 278
Wurtz, Edna, 120

www.ingramcontent.com/pod-product-compliance
Lightning Source LLC
Chambersburg PA
CBHW050623300426
44112CB00012B/1633